Moving Money

D0540125

Moving Money analyzes the influence of politics on financial systems. Daniel Verdier examines how information asymmetry and economies of scale over time have created a redistributional conflict between large and small banks, and financial centers and their peripheries, and he discusses how governments have attempted to arbitrate this conflict. He argues that centralized states have tended to create concentrated, internationalized, market-based, and specialized financial systems, whereas decentralized states have favored dispersed, national, bank-based, and, with a few exceptions, universal systems. Verdier then sets out to uncover the sources, political and economic, of cross-country variation in financial market organization, examining a growing number of OECD countries from 1850 onwards.

DANIEL VERDIER is Associate Professor in the Department of Social and Political Science at the European University Institute. He is the author of *Democracy and International Trade* (1994) and has published articles in *International Organization, Politics and Society,* and *International Studies Quarterly.*

Moving Money

Banking and Finance in the
Industrialized World

Daniel Verdier

European University Institute

PUBLISHED BY THE PRESS SYNDICATE OF THE UNIVERSITY OF CAMBRIDGE
The Pitt Building, Trumpington Street, Cambridge CB2 1RP, United Kingdom

CAMBRIDGE UNIVERSITY PRESS
The Edinburgh Building, Cambridge, CB2 2RU, UK
40 West 20th Street, New York, NY 10011-4211, USA
477 Williamstown Road, Port Melbourne, VIC 3207, Australia
Ruiz de Alarcón 13, 28014 Madrid, Spain
Dock House, The Waterfront, Cape Town 8001, South Africa

http://www.cambridge.org

First published 2002

Printed in the United Kingdom at the University Press, Cambridge

Typeface Plantin 10/12 pt.   *System* LaTeX 2$_\varepsilon$ [TB]

A catalogue record for this book is available from the British Library

ISBN 0 521 81413 8 hardback
ISBN 0 521 89112 4 paperback

To the memory of my dearly loved wife,
Audrey Paige Verdier

Contents

Appendixes

Figures

Tables

Preface and acknowledgements

For the past eight years, I have been searching for what accounts for factor mobility or its opposite, factor specificity. It began with my 1995 *Comparative Political Studies* article, in which I advanced the idea that factor mobility is a sociopolitical construct, reflected in asset holders' membership in sociopolitical networks. In this book, I further probe this insight with respect to the capital factor, providing an institutional backbone for (or rather an explicit specification of) the generic and softer notion of network.

This book was written while I was at the European University Institute in Fiesole. The research was financed by the Institute and conducted in collaboration with Elisabeth Paulet. I also benefited from the tutoring of Benoit Friguet, Marcel Jansen, and Ludovic Renou, and from the advice of Giovanni Peri. Thimo de Nijs and Roland Ruittenbogaard contributed information on the Dutch case.

The book required the drudging compilation of a database, established in collaboration with Elisabeth Paulet. We thank Andrew Clayton from the Bank of England, Paolo Garofalo from the Banca d'Italia, Dr. Gabriele Jachmich from the Institut für Bankhistorische Forschung eV, Mr. Nougaret from the Crédit Lyonnais, Dr. Francesca Pino from the Banca Commerciale Italiana, Dr. Sbacchi from the Credito Italiano, and Petros Valamidas from the Bank of Greece for kindly and generously responding to our requests for documentation.

Among the many friends, colleagues, and acquaintances whose advice was a great benefit are Stefano Bartolini, Thomas Bernauer, Richard Breen, Richard Deeg, Marcello de Cecco, Cedric Dupont, Douglas Forsyth, Peter Hertner, David Laitin, Dale Murphy, Calum Macdonald, Larry Neal, Thomas Plümper, Jaime Reis, Ronald Rogowski, Gerald Schneider, Herman Van der Wee, and Jonathan Zeitlin. I especially thank Douglas Forsyth and the participants in the 2000 EUI conference on "The Origins of Universal Banking" for a stimulating discussion: Marcello de Cecco, Richard Deeg, Alfredo Gigliobianco, Joost Jonker, Sverre Knutsen, Michel Lescure, Ranald Michie, Alessandro Polsi, Jaime Reis,

Don K. Rowney, Hans Sjögren, Norbert Walter, and Dieter Ziegler. Giuliano Amato, Antonio Pedone from Crediop, Franco Cotula at the Banca d'Italia, and the board of the Association of European Banking History helped with the funding. Prior iterations of present chapters were presented at the Banca d'Italia, the University of Konstanz, the Graduate Institute of International Studies in Geneva, the Swiss Federal Institute of Technology in Zürich, the Academy of International Business, the American Political Science Association, and the International Studies Association; I wish to thank the participants in these meetings for their questions and comments. At these numerous meetings, I was fortunate to have discussants such as William T. Bernhardt, Spyros Demetriou, Barry Eichengreen, Torben Iversen, Michael Mastanduno, Fiona McGillivray, Jeannette Money, Dale Murphy, Louis Pauly, and Beth Simmons. I am indebted to Peter Gourevitch and David Lake who, as editors of *International Organization*, consistently provided thorough and substantive comments on the many papers that I submitted for review. Jim Caporaso, as editor of *Comparative Political Studies*, Philipp Cottrell, as editor of the *Journal of Financial History*, and John Bowman at *Politics and Society* played a similar role. There is finally the army of anonymous reviewers who were ever generous with their criticisms.

Still, the person I talked finance the most with, one with a practical understanding of banking, who could associate human faces with corporate names as well as find her way through actual bank balance sheets, was Audrey Paige Verdier, my beloved wife, who left this world a few weeks before this book was completed. Finance was her profession, her hobby, her life. My debt to her is eternal.

Introduction

> Politicians strut and fret their hour upon the stage, and then are heard
> no more. The real moving forces in the development of the economic
> and financial systems lie elsewhere. *The Banker* April 1996, 96.

This book is about moving money within and across countries. It raises
the following question: are the few percentage points of my income that
I save each month lent to a firm in my neighborhood or do they end
up refinancing the short-term debt of the Republic of Mali instead? The
answer to this question does not depend on technology, for, since the
telegraph was invented, money has had the capacity to move to almost
any urban area in the world at the speed of electromagnetic waves. Nor
is the answer more likely to be found in economic reasoning. The local
firm and the foreign government, holding risk constant, will pay the same
interest on the sums they borrow. The answer, instead, is political. My
savings are more likely to help fund production in my local industrial
district if I live in Germany, Italy, Canada, or the United States, but to end
up in Timbuktu if I live in Britain or France. Mobility of capital reflects
the degree of centralization of the state. It is the structure of the state
that determines the outreach of the "great go-between," Bagehot's phrase
for Britain's financial system, to which he ascribed the responsibility for
moving money.

Many books are written on moving money, cross-border flows, and
the mobility of the "K" factor – capital. But while most books associate
capital mobility with global financial flows, currency markets, and direct
foreign investment, the present work makes the unusual claim that capital
mobility begins at home, between cities, between regions; mobility across
districts is a prerequisite for mobility across countries.

It is easy to forget in these days of global market expansion that financial
systems are nested in the politics of their respective nation-states. Irrespective of whether the state intervenes or not in the allocation of credit,
whether *politicians strut, fret*, or *are heard no more*, politics is omnipresent
through its institutions. The reason is that markets are not neutral, but

create winners and losers. Even in the best-ordered society, market discipline is not a credible mechanism for the allocation of wealth unless politicians manage the redistributional conflict, and deflect, accommodate, or buy off the victims' resistance to market competition. This reliance on politics accounts for the differences between financial markets. Different political institutions, reflecting different historical trajectories, articulate redistributive conflicts differently, shaping peculiar financial rules and structures.

This is a comparative study of how banks and financial markets are organized. The argument is that the degree of centralization of the state shapes how financial markets are organized. The level of state centralization is determinant because financial markets are centralizing mechanisms. Banks tend to cluster in financial centers. The savings that move to the center do not always flow back to the periphery to fund local, generally small investments. Capital mobility, instead, tends to be one-way. Financial centers drain the local economies of their financial resources, leaving behind a periphery of aggrieved local borrowers, banks, taxpayers, and governments. Decentralized state institutions empower these local peripheries, whereas centralized institutions do not. A good part of bank and financial regulation is designed to hinder the development of the center at the expense of the periphery, and this regulation is mostly found in decentralized countries. It is the centralized countries that regularly reach the highest levels of market liberalization – they have a financial center characterized by breadth, depth, functional specialization, and internationalization.

In contrast, decentralization foils financial liberalization. Decentralized countries rarely reach high levels of market liberalization. Their banks are dispersed, and market-induced specialization among banks is often circumscribed. Stock markets are shackled and internationalization is reduced. The US financial system is no exception to this rule. The United States is home to the largest concentration of bank assets and the largest stock capitalization in the world. But it owes its leading position to the absolute size of its economy and the wealth of its citizens, not to financial regulation.

This book tells a story. The prologue, which, as in children's tales, is brushed with sufficient historical imprecision to provide a convenient background to the unfolding drama, presents a tranquil era in which short-term bank resources took the form of banknotes and current accounts. The sudden arrival of the deposit, along with the check, opened up the first period of market expansion (1850s–1913), followed by a period of market contraction (1914–1960s), and then another period of market expansion (1960s–present). The first and last periods show remarkable similarities. Competition intensified, banks grew larger, and geographic concentration in the sector increased. Domestic markets were opened to foreign influence, foreign investment surged, and money and equity markets boomed. Parallels between 1900 and 2000 are striking enough to make the study of the past directly relevant to understanding the present, and to make us wonder if the past will keep repeating itself.

How financial systems are organized

In this work I shall consider four organizational dimensions along which financial systems are ordered: spatial concentration, internationalization, market development, and specialization. Financial systems vary, first, in terms of banking concentration. In Britain, France, and other centralized countries, a handful of very large banks manage nationwide *branch* networks. In contrast, in Germany, Italy, and other decentralized countries, more than half of the loan market is on the books of savings banks – institutions with a quintessentially local reach. In the United States and Norway – two decentralized countries – one still encounters cases of *unit* (single agency) banking.

The second dimension that is considered in this book is the degree of *internationalization* of the capital market. The capital market is highly dependent on cross-border capital flows in Belgium, Portugal, and Britain, whereas it is closer to self-sufficiency in Japan, Iceland, Germany, and Italy.

The third dimension is *intermediation* – the importance of banks relative to securities markets in the supply of external finance to firms. In centralized Britain, France, and the Netherlands, markets have traditionally been dominant, whereas in decentralized Germany, Italy, and Scandinavia, banks have acted as intermediaries between investor and borrower.

The last dimension is the degree of *specialization* of banking. In centralized countries, Britain especially, banks traditionally specialize in one or two activities – commercial paper, lending, flotations, savings, mortgages, and so on. However, in many, though not all, decentralized countries – Germany is a good example – banks have traditionally been *universal*, providing almost all services under one roof.

Concentration, internationalization, market development, and specialization are the four dependent variables of this study. The explanatory power of state centralization, however, does not stop at these four dimensions. I have written elsewhere on the role played by state structures in determining the relative importance of *state banking* – when the state is directly involved in the allocation of a substantial share of loans. I have also touched on the notion of financial *stability* – when banks show resilience in the face of liquidity crises. Linked to the notion of stability is the early establishment of central banking and *lending-of-last resort* across countries.[1]

Case selection and methodology

The method is comparative. I look at financial systems in fifteen to twenty advanced industrial countries, depending on the period. Case selection is dictated by data availability, which, in turn, is a function of financial development itself. Fifteen to twenty is a methodologically inconvenient number of cases. I have attempted to mitigate this problem by relying on the graphic representation of bivariate relationships and using small-n-friendly statistics. To present results and identify outliers, I rely on partial regression plots – the multivariate analog of the bivariate scattergram.[2] When the variables are asymmetrically distributed and/or the number of observations drops too low, I bootstrap the statistics.[3] Given data limitations, it would be a mistake to try to squeeze too much out of the data. Conviction, if it will come at all, will not come out of any single statistics – none was designed to withstand econometricians' scrutiny – but from considering the entire body of evidence together.

Merely adding new cases does not always make good econometric sense. Including a handful of undeveloped countries would, in addition to adding imprecision to the data, raise the risk of non-linear and poorly understood variations, expanding the dataset to be sure, but not necessarily adding meaningful degrees of freedom. It would also increase the degree of interdependence between observations. The greater the developmental gap between countries, the less independent are the observations. Banking in Argentina at the turn of the century exhibited the same structural traits as British banking, not because domestic conditions were identical in the two countries – they were not – but because banking in Buenos Aires was run by the local branches of British banks.

[1] On state banking and financial stability, see Verdier 2000 and 1997 respectively.
[2] Each plot generates a coefficient and a fit that are equal to the coefficient and fit of the dependent variable against the chosen right-hand-side variable, while simultaneously controlling for the effect of the other right-hand-side variables on both variables. See Bollen and Jackman 1990.
[3] Bootstrapping is a non-parametric technique that makes it possible to get around the size constraint ($n > 30$) imposed by the central limit theorem. Bootstrapping is also useful in the presence of variables that are distributed asymmetrically, multimodal, or truncated – a common occurrence in small samples. See Mooney and Duval 1993.

British international influence breached rule number one of comparative analysis – the independence of cases.

Of course, few cross-sectional observations in comparative politics are ever entirely independent, as governments learn from one another, mimicking policies that seem to work elsewhere, while screening out those that fail. This is especially true in matters of finance, and even more so when cash crosses borders. Yet the ongoing globalization of the world economy does not disqualify the use of the comparative method in this research. My argument is that variations in political institutions explain variations in financial structures. This claim is untestable only if case contamination affects the institutional variable, not if it affects financial structures. If globalization is strong, then financial structures should converge despite any parallel lack of change in institutional features, thereby weakening or falsifying my working hypothesis. Economic convergence does not make the present research spurious, but merely presents it with a rival hypothesis.

At any rate, I do not argue that political institutions explain all, or even most, financial structures. Other aspects matter, such as wealth and economic growth. At most, the empirical regularities that I shall identify may serve to suggest the plausibility of the argument. Although I will not refrain, whenever the opportunity arises, from pointing out the limitations of rival arguments, my sole aim is to introduce a new variable into the field of financial studies – a variable with a distinctive political content.

Organization of the book

The book has three parts. The first part is theoretical. It includes a survey of the literature on banks and financial markets and a statement of the full argument. The second and third parts cover the two golden periods of financial expansion: the market expansion of 1850–1913 and the market expansion of 1960–2000.[4] These two parts each have four chapters, respectively dealing with geographic concentration, internationalization, intermediation, and product specialization.

---

[4] The 1914–59 period was excluded from this book for methodological reasons that are given in chapter 2. For an account of this period, see Verdier 1997 and 2000.

Part I

Theoretical conjectures on banking, finance, and politics

1 Capital scarcity, capital mobility, and information asymmetry: a survey

Finance is a rich field of study, pooling contributions from historians, political scientists, and economists. My goal is not to draw up an exhaustive inventory of the existing literature, but merely to situate the approach adopted in this book. I successively look at (1) the historical debate on capital scarcity, on which I offer a new perspective; (2) the use by political economists of the notion of capital mobility, which I try to clarify; and (3) the economic literature on information asymmetry, on which I build my argument.[1]

Capital scarcity

In an article published in 1952, Gerschenkron provided the most ambitious explanation yet offered of why financial structures differ across nations. The more capital was needed in a short amount of time, he argued, the less equity markets could cope with the task of allocating long-term financial capital; instead, banks and state had to step in. Hence the "orderly system of graduated deviations from [the first] industrialization":[2] British industrialization was self- and market-financed, manufacturers ploughing back profits into their own factories; French industrialization (the 1850–70 spurt) was financed by investment bankers, who raised long-term capital and lent it to factories; German industrialization was financed by universal bankers, intermediating between depositors and factories; and Russian industrialization was financed by the state, raising capital from taxpayers and foreign lenders to distribute it to banks and factories. The need for banks or state intervention reflected economies of scale. Economies of scale were characteristic of late industrialization; the period was also lacking in standards of honesty and in adequate mechanisms for the enforcement of contracts.

---

[1] In a more diversified survey (Verdier 2002), I review eight additional approaches: (1) developmentalism, (2) fixed costs, (3) social capital, (4) institutional commitment, (5) legal origins, (6) market segmentation, (7) curb market, and (8) global convergence.
[2] Gerschenkron 1962, p. 44.

Gerschenkron's theory is a two-step argument. The first step links backwardness to the timing of industrialization. The second step links this timing to the organization of the financial system – the relative degrees of market, bank, and state intermediation in the provision of long-term capital. The first step has been heavily criticized on the grounds that not all backward economies industrialized, nor did all do so in a "big spurt."[3] The second step, the contribution of markets, banks, and the state to industrialization, has better stood the test of time. To be sure, the fit between the timing of industrialization and the type of credit system is far from perfect; there are cases (Italy and Austria) that exhibited the banking traits of late industrialization, despite the fact that their big spurt, by Gerschenkron's own admission, petered out. There is also Denmark, an economy that grew faster than Germany in the prewar decades and that developed universal banking, but without large-scale, capital-intensive industrialization.[4] Despite these limitations, historians have offered no generalizable alternative to Gerschenkron's argument.[5]

Zysman (1983) applied Gerschenkron's insights to the study of industrial policy in the postwar period. He proposed a threefold typology of banking systems, distinguishing between the French "state-led" model, the Anglo-Saxon "market-based" model, and the German-like "private-bank-organized" model.[6] This typology is very similar to Gerschenkron's triptych, with the difference that France, rather than Russia, is offered as the paradigm for state banking. The rationale for the choice of France reveals a key modification that political scientists brought to Gerschenkron's synthesis when they imported it. Of course there was a strong demand in postwar France for a quick rebuilding of the economy. But this was also the case almost everywhere in Europe. What made France paradigmatic in its credit policy was the specific institutional makeup of the French state – a "strong" state, in Zysman's terminology. For Gerschenkron, the

[3] Gerschenkron (1962, p. 234) himself grappled with the Bulgarian case, coining for the occasion the notion of "missed opportunity." For a thorough review of new developments in growth time-series since Gerschenkron, see Sylla and Toniolo 1991.

[4] Bairoch's (1993, p. 8) data for 1890–1913 show a 2.3 percent annual growth in GNP per capita for Denmark against 1.7 percent for Germany. On Denmark, see Gerschenkron 1962, pp. 16, 361.

[5] Gerschenkron's proposition that industrial capital shortage made continental banking less specialized than British banking is widely shared among economic historians. In a recent review of Gerschenkron's contribution, Sylla and Toniolo (1991, p. 24) wrote that "the 'loose' version of Gerschenkron's paradigm still offers a good first insight into [the problem of European industrialization] and provides a powerful guide in framing the meaningful questions that scholars should ask." Still, very few historians have endorsed Gerschenkron's synthesis. An exception is Jon Cohen (1967).

[6] For a similar argument, see Hu 1984. Knutsen (1997, 108) endorsed Zysman's typology in his study of postwar Norwegian banking.

state is a possible substitute for market failure that is a priori identically available across nations. For Zysman, and for Shonfield (1965) before him, states differ in their capacity to intervene in the economy in general, and in capital markets in particular, and this difference, very much like capital endowment in Gerschenkron's theory, is the fruit of a historical legacy.[7]

Gerschenkron left the causes of capital scarcity underexplored. Although it could be a shortage of capital in the national economy as a whole, the problem was most often a shortage of capital flowing to industry. Prussia is a case in point. No overall capital shortage existed there during the first half of the nineteenth century – in fact, Prussia exported capital. But this capital was not readily available to industry, as investors preferred government bonds.[8] To account for this fact, one needs to shift the emphasis away from the firms' demand for bank loans (in accounting terms, the assets side of a bank's balance sheet) toward the savers' supply of cash to banks (the liabilities side). Financial systems vary, I argue with Gerschenkron, because they enjoy differential access to capital. The cause of scarcity, however, does not lie in a temporary surge in the demand for capital, but in the sustained Malthusian regulation of centripetal capital flows in countries where local governments are politically powerful. In relation to the Gerschenkron–Zysman synthesis, the present study concurs that state structures matter as an explanatory variable. The question is: which aspect of state structures? Political scientists working in Zysman's footsteps have so far put much weight on the elusive notion of state autonomy and political insulation. Instead, I emphasize the intuitive and measurable notion of state centralization.

Capital mobility

Capital is a factor of production, and factor mobility is a key parameter in political economy models. Such models typically seek to derive the regulatory outcome from a policy process in which firms, factors, and

[7] The notion that state allocation of credit is superior to market allocation in situations of industrial catchup has been qualified by Loriaux (1991) in a study of postwar France and Pérez (1997a) in a study of postwar Spain. The Gerschenkron–Zysman synthesis generally found greater support in studies of East Asian finance; see Wade 1985 and Woo 1991. Yet, even there, Haggard and Lee expressed caution about the risks of "predation and patrimonialism" (1993, p. 20). The works of Rosenbluth (1989) and Calder (1993) on the Japanese financial system sought to debunk the myth of the "strong" Japanese state. The debate critically hinges on the definition of state strength, a synthetic and tautology-prone concept.

[8] See Barrett Whale 1968, p. 11; Tilly 1967, p. 156; Schmoller 1904, vol. II, p. 182; Joseph Hansen 1906, vol. I, pp. 580–86; Beckerath 1954, pp. 7–14; Borchardt 1961.

politicians pursue their respective policy preferences.[9] Factor mobility usually enters the model as a parameter in the determination of economic actors' policy preferences. If mobile across sectors, capital merely exits from a sector that becomes unprofitable. In contrast, if capital is specific to a sector, it faces a choice between retooling the sector or lobbying for government support for that sector.

Some studies try to determine the causes of capital mobility or, inversely, capital specificity. This "asset-specificity" literature, as it is known, typically points to sectoral barriers to entry. Instances of entry barriers include sunk investment costs, R&D intensity, learning by doing, brand names, and patents.[10] In a study of Norwegian firms, Alt et al. argue that firms with large R&D expenditures create specific assets for the manufacture of products with no close substitutes, which are difficult to dispose of if there is no demand for the product. As a result, Alt et al. argue, R&D-intensive firms have a clear propensity to lobby for subsidies or market protection.[11]

The asset-specificity literature rests on a notion of capital that is made up of dissimilar elements. Capital comes in two forms: (1) *production* capital, which comprises machinery, stock, and the buildings that house them, as well as intangibles like patents, and (2) *financial* capital, referring to all financial assets, long and short. The asset-specificity literature does not deal with the dichotomy well. Either that literature shuns financial capital to concentrate its attention on production capital exclusively;[12] or, alternatively, it treats production and financial capital as separate factors of production, with the latter more mobile than the former.[13]

Treating finance as an intermediate sector between savers and borrowers brings clarity to the analysis. Physical capital is, almost by definition, fixed. Unbolting a piece of machinery for relocation is a costly business

---

[9] For a useful typology of models, see Rodrik 1995.

[10] See Frieden 1991, Hiscox 1997, and Alt et al. 1999.

[11] Alt et al. 1999, 109. The literature also identifies political determinants of capital mobility. Alt and Gilligan (1994) argue (though do not show) that the electoral rule shapes the scope of public policy and the degree to which a firm will invest in specific assets. If members of parliament are tied to single-member districts, they provide the protection that keeps firms tied to a specific location. If they do not represent geographically based constituencies, but are elected from a national list of candidates, they may still provide protection, yet not of the kind that ties firms to a location. I have argued elsewhere that factor specificity is a sociopolitical construct, reflected in asset holders' membership in networks (Verdier 1995).

[12] See, for instance, Frieden and Rogowski 1996, p. 27.

[13] For instance, Frieden (1991, 438) writes: "it is consonant with the specific-factors approach to assume that...financial capital is mobile among industries, while physical capital is industry-specific." Frieden further separates financial capital into bonds and debt, said to be mobile across countries, and stocks, which are less so (ibid., 429).

proposition with limited empirical relevance. What gives a country a long-term comparative advantage in capital goods is not the stock of physical capital per se, which becomes obsolescent in ten or twenty years, but the flows that this stock generates in the form of savings and depreciation allowances. Savings are the share of factor reward that is not consumed; depreciation allowances are the share of revenues set aside to pay for fixed costs. These two flows are a function of two variables, economic growth and policy regulation. A fast-growth economy releases more savings and capital allowances than a slow-growth economy. Holding growth constant, the government can encourage savings and capital allowances through fiscal incentives and the regulatory promotion of a competitive and well-developed financial market.

In the absence of a financial market, savers, investors, and creditors have concentrated stakes in only a few firms and even fewer sectors; they cannot easily exit a money-losing investment in specific (low-liquidation-value) assets, nor enter a profitable one, making lobbying for the regulatory protection of that investment a plausible option. In contrast, in the presence of a financial market, investors and creditors each own a diversified portfolio of financial instruments.[14] Little lobbying is likely to come from a large number of small claimants; they are more likely to reduce – or write off – a stake in stagnating sectors and concentrate future investments in growth sectors.[15] The initiative to lobby, if any, is more likely to come from management (and labor), whose loyalty to the firm is higher than that of the investors and the bankers, in order to prevent both the latter from walking away from the firm.[16]

This financial approach provides a better empirical referent to the notion of capital mobility than the asset-specificity literature. That "an automobile factory cannot costlessly be converted into a brewery," to use

---

[14] The argument was first made by Schonhardt-Bailey 1991 and Schonhardt-Bailey and Bailey 1995. They argue that financial capital can effortlessly cross sectoral boundaries only in the presence of a well-functioning corporate securities market. Absent such a market, individuals willing to adjust their portfolios – that is, to liquidate assets in declining sectors and/or acquire some in rising ones – face discouraging transaction costs.

[15] Bankers, unlike equity holders, may be few enough to overcome the collective action dilemma. However, in the presence of a broad capital market, their claims typically take the form of senior debt, secured by the firm's capital and unlikely to induce loyalty in the firm or the sector.

[16] This is a standard result in models with multiple factors, some of which are mobile across sectors, others specific. The specific factor's marginal productivity increases with an inflow of mobile factors into the specific factor's sector of employment and declines with an outflow. This is also a central feature of the core–periphery model of chapter 2. For an application to cross-country capital flows, see Hiscox 2000.

Frieden's formulation, would indicate that capital is specific only in a non-monetary economy.[17] In a monetary economy, the liquidation value of the former could in theory suffice to pay for the latter. More realistically, the profits generated by car manufacturing may be invested in the construction of a brewery if brewing is expected to be more profitable than the assembling of cars. The same outcome is instantaneously reached in the presence of a financial market through institutional investors modifying their relative holdings of stocks in each sector. The induced change in relative share values allows the rising sector to incur new debt, while forcing the declining sector to reimburse past debt.

One is reminded of Bagehot's description of the functioning of Lombard Street 125 years or so ago:

Political economists say that capital sets towards the most profitable trades, and that it rapidly leaves the less profitable and non-paying trades. But in ordinary countries this is a slow process, and some persons who want to have ocular demonstration of abstract truths have been inclined to doubt it because they could not see it. In England, however, the process would be visible enough if you could only see the books of the bill brokers and the bankers . . . If the iron trade ceases to be as profitable as usual, less iron is sold; the fewer the sales the fewer the bills; and in consequence the number of iron bills in Lombard Street is diminished. On the other hand, if in consequence of a bad harvest the corn trade becomes on a sudden [sic] profitable, immediately "corn bills" are created in great numbers, and if good are discounted in Lombard Street. Thus English capital runs as surely and instantly where it is most wanted, and where there is most to be made off of it, as water runs to find its level.[18]

Only if the financial system is undeveloped – in "ordinary" countries, as Bagehot calls them – is the transfer of resources from declining to rising sectors dependent on whether entry by new firms is or is not possible. If entry is not limited (low asset specificity), then financial capital crawls to growth sectors in the form of direct investment financed through profit retention by non-financial companies. If entry is limited (high asset specificity), then financial capital is sector-bound and capital mobility approaches zero. There, low mobility reflects the ordinarily low liquidation value of physical assets or the usually high conversion costs of these assets.

The relationship between financial market development and capital mobility with respect to a given sector is thus quasi-linear. Holding growth constant, financial development can be said to be, without significant loss of generality, a necessary condition for capital mobility.

[17] Frieden 1991, 436.   [18] Bagehot 1991, p. 6.

Information asymmetry

Current microeconomic applications of information asymmetry to banking illuminate the choice between direct and intermediate finance along with providing a rationale for the existence of banks. This literature justifies the existence of a close bank–firm relationship for firms that are small or young. It can also be used to rationalize state promotion of non-profit banks. Yet, information asymmetry only takes us so far. It justifies the existence of diverse financial institutions, but is silent on the relative occurrence of each.

Entrepreneurs are better informed than investors about the quality of the projects they want to develop. This is a classic adverse selection problem, which causes the price of projects to be evenly low irrespective of quality.[19] As a result, only the bad projects get external finance; entrepreneurs with good projects are better off financing them themselves. This inefficient outcome sets the stage for the role of monitor. An individual who monitors a borrower – by screening projects, or preventing opportunistic behavior, or performing ex-post audits – could mitigate the adverse selection problem. Either this monitor could be an analyst, certifying to investors that a borrower is sound, or he could be a sophisticated investor, whose stake in the borrower's project would signal that the project is sound, or a bank, lending to the borrower its customers' deposits. How can we make sure that the monitor is doing the job properly? Reputation suffices to discipline the analyst. The personal stake signals the sophisticated investor's credibility. Diversification into a large number of independent projects guarantees the solvency of the bank. If there are scale economies in monitoring projects, as Diamond (1984) claims, then the bank is the most efficient monitor. Therefore, banks exist, according to Diamond, in order to serve as *delegated monitors*.

Since markets and banks coexist, it is worth asking in what circumstances entrepreneurs will prefer direct finance to intermediate debt (commercial paper, bonds, and equity are direct finance; loans are intermediate debt). Two complementary solutions are present in the microeconomics literature.[20] Both assume that direct debt is less expensive than intermediate debt – a fact that is verified in practice. The first model, by Diamond (1991), rests on a firm's track record. New borrowers borrow from banks initially. If, in the process, they acquire a good credit record, their reputation eliminates the need for monitoring. They may issue debt directly, without using an intermediary. Lower-rated borrowers, in

---

[19] The classic formulation is Akerlof's (1970) used car dealer, transplanted to finance by Stiglitz and Weiss (1981).
[20] I draw on the excellent textbook by Freixas and Rochet (1998, ch. 2).

contrast, will still be suspected of bad credit-worthiness and thus remain dependent on bank loans and monitoring. The very-low-rated ones will be screened out. In the second model, by Hölmstrom and Tirole (1997), the firms overcome the moral hazard problem through partial self-financing. By investing its own resources in its own project (that is, by having a large "capital"), the firm credibly signals its private information on the high quality of the project along with its commitment to make it work. Uninformed investors are willing to advance the residual funding without monitoring. In contrast, if the firm is capital-constrained and unable to self-finance part of the project, it must fall back on bank monitoring and make do with dearer intermediate finance.

Despite their differences and respective limitations, the two models concur with casual observation of reality. Information asymmetry creates a *pecking order* among firms that compete for external funding.[21] Firms that get access to money markets tend to be old and to have a good track record, as Diamond's analysis suggests. This fits quite nicely with the common idea that a firm's funding requirements go through a lifecycle: startups have to rely essentially on internal funds, then on bank assistance as they grow larger, and finally on commercial paper and equity once they are sufficiently established to enable individuals to evaluate their earnings with a modicum of confidence.[22] Furthermore, as Hölmstrom and Tirole argue, firms that get access to markets tend to be large and well capitalized. Firms that are small and collateral-poor, in contrast, typically fall back on bank loans. In a period of credit crunch, when banks find themselves to be overextended and start curbing lending, the small, poorly capitalized firms are hit the hardest. The large firms can either renegotiate their loans or go directly to the markets.[23] In sum, both reputation and capital are substitutes for monitoring. In fact, reputation and capital tend to coincide.[24]

Small and young firms are particularly at risk in periods of credit crunch, when banks rein in loans. Firms can insure against this risk, Petersen and Rajan (1994) argue, by entering a long-term, exclusive relationship with a bank. *Relationship banking* – a durable relationship spread across a wide array of products – informs the bank about the credit-worthiness of the firm, thus reducing the cost of lending. The firm commits itself to remain a client of the bank over the long run, and the

---

[21] The phrase is Calomiris' (1995).

[22] See Lamoreaux 1994, p. 154 and Calomiris 1995, p. 262.

[23] See Gertler and Gilchrist 1994.

[24] With the possible exception of banks, which until recently were able – but are not allowed any more – to operate on very low capital bases. The strong regulatory harness under which banks operated may have been responsible for this anomaly.

bank smoothes out the cost of capital to the firm over the firm's lifecycle. The bank subsidizes the firm when young and is repaid later. The bank also tides the firm over during credit crunches.

However, borrowers cannot credibly commit to relationship banking in the long run. They have an interest at some later stage, once they have established a track record with their initial bank, in breaking the relationship with the bank and borrowing from competing lenders, who can thus take advantage of the initial bank's efforts. Unable to recoup its initial investment in information gathering, the initial bank abstains from making that investment in the first place.

This problem of time inconsistency has several institutional solutions. A first is the existence of a local banking monopoly, able to enforce exclusivity over the long run – this may account for restrictions on branch banking of the *unit banking* type.[25] A second related solution is joint membership in a social network – this may account for the existence of *credit cooperatives*, in which members are liable for any loan on which the cooperative defaults and thus have an incentive to monitor their peers.[26] A third solution is to allow the bank to take an equity position in the firm, enabling the bank to share the surplus to which its lending contributed – this may account for the existence of *universal banking* (that is, universal banking for the small, of course). It is difficult to build an information asymmetry argument that would make universal banking pertinent to large firms. Large firms need no bank monitoring, unless they are denied access to markets for reasons unrelated to information asymmetry.[27]

The information asymmetry paradigm provides solid microeconomic foundations for the study of financial institutions. It provides a unified explanation for the diversity of financial intermediaries based on a pecking order between borrowers: large and respectable borrowers directly tap the markets, whereas medium- and less-capitalized firms borrow from intermediaries. Small and undercapitalized borrowers are willing to sacrifice their long-term independence and commit to an exclusive relationship with a bank in exchange for steady financial support. The very small put up with the collectivist atmosphere of a local cooperative. The further one

---

[25] See Petersen and Rajan 1995.

[26] See Banerjee et al. 1994. Still another solution, according to Haggard and Lee (1995), is a "strong" state. This is how they describe the functioning of capital markets of newly industrialized countries in the Far East. Decisions are made hierarchically and firms are monitored and coordinated by bureaucrats. Bureaucratic coordination helps economize on communication expense and reduce uncertainty.

[27] For an opposite view, see Calomiris 1995. Calomiris argues that project diversification and scale economies in monitoring allowed the big German banks to price debt lower than English direct finance, even for the largest firms.

moves down the hierarchy, the more pervasive and intrusive monitoring gets.

However, the information asymmetry literature says little about the relative importance of direct and intermediate debt, of center and local banks, of specialized and universal banks, or of banks and cooperatives. The size and age of firms are not good determinants of what type of funding is obtained, for it is partly determined by what kind of funding is available. Furthermore, many categories overlap. Deutsche Bank – a deposit bank – monitored firms in Germany at the turn of the century in the same way that J. P. Morgan – an investment bank – did in the United States.[28] Last, and most importantly, microeconomic efficiency operates within the limits of *exogenous constraints*. How else can we explain that historical accounts of bank–firm relations under turn-of-the-century German and postwar Japanese universal banking systems so closely match the description of relationship banking, even though the firms and banks involved in these relationships were large enough to qualify for direct finance?

I argue in the next chapter that the principal exogenous constraint was political. It is not that politicians were invented to ruin market efficiency – quite the contrary. But freely functioning financial markets generated externalities that threatened the stability of political institutions, something which politicians were concerned about.

Conclusion

The three foregoing approaches help situate the one offered in what follows. Gerschenkron and his followers explained variations in financial organization by focusing on the temporary capital scarcity provoked by surges in the demand for loans. Instead, I emphasize the long-term scarcity caused by the regulation of competition between various types of banks vying for cash. The asset-specificity approach seeks to explain capital mobility without the help of a financial sector. Instead, I conceptualize capital mobility as a function of financial development. The information asymmetry approach offers a rationale for bank variety, but cannot derive the relative importance assumed by each variety. I remedy this problem by adding structure to the information asymmetry approach.

---

[28] Contrast Calomiris' (1995) account of monitoring by the *Berlin Großbanken* with de Long's (1991) account of J. P. Morgan. The difference corresponds with the distinction between "intermediation" and "certification" made by Hölmstrom and Tirole (1997, 675).

2 The institutions of capital mobility

Lombard Street is the great go-between. Bagehot 1991, p. 5.

The argument of this book is that a freely functioning financial sector can split an economy's financial geography into a center and a periphery, redistributing income from location-specific factors in the periphery to those in the core. It may thereby modify the fiscal apportionment between local and central governments, and thus the very makeup of the state. Consequently, and in anticipation of this occurrence, the financial market elicits political resistance and incurs regulatory curbs in countries that are not fully centralized.

Consider an economy featuring a financial sector distinct from non-financial sectors. The financial sector raises *capital* (the factor) to make *finance* (the product).[1] Capital is an input that is specific to the financial sector, but it is not location-specific, at least not to the same extent as labor, machinery, or skills are, but instead easily moves around. A financial product, in contrast, is the output of the financial sector. This output is used as input by non-financial firms (in the form of loans and underwriting) and financial firms – banks are the largest consumers of day-to-day loans, bond issues, and derivatives. The output is also consumed by final consumers in the form of mortgages and credit for consumption.

Unlike capital, financial products are not necessarily free to move around, but see their geographic mobility hampered by *information asymmetry* – the fact that investors cannot trust borrowers to tell them the truth about the profitability of their investment. Information asymmetry generates a transaction cost, which, when it is too high, prevents the transaction from occurring.

---

[1] A terminological note: I use the word "capital" to refer to the external liabilities of banks (deposits) and insurance companies (insurance premiums). These liabilities, together with financial assets (loans, mortgages, bonds, stocks), form what I referred to in chapter 1 as "financial capital." In contrast, "physical capital" is made up of the buildings and machinery that figure as assets on the balance sheets of non-financial firms. Capital is sector-specific – it is specific to the financial sector – but not location-specific; physical capital, like labor, is both sector- and location-specific.

Information asymmetry, though relatively constant over time, is not parametrically given, but instead is a function of location. Information asymmetry reflects the geography of *information networks*. An information network is a social construct which may take various concrete forms – a street, as in Lombard Street or Wall Street, a national trade association, a chamber of commerce, a country club, a parish, and so forth. Two ideal types are conceivable. In one case, a dominant, core-based network outclasses a multiplicity of small, barely active local networks. At the other extreme, a collection of dense local networks blocks the growth of the financial core. Consider a possible transaction between a firm located in a periphery and a bank located in the core (or in another periphery). In the former case, that of the dominant core, information flows freely between the firm and the bank. In the latter case, that of the fenced-in core, information is trapped in local networks, inaccessible to outsiders.

Why would financial information be trapped in local networks as opposed to flowing freely to the core? Because regulatory barriers stem the flow. A well-functioning financial market may inflict great harm on *location-specific factors*. Financial markets indeed are powerful centralizing mechanisms, emptying peripheries of resources to the benefit of the center and impoverishing local factors – labor, services, local governments. Such a peripheralization skews both the localization of firms and the allotment of tax revenues in favor of the center, putting peripheries on the defensive. The great go-between is equally great at going up and over. As a result, whenever the potential victims of financial agglomeration enjoy enough political power to defend local banks against competition from the center, either by regulating entry or by subsidizing local banks, investment information will be trapped in local networks. The power of the periphery is the only exogenous variable in the model – it reflects the constitutional organization of the state. Information asymmetry across geographic networks is an inverse function of the degree of *centralization of the state*.

In the following, I develop the key ingredients of the model – economies of agglomeration, information asymmetry, financial regulation, fixed factors, and state centralization. I present a formal model of core–periphery relations. I conclude part I with a summary of the argument and a preview of the empirical chapters.

Economies of agglomeration

The financial sector tends to agglomerate in one place because it combines internal scale economies with forward–backward linkages.[2] First,

[2] Internal scale economies and forward–backward linkages are sufficient, though not necessary, conditions to produce economies of agglomeration. See Krugman 1991 and Fujita

financial centers display internal scale economies – the higher the volume, the more efficient the pricing, and the more attractive to buyers and sellers the market is. This is true for both the long-term and the short-term segments of the market. The long-term segment, commonly referred to as the "primary capital market" – primary because bonds and stocks are traded for the first time – pools the largest issuers in the economy. The issuing of a security presents steep fixed costs, favoring large over small issues. The short-term market, the so-called money market, on which currencies, commercial paper, notes, and certificates of deposit are traded, also thrives on volume. The money market is reserved for banks, institutional investors, and large firms.

Second, the various components of the financial district link up in a circular fashion. The capital market and the money market are connected via two institutions: the "secondary capital market" and the money center banks. For the sake of clarity, consider figure 2.1, showing the four components, linked together in a circuitous way. The arrows indicate the flow of funds. Start from arrow 1. The money market depends on banks for the supply of cash. Until recently, cash essentially took the form of savings deposits, which the banks would lend to brokers and market makers, pledging securities as collateral. With money-market and mutual funds now displacing savings deposits, banks are rushing into brokerage and asset management to serve as liaison between investors and market.

Then move to arrow 2. The breadth of the secondary market – the place where stocks bought on the primary market can be resold – is determined in part by the depth of the money market. A deep money market lets brokers, securities dealers, and arbitrageurs of all types borrow the cash they need to finance the short-term positions they repeatedly take, either to make markets for securities or merely to speculate.

On to arrow 3. Investors value depth in the secondary market – they value the liquidity that it offers and are willing to pay a premium for it. This premium, in turn, is attractive to issuers. Arrow 4 last. Banks depend on the capital market to transform long-term loans to industry into securities, recoup their liquidity, and lend anew. The great go-between looks like a merry-go-round.[3]

et al. 1999. The concept of economy of agglomeration was first introduced by Alfred Marshall (1920, p. 271), who illustrated it with the Sheffield cutlery "industrial district." The notion of industrial district has received much attention from social scientists looking for a viable alternative to corporate hierarchies; see Bagnasco 1977, Piore and Sabel 1984, Zeitlin 1995, Herrigel 1996.

[3] The reality is more complex that this simple graph suggests. Almost every component is linked to the others through a series of circular relations. For instance, stocks serve as collateral to call loans. It is also impossible to separate linkages into forward and backward in the absence of any obvious linear ordering of production from intermediate to final.

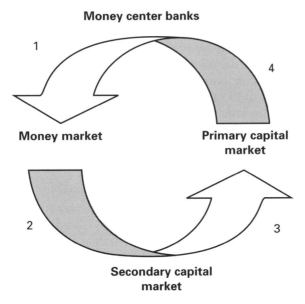

Money center banks

Money market

Primary capital market

Secondary capital market

Note: Arrows indicate the flow of funds:
1. Banks channel individuals' savings and firms' current accounts to the money market;
2. The money market leverages the secondary capital market;
3. The secondary capital market makes the primary capital market attractive to investors;
4. Corporations repay bank loans by issuing equity on the primary capital market.

Figure 2.1. The circuitous center

The above circularity, combined with the internal scale economies that characterize the functioning of the market, generates economies of agglomeration. It explains why the financial center is the place where all the largest and most profitable banks in the economy are headquartered. It accounts for why financial centers have a proclivity to develop at the expense of their peripheries.[4]

---

[4] There are several additional incentives for agglomeration in financial centers, reminiscent of Marshallian districts. Geographic concentration supports specialized local providers of inputs – lawyers, accountants, messenger services, public relations firms, and computing services to name just a few. Geographic concentration also supports a well-supplied labor market. Employees, who are usually well-paid and qualified, are less likely to remain unemployed if their employer does badly and they lose their jobs, and firms can recruit more easily and from a wider range of expertise if they do well. An active labor market also facilitates the diffusion of product innovation among financial institutions. Last, geographic concentration facilitates the spread of more reliable information, usually through personal contact and well-established relationships. The pricing of untested products (as in primary issuing) is sensitive to private information.

Economies of agglomeration make explaining cross-sectional variations in financial centers easier than it seems. Since long and short
communicate – capital markets are leveraged by demand deposits and
money-market accounts – and since debt and equity are complementary – higher equity value increases the capacity to borrow – it follows
that these components all expand or contract together. Explaining the
size of one component is no different from explaining the size of another
or that of the system as a whole.[5]

Information asymmetry

Clearly, there are limits to financial agglomeration. Agglomeration is unlikely to go on until the periphery totally empties out; it probably reaches
an upper bound in the form of rising opportunity costs.[6] More importantly, information asymmetry has opposite, centrifugal effects. We saw
in the previous chapter that small firms tend to fund their long-term
needs using local bankers. The comparative advantage of local banks lies
in their access to local information, which they collect through membership in local social networks – the chamber of commerce, city hall, and
other relevant local organizations. Good investment information allows
local bankers to monitor their clients' credit-worthiness and overcome the
information asymmetry that otherwise characterizes investor–borrower
relations.

In theory, large banks, provided that they want to, have the capacity to
serve the needs of local, small firms through their local branches. The pro-
viso matters, for quite often center banks do not want to bother with the
smaller and lesser-known. Their comparative advantage lies in their physical proximity to the financial market, leading them to place the emphasis
on lending standards, high volume, and large deals. Central headquarters also want their local agents to be in the position, if need be, to meet
liquidity requirements that keep changing with the overall position of the
bank. In sum, high opportunity costs may make the local branches of
center banks less free than local independent banks to meet the financial
needs of local firms with adequate consistency. But assuming that they set
their mind on including local firms among their clientele, center banks

---

[5] Clear to earlier observers (Goldsmith 1969), the bank–market complementarity is un-
deremphasized in the more recent literature. Banks are portrayed as rivals to markets
(Zysman 1983, Sylla 1997).

[6] Financial centers become congested, office space gets expensive, and the wages paid rise
out of line with the rest of the country. Screen trading and the linking of markets enable
banks to relocate activities pertaining to trading on secondary markets in suburbs or
second-tier cities. However, primary issuing and most investment-banking type services,
which require a large input of specialized providers and information, do not easily relocate
to the periphery.

can certainly do what it takes to develop local intelligence – appointing a local to manage the branch, accumulating relevant information, lavishing donations on local charities, and so forth.

The only reason why center banks might fail to penetrate the periphery lending market is if the local banks are already well established. Center banks rarely penetrate self-governed industrial districts. Banks situated in industrial districts, in which a large chunk of the tax base is collected by a local government that plows these revenues back into the local economy, are in a good position to resist competition from the center. Indeed, serving the financial needs of both the private economy and the government, the local bankers are omnipresent and omniscient in relation to that economy. In contrast, banks located in regions where local firms are subsidiaries of national firms, or where local governments have no independent resources, or where local procurements are decided by the political center, are privy to no special intelligence that a center bank could not acquire on its own.

The sociological literature on social networks is particularly apt at characterizing the source of the local banker's physical advantage over the local agent of a center bank.[7] Information asymmetry between investor and borrower can be overcome through relational information – regular dealings, direct and indirect, in various venues. Social networks function by channeling relational information to insiders, while denying it to outsiders. Being part of the local elite, local bankers are consummate insiders. The symbiosis with the local community is nowhere better expressed than in the following statement by the chairman of a powerful Roman savings bank: "We nearly always find something for the parish priest to repair the church roof."[8] Local banks are parochial banks.

In sum, center banks may enter local investment markets if they manage to penetrate the information networks, but are unlikely to succeed if the local banks are strong. Center banks cannot get around this difficulty by relying on their generally greater cost efficiency. Aggressive underpricing, in the absence of first-hand credit intelligence, is good at attracting only the poor-risk entrepreneurs, those whose credit needs elicit no response from the better-informed local bankers. Information asymmetry across various locations, therefore, is an endogenous variable. It has a high value for those banks that do not – or cannot – make the effort to enter a long-term relationship with local firms and get access to appropriate information networks. Information asymmetry is irreducible for a

---

[7] For a review of that literature and its application to politics, see Verdier 1995.
[8] Pellegrino Capaldo, chairman of the Cassa di Risparmio di Roma, 1986; quoted in *The Banker* April 1992, 13.

center bank trying to develop its portfolio of loans in a periphery already controlled by a few local banks working closely with the local government. What determines the relative strength of local information networks?

Regulatory protection

Local government autonomy is a necessary condition for the existence of a strong banking community. Local banks cannot survive without regulatory help. Information asymmetry has a centrifugal effect only on the assets side of the bank's balance sheet (lending), not on the liabilities side (borrowing). Information asymmetry inconveniences branches when they try to get a foothold in the local investment market, but not when they seek to collect local deposits. Savers and corporate treasurers with excess cash on their hands have no qualms about sending this cash to the center – indeed, they may prefer to do so on the grounds that center banks have a greater reputation than local banks and can be trusted not to fail as often. Center banks may also have more savings and investment opportunities on offer than local banks. Information asymmetry affects loans, not deposits.

Local banks and money centers compete for cash. In the past, cash primarily took the form of individual deposits. Local banks reinvested deposits in loans to local industry (directly or by financing local government projects), whereas center banks, at least until the 1930s, drained most of it to the money market. Center banks enjoyed a competitive advantage over local banks, for they were able to offer investors a wider range of products and higher returns. This competitive advantage is even more pronounced today due to the generalization of money-market accounts, by which banks do not keep savings on their books, but merely pass on to depositors the money-market rate in exchange for a fee. All banks now have to finance their investments on the money market, at a price that varies with their credit ratings. Dependence on credit ratings is a thorn in the side of the local banks, for it means that banks must refrain from lending to clients with little or no public visibility – the local banks' traditional and most logical line of business. Otherwise, credit-rating agencies and specialized news media will weight too heavily the risk presented by these loans, and force the bank to increase capital in order to avoid a downgrade and higher financial costs. Local banks are at a comparative disadvantage when it comes to financing their investments. That is why they need the regulator to help.

Regulatory help may come in the form of a legal interdiction on entering local markets, tax subsidies, or a state guarantee of deposits. Territorial prohibitions existed in the United States until 1994, when an Act of

Congress legalized interstate banking. They still exist in many European countries, where hostile bids are ruled out by unwritten rules of conduct. Under such conditions, no large bank can enter a local market without securing the consent of the relevant local government.[9] A second way for government to help local banks is to maintain their non-profit status. In Germany, Austria, Scandinavia, Italy, Spain, and Japan, the local banks are non-profit banks – savings banks and credit cooperatives – paying limited or no taxes and enjoying a state guarantee on liabilities. In the presence of a guarantee, the bank gets the credit rating of the guarantor, which is as high as it can be when it is the state. The state guarantee enables local banks to refinance more cheaply on the Euromarkets than the private banks – despite the fact that they make riskier loans.

More generally, entry barriers, subsidies, and the deposit guarantee constitute the second line of defense that local banks erect against the center banks. For banks are vulnerable on two sides simultaneously: on the assets side and on the liabilities side. Monopolistic control over local information informally shields them from centripetal competition on the assets side, but does little to guard against a hemorrhage on the liabilities side. The latter is the task of explicit government regulation.[10]

Fixed factors and local governments

The need for regulatory help is not specific to local banks; it is also felt by local firms and local governments. If local banks either concede local deposits to center banks or try to shore up their credit ratings, they cannot finance local entrepreneurs. Falling back on the center for financing would certainly mean (holding extant structures constant) absorbing a

---

[9] The fixed costs of establishing a retail network are so high that entry usually proceeds by way of takeover.

[10] Why do banks need protection on more than one side of their balance sheet? Answering this question will prove useful to the modeling exercise below. If information asymmetry prevents center banks from making loans to firms located in the periphery, such banks should have no use for the savings of the periphery; conversely, the local banks should have no need for government regulation to protect their deposit markets. Therefore, a high level of information asymmetry makes financial regulation redundant. This redundancy will prove convenient in the modeling exercise below, sparing us from piling financial regulation on top of information asymmetry. Nevertheless, the redundancy obtains only if two conditions are met: autarky and static growth. If we allow the center to invest abroad, then center banks have a readymade use for the capital of the periphery. Similarly, if we think of growth as a dynamic process, then the capital of the periphery may go to the industry located in the center. For the sake of convenience, the model that I offer below disregards these two possibilities, assuming instead autarky and static growth. However, historical reality is saturated with openness and dynamic growth; the regulatory protection of the deposit market was a necessity for the survival of local financial sectors.

higher cost of finance. To offset this drawback, local firms would reduce rewards to the other inputs, labor and dedicated local service suppliers. By extension, local governments are unable to maintain a strong tax base if local banks, local entrepreneurs, and local factors are impoverished. There is indeed a triangular interdependence between affluent local industries, well-entrenched local banks, and politically powerful local governments. Local industries need local banks to sustain local investment, local banks need the political protection of local governments to hold back the competition for resources from the center banks, and local governments need prosperous local banks and industries to maintain their relative fiscal independence from, and power vis-à-vis, the central government.

Of course, not all peripheral districts will necessarily suffer from the centralization and globalization of capital markets. Those districts that accommodate the rise of firms large enough to efficiently tap equity markets are not necessarily harmed by the decline of local banking. One would expect these districts and the firms to which they are home to espouse the cause of centralization or, at least, be conflicted – although the large firm provides local employment, its interest in the welfare of its local host is circumstantial and reversible.

With this caveat made, local bankers have allies outside financial circles: they are the natural partners of fixed factors – labor and service providers – and their local government. Through the subnational level of representation, these local coalitions may ask for and perhaps get legislation regulating competition with center banks. Fixed factors located in the financial center are in the opposite situation. They work for non-financial firms that welcome the relative drop in the cost of finance that would follow from a concentration of capital in the center. They largely benefit from the peripheralization of the rest of the economy. They are likely to resent financial regulation of the type presented above, siding instead with the center banks.

Centralized and decentralized states

However widely it may be felt, the need for regulatory help is insufficient in and of itself to translate into actual regulatory help. The potential losers must get together and overwhelm the political power of the financial center. Too few to make a difference electorally, yet much too scattered to act collectively, especially against a geographically concentrated opponent, local banks and firms have solely the local government connection as viable political channel, and this only in those countries where local governments enjoy a modicum of political power – in decentralized countries. Local governments in federal and otherwise decentralized states can use the right to veto certain policies within their jurisdiction. They can also use their collective veto in the upper chamber – if any – to block financial deregulation, or whatever formal or informal access to the upper echelons of the administration that they enjoy. In contrast, they are powerless in centralized states. The more decentralized the state, the more politicians are sensitive to the interest of the periphery in center–periphery conflict.

It is a stylized fact that information asymmetry increases with distance.[11] Yet the reason why that is the case, especially today, has eluded the financial literature. It has little to do with information technology or transportation costs. Instead, it essentially reflects the territorial organization of the state. The existence of powerful local governments in decentralized states offers a mainstay to firms and banks that suffer from the development of the financial core and seek to block the emptying of the periphery from financial resources. Investment information networks gel around local governments, only because these local governments offer to the victims of corporate finance easy access to the political system. Such networks are the byproduct of networking and lobbying strategies that the victims of geographic concentration pursue with a view to maximizing the expected benefits of regulatory protection subject to an institutional constraint.

State centralization is measured by the proportion of government revenues drained by the central government (see appendix 3 for details). I preferred this measure to the standard dummy variable differentiating federal from non-federal systems because it is continuous. It is also a more precise measure of decentralization than federalism, which places Belgium and Spain in the same league as Switzerland, Germany, and the United States. The distribution of expenditures across levels of government is a good indicator of the distribution of power across levels – of which federalism is one determinant, along with electoral rules, the party system, and the internal organization of the public administration.[12]

The fiscal measures in selected years are reported in table 2.1. According to the measure, Belgium, France, the Netherlands, and the United Kingdom consistently come out among the most centralized in the sample, whereas Switzerland, the United States, and Germany are among the most decentralized. Although levels vary over time, the ranking is rather stable across countries. Only two cases, Canada and Italy, show a long-term change, Canada toward greater decentralization, Italy toward greater centralization. In all other cases, the actual proportions vary, but the overall cross-sectional distribution does not. This is a remarkable

[11] This fact is especially emphasized in studies of late nineteenth-century banking.
[12] The fiscal decentralization variable has already been successfully used as proxy for political decentralization in Chhibber and Kollman 1998 and Treisman 2000.

Table 2.1. *Political centralization ratio, selective years*

	Circa 1880	Circa 1911	Circa 1930	1960	1990
Australia	.25			.80	.73
Austria			.70	.68	.68
Belgium	.85	.81	.90	.91	.90
Canada	.75			.62	.47
Denmark	.64		.58		.70
Finland	.78	.72	.72	.71	.71
France	.83	.80	.95	.92	.81
Germany	.49	.61	.66	.54	.51
Greece				.80	.94
Ireland			.81	.85	.93
Italy	.55	.53	.81	.83	.91
Japan				.74	.64
Netherlands	.87	.78	.72	.94	.89
New Zealand	.60			.92	
Norway	.60	.61	.54	.70	.83
Portugal				.90	.92
Spain	.79				.81
Sweden	.64	.59	.57	.70	.67
Switzerland	.37	.37	.39	.45	.37
United Kingdom	.70	.63	.81	.85	.90
United States	.33			.67	.56

Note: See appendix 3 for data description and sources.

feature, justifying the modeling of state centralization as an exogenous variable.

The unexplained residual

The theory advanced in this volume privileges the organization of the state at the expense of the composition of the party system. This bias limits the scope of application of the theory. In particular, it restricts its historical relevance to the two periods studied in this volume – 1850–1913 and 1960–2000 – missing important financial developments that occurred during the intervening period stretching from World War I to the 1960s.

If, as I argue, information networks reflect strategies maximizing benefits subject to the constraint of a given institution, it logically follows that a change in the nature of the institution is likely to cause a change in the type of preferred networking strategy and, in turn, a change in the configuration of the resulting networks. For instance, if political institutions recognize interests better when such interests are organized as sectors

Table 2.2. *A typology of banking sectors*

	For-profit	Non-profit
CENTER	*center banks* (joint-stock, partnership)	*state banks* (postal savings, national savings schemes, credit state agencies and assimilated)
PERIPHERY	*country banks* (joint-stock, partnership)	*local non-profit banks* (savings, cooperatives, mortgage, local government-owned banks)

than when organized as territorial districts, it is logical that the victims of financial development will coalesce sector by sector to extract regulatory protection, justifying the creation of sector-based information networks. More generally, the conflict that is triggered by the functioning of the financial sector is primarily a conflict between the big and the small, a conflict that may, but need not, be articulated as a center–periphery cleavage by the political system. Being an issue with a socioeconomic content, financial regulation might very well surface as a partisan cleavage, between political parties seeking the vote of the median voter. Hence, politicians may articulate the conflict between local and center banks in at least two different ways – as a vertical dispute between levels of government, or as a horizontal debate between vote-seeking parties.

One is easily convinced of the plausibility of this conjecture by looking at how banking systems are organized in reality. Table 2.2 provides the basic breakdown of a generic banking system. Such a system typically displays a first category of center banks, which can either be commercial or run by the state, and a second category of local banks, which can also be commercial or run by the local government. There are two intersecting dimensions: center/periphery and for-profit/non-profit. From this typology, and anticipating the next chapter to some extent, it is not difficult to infer what is going on. In decentralized countries, small borrowers rely on local banks, and financial politics is articulated by the center–periphery cleavage. In centralized countries, in contrast, small banks, small firms, and local districts cannot seriously rely on local governments to champion their interests with the lawmakers. Instead, the regulatory debate is likely to focus mainly on the relative importance of state and center banks, with small business supporting the establishment of state-funded credit agencies against the opposition of large private (or nationalized yet run like private) banks. Such state agencies were called "special credit banks," with the word "special" standing for "sectoral."

The theoretical apparatus presented so far documents the former cleavage, but says little about the latter and its policy offspring – the state banks. This limitation will force us to leave aside an important aspect of banking history: the rise of state banks during the period 1914–59 and their collapse afterward. What accounts for the timing of their rise and fall? I have argued elsewhere that the class polarization of party systems in most countries empowered groupings such as farmers and small business with no strong allegiance to labor or capital.[13] Governments, mostly those in centralized states, typically responded to this redistribution of power by chartering special credit banks. The dilution of the class cleavage in the postwar era eventually undermined the electoral power of these middling groups, with the result that most of the special banks were dismantled and privatized. I have decided to leave such considerations out of the present volume, for reasons of analytical tractability and, above all, testability. This is why the present volume focuses on the two golden periods of financial market expansion – 1850–1913 and 1960–present, skipping the years that fall in between.

The core–periphery model of the financial sector

The present argument holds two propositions, one political and one economic. The political proposition posits a bivariate relationship between state decentralization and information asymmetry; this relationship is straightforward and requires no special modeling. The economic proposition says that high information asymmetry protects local banking whereas low information asymmetry causes a relocation of the financial sector to the center. The relationship is multivariate and causally complex. It is also counterintuitive, for, if finance concentrates in the center, ceteris paribus the return to capital will drop in the center and increase in the periphery, causing capital to return to the periphery (or not to leave it in the first place). Only a formal model can help us sort out the two effects and provide the conditions under which one prevails over the other. I use the core–periphery model developed by Fujita, Krugman, and Venables (1999, ch. 5), modified to take into account the specific traits of the financial sector. Below, I present the basic assumptions of the model, discuss its relevant features, and summarize the results. The reader will find the full presentation, along with formalization and simulation, in appendix 1.

The model has two regions, which, in equilibrium, may either be symmetric or differentiated into core and periphery. In each region there are

[13] Verdier 2000.

two sectors, a financial sector and a manufacturing sector. The financial sector displays the two ingredients of economies of agglomeration: scale economies (the average cost of production decreases as the quantity produced increases) and circularity (in addition to capital, the sector uses part of the financial goods it produces). The financial sector produces a variety of differentiated financial goods, which are purchased by consumers, firms active in the financial sector, and firms in the manufacturing sector. The manufacturing sector uses a mix of financial inputs and a variety of fixed factors, which I refer to as labor. Without loss of generality, manufacturing is assumed to be constant-scale and its products homogeneous. The manufacturing sector sells only to consumers (a simplification with no bearing on the results). Consumers are merely the two factors that were already introduced, capital and labor. As indicated, they consume two types of goods, financial and manufacturing, spending the income they draw from their respective sector of employment. Both in fixed supply, capital and labor differ in one important respect: capital can flow freely between the two regions, whereas labor is region-bound.[14] Last, the two regions together form a national economy and no tariff hampers the circulation of either financial or manufacturing goods. Nevertheless, financial transactions incur a cost, as bankers and financiers need to gather information about investors. This cost varies between a nominal amount (it is never zero) and an infinite one, reflecting the degree of decentralization of the state.

The model enacts the tension between the centrifugal and centripetal forces at play in the financial sector. On the one hand, keeping finance at the periphery is the fact that two categories of its consumers, labor and manufacturing firms, are fixed; were capital to concentrate in one region, the financial sector would incur an information cost on the sale of its products to half the national pool of manufacturing and labor in a two-region economy, more in an n-region economy. On the other hand, pulling finance to the center is the lure of lower production costs.

The model yields the expected outcome. At sufficiently high levels of information costs, there is a unique stable equilibrium in which finance is evenly divided between the two regions. When information costs fall below some critical value, the symmetric equilibrium breaks down. A new stable equilibrium emerges, in which all finance is concentrated in

---

[14] To reiterate the point made in n. 10, I take advantage of the fact that, under autarky and no-growth assumptions, a high level of information asymmetry is sufficient to deter capital from leaving the periphery. Although these assumptions do not hold in reality, they are simplifications of no consequence to the results of the model. Information asymmetry and regulatory protection systematically covary, since both are (inversely) determined by the state centralization variable.

one region. A drop in information costs tilts the scales in favor of the region with the higher initial capital endowment. The model also unambiguously shows the redistributive effect of financial agglomeration on the fixed factors: labor at the center is better off, while labor at the periphery is worse off. The model finally shows that geographic concentration is more likely to occur when the relative demand for financial goods by consumers, industry, and the financial sector itself is greater. Concentration also takes place for a wider range of information symmetry values if financial firms have firm control over their markets or enjoy greater scale economies.

Fujita, Krugman, and Venables have shown that the main conclusions of the core–periphery model are robust to a variety of specifications. I show in appendix 1 that the present specification, which is notable for its built-in asymmetry between the two sectors (finance sells to manufacture, but manufacture does not sell to finance), is further evidence of that robustness.

Summary of the argument

I shall recapitulate the argument of the present and preceding chapters. From chapter 1, I incorporated the idea that information asymmetry creates a pecking order among borrowers, with large ones enjoying access to markets and competitive bank rates, and small ones left to enter into a long-term relationship with their local banker. In this chapter, I proposed to make information asymmetry an endogenous variable. Although information asymmetry provides local banks with a raison d'être, such banks, by monopolizing local banking, contribute to an increase in the information gap between peripheral firms and center banks. Local banks are able to establish a monopoly on local banking when they can rely on the support of powerful local governments. State decentralization does two things for local banks. First, it provides them with a relatively coherent local political economy, one in which their omnipresent role allows them to build information networks shutting out outsiders. Second, local governments together have a common interest in ensuring that minimal regulatory measures exist to place local capital out of reach of the center banks. In contrast, centralization leaves local banks without a significant information advantage over center banks and without a regulatory lifesaver, causing the banking system to concentrate in the center. Many of the financial regulatory issues that have agitated financial systems during the past century and a half are reducible to a competition for market share between center and periphery. The rest of this chapter previews the upcoming chapters.

Preview of upcoming chapters

Our story begins in the middle of the nineteenth century. The rise in individual savings, afforded by the spread of wealth associated with industrialization, caused a revolution in the short-term segment of the money market. Bankers started to use savings to open lines of credit to firms. Coupled with the right given to banks to incorporate and open branches countrywide, this innovation gave the largest banks the capacity to create a vast internal payments system involving no actual transfer of money, only bookkeeping entries. This technology threatened to displace the local banks. The regulatory debate concentrated upon the right of center banks to open branches outside their districts of origin and on the right of the savings banks to match these innovations. The outcome of this tension is studied in chapter 3. That chapter provides systematic evidence for the relationship between state centralization and banking agglomeration.

The elimination of currency risk, made possible by the generalization of the gold standard, led to the internationalization of the money and bond markets. Internationalization created lending and placement opportunities for the largest center banks at the expense of local banks. Financial internationalization reinforced the core–periphery pattern in centralized countries; it remained limited in decentralized countries. Financial internationalization is addressed in chapter 4. That chapter provides systematic evidence for the relationship between state centralization and financial internationalization.

The extension to private firms of the right to incorporate caused a growth in corporate securities markets, thanks to which firms could repay bank loans by issuing securities. Like branch banking and internationalization, securitization favored the largest banks and borrowers at the expense of other interests, triggering opposition to the unencumbered development of corporate securities markets in the form of taxation and anti-speculation legislation. The origins of stock markets are studied in chapter 5. This chapter provides systematic evidence for the relationship between state centralization and stock market development.

The degree of specialization of banks was a function of the size of the financial center and thus of the degree of centralization of the state. Concentration favored specialization, fragmentation, universal banking. The relationship between state centralization and bank specialization was not linear, though. A complicating factor was the long-term instability of universal banking. Governments generally helped banks remain liquid during crises by creating lenders of last resort in the form of a permanent rediscounting window at the central bank. Although this reform made universal banking practicable in countries where markets were too fragmented to justify specialization, the timing of its adoption reflected state centralization. Therefore, the relation between state centralization and universal banking was non-linear. Universal banking was most likely to emerge in states that were neither so centralized that center banks displaced local banks, nor so decentralized that there was no central bank. The origins of universal banking form the subject of chapter 6, concluding part II. That chapter provides systematic evidence of the non-linear relationship between state centralization and specialization.

It is worth repeating that these four empirical chapters deal with the expansion of the financial market. World War I and its aftermath led to the unraveling of half a century of financial innovation. The war curtailed internationalization, destabilized currencies, and forced central banks to retract prewar liquidity commitments to their own banking systems. The stock market crash of 1929 was the last straw. There then ensued the longest financial contraction in modern history, along with the return of the state to domains where markets had reigned supreme. State regulation provided small business with a new opportunity to reclaim the financial ground lost to large firms. Governments chartered state credit banks, specialized in the provision of medium- and long-term credit to small and medium-sized firms. This period is not covered in these pages, but has been addressed elsewhere.[15]

Starting with the 1960s, history began to repeat itself. Deregulation brought in its wake the four siblings of financial competition. The first was banking agglomeration. The money center banks regained the ground lost to state credit banks in the previous period. However, local banks – especially non-profit local banks – successfully resisted the onslaught in decentralized countries, where they were well entrenched to begin with, both in the market and the polity. Banking agglomeration in the second half of the twentieth century forms the subject of chapter 7. This chapter provides systematic evidence for the persistence of the relationship between state centralization and bank agglomeration.

The second manifestation of competition was internationalization, epitomized by the development of the Euromarkets. After emerging offshore, in the breach of Keynesian macromanagement, internationalization became a deliberate policy in the 1980s, which governments pursued to improve the efficiency of domestic financial systems. The global money market transformed the way banks did business – moving them away from intermediation toward market facilitation. It also transformed the way they financed their investments – away from deposits toward borrowing on the money market. After recalling recent political conflicts about

---

[15] See Verdier 1997 and 2000.

foreign bank entry, chapter 8 shows that decentralized countries exhibit a systematically lower level of financial internationalization.

The third trait of modern finance is the growth of securities markets. The deregulation of stock markets, the so-called Big Bangs, broke open the last barrier to the geographic concentration of finance, causing resistance in decentralized countries. Chapter 9 investigates the relation between securitization and state structures. The past relation still exists, but its visible effect is suppressed by a new relationship between centralization and state control of industry, inherited from the 1930s–1950s, with negative effects on market growth. This chapter brings to light the hidden relationship between state structure and the stock market.

Finally, chapter 10 raises the issue of the product mix adopted by banks. Banks, once again, enjoy the liberty to offer just about any financial service to anyone, including brokerage and insurance. Although many have interpreted these reforms as signaling the triumph of the universal model of banking, I make the counterargument that market competition will beget a new form of specialization between retail and investment banking. Although it is premature to submit this prediction to testing, I point to early signs that it may be happening. I also raise the issue of the role of institutional structures in shaping the product mix.

Part II

The first expansion (1850–1913)

The second half of the nineteenth century saw the advent of modern finance. This is when the first joint-stock banks, financed by deposits rather than equity alone, opened their vast and sumptuous offices in London, Paris, New York, and other financial centers (chapter 3). This is when the first true international market for capital, backed by the most stable fixed-exchange-rate system ever to exist – the gold standard – emerged (chapter 4). This is when corporate stock markets opened their doors to the masses of individual investors (chapter 5), and when financial sectors across the industrializing world began to feel the need for product specialization (chapter 6). Except for automated tellers and internet connections, what we know of the financial sector today was already in place by the beginning of the twentieth century.

3 The advent of deposit banking

> Compared to recent financial innovations, the rise of deposit banking systems in the nineteenth century was a veritable revolution.
>
> De Cecco 1987b, p. 1.

Modern banks were founded in the nineteenth century. Unlike Gerschenkron and, more generally, the Saint-Simonian approach to credit, which views the origins of these banks as a response to industrialization, I argue that these banks were the outgrowth of an innovation in the payments mechanism. It consisted in the gradual displacement of commercial paper, traded at a discount in a centrally located market, by drafts and deposits, offered by a handful of joint-stock banks, each running a countrywide network of branches. This transformation began in earnest in the 1820s in Britain, and in the 1860s on the continent, reaching its present format by 1900.

The rise of deposit banking signaled a rise in financial agglomeration, for it triggered a trend toward branch banking. Joint-stock banks headquartered in the center threatened to turn local banks into local branches. Deposit banking also meant a concentration of the banking sector, though not necessarily the financial sector as a whole, as the consecutive expansion of the market spawned new functional specialization in the areas of issuing, brokerage, market making, and so forth. Branch banking did not develop uniformly across countries. Branch banking met the political opposition of local banks. In decentralized countries, local governments used their political power to stem branching, restrict deposit banking to the local economy, and stem the flight of local savings to the center. Only in centralized countries did branch banking enjoy a free run.

I first sketch the situation of the deposit market by mid-century. I present the rise of deposit banking, the ensuing liquidity problem faced by for-profit banks, and their market response in the form of consolidation and branch banking, teeing off a regulatory dispute between banking sectors. I then argue and show that the regulatory dispute was won by local banks in decentralized countries, but by center banks in centralized countries.

Prior to checking accounts

By the 1820s in Britain, the 1830s in Belgium, and mid-century for the rest, the market for individual deposits was still divided into current accounts, supplied by private banks, and savings accounts, offered by savings banks. Current accounts were held by traders, shippers, and all businesses involved in the exchange of goods and services. They were designed to facilitate commerce, credited whenever the client discounted a bill of exchange, debited whenever he settled a debt due on a previous purchase. In contrast, the market for individual savings was controlled by savings banks. Savings accounts were opened by individuals, not businesses, and were always creditor – they could not be used to borrow money. The two deposit markets were separate, except in the case of princes and principates, monarchs and governments, and wealthy private persons, who already deposited their wealth with the *haute banque*.[1]

More will be said on current accounts in the next section. In this section, I concentrate on the savings banks. My main point is that savings banks enjoyed a stronger market position in decentralized than in centralized countries. The reason is that savings banks were regulated by the central government in centralized polities but by local governments in decentralized polities. Moreover, central government regulation was less conducive to the expansion of the savings banks than local government regulation.

Initially, savings banks were non-profit organizations, created in the early 1800s by philanthropic individuals and local municipalities to instill the saving habit among the urban poor. Savings banks invested their customers' savings in mortgages and safe government paper. Soon, however, the breakout – or sheer anticipation – of crises raised the question of government supervision. The nature of the answer reflected state structures. In centralized countries, such as Britain, France, and Belgium, the solution to the savings banks crisis came from the center. In Britain, the 1817 statute provided for the mandatory deposit of all savings banks' resources in an account with the Bank of England.[2] In France and Belgium, the savings banks first spontaneously invested all their deposits in *rentes sur l'Etat*. This initial solution proved illusory when this asset began to depreciate. Anticipating the reversal, the Caisse d'épargne de Paris petitioned and obtained the right in 1829 to redeposit all its

---

[1] See Gille 1965.   [2] See Horne 1947 and Moss 1997.

resources in a current account earning a fixed rate of interest with the Royal Treasury.[3] The Belgian solution was more radical: the failed savings banks were allowed to be taken over or displaced by the two largest joint-stock banks.[4]

State custody was not favorable to the long-term expansion of the savings banks. State officials in Britain and France harbored mixed feelings: they benefited from managing the savings banks' ample resources but had little control over their operating costs. Support existed at the ideological level – succor the poor, combat poverty. But that aura of charity, which was duly invoked by the central government whenever a new statute regulating the savings sector was adopted, in the end worked against the savings banks. It prevented them from becoming the bank of the rising middle class. The British and French governments chose to contain rather than promote the development of savings banks, reducing the interest rates that these banks could pay to their depositors and capping the amount of each account.

Similar financial setbacks in decentralized countries drew the opposite response. In Germany, Italy, and Switzerland, among others, the savings banks were rescued by, and became the *chasses gardées* of, fiscally strained local governments. The banks invested their profits in local government projects, and their resources (individuals' deposits) in mortgages (local land).[5] In some areas, they also held communal bonds among their assets. This was current practice in Italy and Prussia in the early part of the century.[6] In Geneva, the cantonal Caisse d'Epargne held more city bonds than state bonds until 1873.[7] In Austria, the savings banks were allowed to make short-term loans to towns.[8] In the United States, in Massachusetts and Maryland, savings banks were prohibited from investing in bonds of other states.[9] In Denmark, until the end of absolutist rule in 1848, the savings banks were forced to place their deposits at interest in the treasury; the following liberal governments discontinued the practice, and savings resources thereafter were mainly invested in mortgages.[10]

---

[3] On French savings banks, see Passion 1991, p. 102, and Vogler 1991a. Located further away from the center than the Paris savings bank, the Caisse des Bouches-du-Rhône voiced its opposition to the centralization; see Americi 1997, p. 105.

[4] On Belgian savings banks, see Chlepner 1926, p. 96. Witte writes that "dans les petites villes, les Caisses, en concurrence avec les banques, avaient du fermer leurs portes" ("in small towns, the savings banks that were competing with deposit banks were forced to shut down"; 1991, p. 174).

[5] Cahill (1913, p. 75) reports that in 1911 German savings banks still invested about 60 percent of their deposits in mortgage loans.

[6] On Italy, see Polsi 1993, pp. 234, 249; on Prussia, Thomes 1995, p. 151.

[7] On Swiss savings banks, see Hiler 1993, p. 188.

[8] On Austro-Hungarian savings banks, see Albrecht 1990, p. 77.

[9] See Vittas 1997, p. 150.   [10] See S. A. Hansen 1982, 590.

Municipalities proved better custodians of the long-term interest of the savings banks in decentralized countries than did the state in centralized countries. For local municipalities, the welfare of the local economy mattered more than that of the poorer classes. Local governments supported the savings banks' administrators when these sought to extend their activities. Although in many cases the local imperative clashed with the central regulator's ideological wishes, the decentralized nature of the regime ensured that local wishes in the end prevailed over those of the central government.[11]

Spain is an intermediate case. Yearning for centralization, the Spanish government in 1853 attempted to centralize savings banks' resources in a French-like central caisse. The attempt miscarried, triggering a run on the savings banks by savers loath to have their money buy Madrid government debt.[12] The Netherlands is a case sui generis, in which a centralized state coexisted with a large local savings sector. The probable explanation, building on Jonker's (1996b) work, lies in the dominance of the money market, which was too centralized to serve the needs of the periphery (yet sufficiently decentralized, as we shall see, to crowd out branch banking).

Australasian savings banks, initially modeled after the British trustee banks, over time became state savings banks in New South Wales, Victoria, and South Australia, while remaining independent in other dominions. With the creation of the Australian federation in 1901 among six of the seven dominions (New Zealand did not join) these savings banks ipso facto became local, non-profit banks.[13] The Canadian experience, in contrast, paralleled the British and French cases. The profit sector quickly outstaged the trustee banks, whereas the government savings banks, which the federal government inherited in 1867 from the four founding provinces, were run like the postal savings system, dispensing cash and patronage to the government.[14] It is important not to forget that Canada initially began as a rather centralized state. Only over time did the confederal structure accommodate regional diversity.

In sum, even though savings banks started off as a local endeavor to succor the poor, by 1850 the local logic had dethroned the class logic in decentralized countries. Only in centralized countries did the philanthropic motive retain pride of place, albeit as a convenient justification for the central treasury's lack of ambition for local savings banks. Central treasuries

[11] For an Austrian instance of continual tension between center and periphery on the regulation of savings banks, see Albrecht 1990.
[12] On Spanish savings banks, see Titos Martinez 1995, p. 108.
[13] On Australia, see Wallace 1964.
[14] On Canadian savings banks, see Stewart Patterson 1932 and Bunbury 1997.

were universally wary of extending their guarantee to deposits collected by organisms over which they had little managerial control. Therefore, local governments controlled the local non-profit segment in decentralized countries, but were excluded from it in centralized countries.

The rise of branch banking

The neat separation between the current account and savings markets was breached by a change in the payments system – the substitution of the check and the wire transfer for the bill market.

Besides establishing a common unit of payments, the payments system plays an additional role, at least in advanced economies – that of shifting liquidity from those who have a surplus of it to those who feel a need for it. This role was met by the "money market." The most developed instance of a money market until the eighteenth century was the market for international acceptances. A London importer would pay a foreign exporter with a letter of credit written by his London bank promising payment in ninety days. The exporter would then cash the bill with his local bank, which would then send it to the London bank for acceptance. Once accepted the bill would become a means of payment which could be held as an investment, since it was earning a fee equivalent to an interest. It could also be sold in the open market as a source of funds, since the banker's acceptance made it as good as cash. When the draft matured, the importer or, in case of default, the accepting bank itself would be responsible for paying the holder of the acceptance. The domestic version of the acceptance, the domestic bill of exchange, followed similar rules.[15] The system could work with or without a central bank; a central bank would merely offer a liquidity guarantee in the form of a rediscounting window at which any bill at any time could be exchanged for cash at a rate fixed by the central bank.

In the course of the nineteenth century, the bill was dethroned by the deposit-cum-overdraft as principal instrument of the money market. The system builds on a simple principle – a firm has a current account with a bank, earning interest whenever the account is in credit, paying an interest whenever the account is in debit. Although the principle is as old as money-lending and was practiced by all banks before the eighteenth

---

[15] Although they were the most common money-market instruments in trading countries, the acceptance and domestic bill of exchange were not the only such instruments available. In the Netherlands during the nineteenth century, the dominant instrument was the *prolongatie*, a month advance against a security (public debt or the stock of a chartered company); see Jonker 1996b. In the postbellum United States, it was the promissory note, a bill without bank endorsement; see James 1978.

century, it was reinvigorated by three related innovations – the joint-stock bank, the branch-bank network, and the individual deposit. A joint-stock bank is a company whose ownership is divisible into shares that are tradable and do not engage the responsibility of their holders beyond the value of the share. It is different from the private bank, whose partners are fully liable on their private assets for an eventual failure. The decisive difference between the two forms of ownership is size; bound by family and personal bonds in the private bank, size is unlimited in the joint-stock bank.

Its capacity for expansion made the joint-stock bank the appropriate vehicle for the second innovation, branch banking, that is, the opening of branches nationwide. The opposite of the branch bank is the unit (single agency) bank. The opening of branches in every town was motivated by the desire to capture the savings of the population in the form of individual deposit accounts – the third innovation. Deposit collection allowed for an even greater size, since a 1-to-5 equity–deposit ratio, say, would allow the bank to be five times as large as its shareholders' investment. The combination of these three innovations resulted in the center bank, that is, a bank financing its investments mostly with individual deposits drawn from all corners of the nation.

Deposit banking grew in part by substituting itself for existing payments mechanisms. Deposit banking took market share away from banknotes and coins, as checks and wire transfers reduced the amount of cash kept on hand for payments purposes. It also cut into the bill market, as banks no longer needed to rely on rediscounting to maintain adequate liquidity. The check and giro[16] facilities afforded by branch-owning banks lessened the need for bills of exchange – albeit bills remained popular with traders, as it provided them with trade credit.[17]

Deposit banking brought within the payments system and the money market three segments of the economy – the periphery, industry, and the middle class – until then excluded. I consider the periphery first. The eighteenth-century bill market was centrally located in Amsterdam, London, Paris, and other capitals. Central location reflected the economies of scale that are inherent to the functioning of any market – volume brought liquidity, and liquidity attracted more business. But central

[16] A girosystem is a central clearing system for wire transfers. Germany and Italy were "wire transfer [giro] countries"; Britain, France, and the United States were "check countries."

[17] For Britain, see Powell 1966, pp. 310–18, and Cottrell 1980, p. 200; for France, see Bouvier 1968, p. 157. Facilitating the spread of the check was that, unlike a bill of exchange, it implied no bank credit to the drawer, and thus could be extended to individuals with no credit history. If drawn on a reputable house, however, it functioned like a bill, being endorsable by as many signatures as hands it passed through.

location also was a source of discrimination against business located on the periphery, for which credit information was more difficult to obtain. Anecdotal evidence of an information gap between center and periphery abounds. For instance, the success met by the country branches of the Banque de France, when it was forced by the government in the first half of the nineteenth century to extend its branch network to the countryside, attests to the limits of the bill market mechanism at integrating the periphery into the money market.[18] Only the British and Dutch money markets may be considered as having been able to overcome this problem. In Britain, scriveners and bill brokers were so efficient at connecting peripheral markets with London that country banks in Lancashire could not get a foothold until the nineteenth century.[19] The same was true of the Netherlands, where even the wide branch network operated by the central bank itself could not compete with the Amsterdam money market. The latter, according to Jonker, also went nationwide through the mediation of local brokers.[20] In most other countries, however, the countryside was left out of the money market until the advent of branch banking.

The second sector to be included in the payments system thanks to branch banking was industry, then on the rise. Manufacturing had a slower inventory turnover than did trade and thus required a type of financing that was not strictly dependent on the shipping of goods to purchasers. The solution took the form of the overdraft. The overdraft was an advance that the bank financed through deposits and that it could thus renew at its own discretion, without having to obtain the sanction of a third party, as was the case with rediscounted bills of exchange.

The third and probably most important group to be included was the middle classes. As the benefits of industrialization began to penetrate deeper into the middle strata, the demand for deposit accounts, both short and long, grew.[21] Risk-averse and uninformed, these new strata at first took their newly earned savings to the savings banks.[22] Deposits in savings banks grew so much, however, that it became conceivable for private bankers to finance investment by tapping the vast store of popular savings. The appropriate vehicle for this strategy was the joint-stock bank, offering deposit and savings accounts to individuals with whom the bank had no

---

[18] See Plessis 1985, p. 158, and Nishimura 1995. The Bank of England's branch network, however, met no such success because it occurred too late, long after the country banks spread the use of check banking in the countryside as an alternative to bill discounting; see Sayers 1976, vol. I, p. 2 and Ziegler 1990.

[19] On Lancashire, see Ashton 1945 and Neal 1994, p. 168.

[20] Jonker 1996b, pp. 105, 183.   [21] See Wysocki 1997, p. 22.

[22] Consult the contributions to Brück et al. 1995.

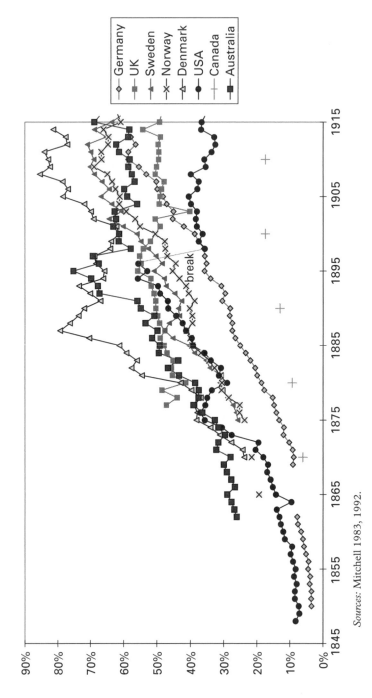

Sources: Mitchell 1983, 1992.

Figure 3.1. Commercial and savings bank deposits weighted by GDP, 1850–1915

previous or other dealings. For-profit banks also saw in deposit taking a way of improving profitability. Depositors typically earned less than bank shareholders; by increasing the share of deposits relative to capital, banks could increase earning on capital. Joint-stock banking effectively brought savings deposits into the payments system, from which they had been previously excluded. Savings banks, the only option available until then, instead, invested deposits in long-term placements such as mortgages and public debt.

The change to which I am referring occurred in a short period. With the exception of North America, in which joint-stock banking was liberalized from the outset in the United States and 1821 in Canada, and the isolated case in Europe of Scottish banks, joint-stock banking was an event of the middle of the nineteenth century. Joint-stock banks first flourished in England and Wales after the passage of legislation permitting joint-stock banking beyond a 65-mile radius of London from 1826 until 1833, and anywhere thereafter. Limited responsibility was granted in 1855. The belatedness of the liberalization owed to the opposition of the Bank of England, which, being the only joint-stock bank in the realm, easily dominated note issuing in England and Wales. Under Peel, the British government granted a de jure monopoly of note issuance to the Bank of England, while allowing other banks to be formed on a joint-stock basis. A parallel evolution occurred on the continent, charters being granted by governments sparingly before 1852 (the Belgian Société Générale and Banque de Belgique in 1822 and 1835 respectively, the Swedish Enskilda banks from 1824 on, Spanish banks in the 1840s). Joint-stock banking was liberalized after 1852, the founding date of the French Crédit Mobilier, which spawned dozens of imitations throughout the continent. It became free sometime after 1860 (1863 in France and Italy, 1864 in Sweden, 1869 in Spain, 1870 in Germany, 1881 in Switzerland). In countries without a note-issuing monopoly, the thus-chartered joint-stock banks were given the right to issue notes as well as collect deposits.[23]

Available data on deposits, albeit quite imperfect, give an indication of the timing of the described change. Figure 3.1 visualizes the importance of bank deposits (commercial and savings) relative to GDP for the countries for which available time-series extend far enough back. Deposits evolved exponentially, starting in the 1850s and tapering off in 1895.

---

[23] That is, prior to 1844 in Britain, 1848 in Belgium, 1864 in the United States, 1865 in Spain, 1893 in Italy, 1904 in Sweden, and prior to World War I in Canada, Australia, and New Zealand. Although Switzerland had no note-issuing central bank until 1905, this right was reserved for the *Kantonal* banks, non-profit banks run by the government of each canton.

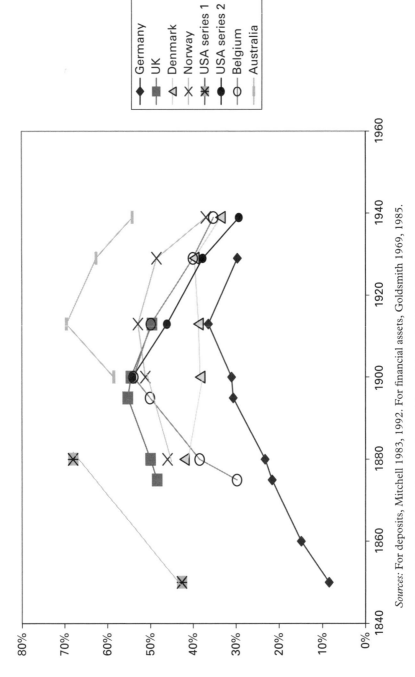

Legend:
- Germany
- UK
- Denmark
- Norway
- USA series 1
- USA series 2
- Belgium
- Australia

Sources: For deposits, Mitchell 1983, 1992. For financial assets, Goldsmith 1969, 1985.

Figure 3.2. Bank deposits as a share of financial assets, 1840–1940

Figure 3.2 shows their growing importance relative to total financial assets for benchmark years. Deposits became the dominant financial asset in the United States, the UK, and Belgium by the turn of the century, and Australia, Norway, and Germany by World War I (the Danish series seems anomalous). In the words of Marcello de Cecco, excerpted at the head of this chapter, the rise of deposit banking was a "veritable revolution."

The liquidity crunch and the demand for short assets

Deposit banking had one potential flaw – it created a liquidity problem for the banks. More specifically, bank assets were becoming less liquid than bank liabilities. Deposits were essentially short-term assets. Although banks tried to lengthen the maturity of deposits by creating term deposits, according to which early withdrawals carried penalties, they could never prevent depositors confronted with the danger of a bank run from cashing their savings rather than facing the risk of losing them all. Furthermore, unlike stockholders, depositors had no insider information on the good management and solvency of banks. They could neither monitor the management nor draw a reliable assessment of banks' solvency. They relied instead on rumor, with the result that banks were subject to "sunspot" panics. Depositors would run to cash in their deposits for no reason other than the mutual fear of being the victim of other depositors' fear of runs. A run on a bank would trigger a run on other banks if it were believed that the collapse of the first bank would weaken the liquidity of the others, as was often the case.[24]

The liquidity problem was compounded by the gradual supplanting of the bill of exchange by overdrafts. Overdrafts were better remunerated than bills, but they were easily renewed, and thus less liquid. Unlike bills, moreover, advances could not be cashed in at the rediscounting window of the central bank.

Relying on more volatile resources (deposits) to finance less liquid assets (overdrafts), banks were caught in a liquidity squeeze. They became aware of it in the wake of a string of banking crises, during which deposits were withdrawn in exchange for coins and central banknotes. Collins (1991) notes that after each crisis in England and Wales, the most severe being the crash of the City of Glasgow Bank in 1878, the banks tended to maintain a higher proportion of very liquid assets.[25] Bouvier (1968) notes that the crash of 1882 in France ended up disqualifying loans to industry

---

[24] The liquidity problems arising from the greater importance taken by deposits in banks resources are underscored in Lamoreaux (1994, p. 107).

[25] Collins 1991, p. 41. An account of the most important crises can be found in Powell 1966, chs. 11–14.

in the eyes of Henri Germain, the director of the Crédit Lyonnais.[26] In Germany, the downswing of 1873–79 led banks to avoid direct share-holdings in firms.[27] In Australia, the 1890s financial crisis led to a de facto separation between commercial and investment banking.[28]

The standard response to a liquidity crisis was for banks to move to a form of banking that was safer. This could be achieved in four ways: first, through standardization – the development of standard lending pro-cedures and thus more interchangeable and negotiable instruments; sec-ond, through internationalization – mostly the development of sovereign lending, a form of lending presenting little risk; third, through securitiza-tion – the promotion of the corporate securities market as a place where banks could transform long-term loans to industry into securities, recoup liquidity, and thus increase asset turnover; fourth, through central bank-ing and the establishment of a lender of last resort. Internationalization, securitization, and central banking will be dealt in chapters 4, 5, and 6 respectively. I focus here on standardization, by far the most important of the four. I proceed to the study of standardization while holding constant internationalization, central banking, and securitization, postponing to later chapters the discussion of how they all fit together.

Banks could mitigate the risk of illiquidity by developing interchange-able and negotiable instruments. They could more easily achieve asset standardization in short-term lending than in long-term lending. Stan-dardization thus amounted to shortening the maturity of most assets. Commercial banks would abandon their initial universality, specializing instead in short-term lending.[29] Short, standardized assets could be used as secondary forms of liquidity, readily disposable in periods of crisis.

But standardized assets had two drawbacks. First, they yielded lower profits. Second, safe paper was hard to find, especially now that overdrafts were displacing trade bills.[30] In London, Paris, Milan, and Berlin, bankers complained about a persistent shortage of "good" paper, increasingly limited to international acceptances, that is, to bills generated by the settlement of international trade.[31] The important role played by good paper in the smooth functioning of the monetary market placed these international centers in competition for the naturalization of the market

---

[26] Bouvier 1968, p. 221. See also Lévy-Leboyer 1976, p. 462.
[27] Edwards and Ogilvie 1996, 429.   [28] Merrett 1997, 182.
[29] On the shortening of bank assets, see Bouvier 1968, p. 162, and Lamoreaux 1994, p. 89.
[30] Only the best trade bills would serve this purpose. Letters of accommodation, a lower-grade paper that a banker would draw on a client to liquidate an advance, which the banker would renew immediately, did not qualify. Such letters could be safely financed with capital only, not deposits.
[31] On the shortage of "good" paper, see Conti 1993, 311; Polsi 1996, 127; Riesser 1977, p. 306.

for acceptances. The Deutsche Bank was organized in 1870 by a group of private bankers to capture a greater share of the foreign short-term credit and payments business.[32] The Federal Reserve was established to develop a market for acceptances in New York.[33] This shortage was also responsible for the revival of competition, noted in several countries, between the central bank and the deposit banks.[34] In France and Britain, the central bank began to discount local banks' paper. In the Netherlands, the non-profit *Kredietvernigingen* (mutual credit societies servicing small business) became the central bank's most loyal customers.[35]

Standardization and the consequent higher demand for good paper brought in its wake two related profit-making strategies – amalgamation and agglomeration. Both aimed at relieving the need for good paper through greater productivity and higher volume. Amalgamation allowed banks to take advantage of the internal scale economies released by the move toward standardization. It is important to note that no such economies of scale existed during the first half of the century, when banking was still a matter of personal connections and when profits sanctioned investments in high-yield, low-volume loans to local industries. It is only after banks had been forced to abandon their long-term positions in local firms and to compensate for low yield through high volume that amalgamation became a profitable strategy. Amalgamation reduced bank capital requirements, improving earning potential. Amalgamation also allowed merging banks to rationalize their asset portfolios, taking over the best paper held by their competitors and liquidating less desirable items.[36]

Amalgamation naturally led to agglomeration – the relocation of bank headquarters in financial centers.[37] Central location gave the joint-stock banks an edge over the local banks, by enabling them to develop new lines of business, from which local banks were excluded. Thanks to their central location, they could handle acceptances and extend call loans to the stock exchange against the collateral of securities. Central location also gave the largest among them access to underwriting syndicates of safe government and railroad bonds. The chairman of a large Irish deposit bank explained to the bank's proprietors in 1915: "[W]e admit that we get money on deposit in Ireland, but we make money in London."[38]

---

[32] On the founding of the Deutsche Bank, see Tilly 1991, p. 93.
[33] On the founding of the Fed, see Broz 1997.
[34] On France, see Nishimura 1995 and also Bouvier 1973, p. 160, and Lescure 1995, p. 318. On Britain, see de Cecco 1974, p. 101, and Ziegler 1990, p. 135. On Belgium, see Kauch 1950, pp. 235, 260. On Italy, see Hertner 1999, p. 196.
[35] According to Jonker 1996a.   [36] See, for instance, Lamoreaux 1994, p. 144.
[37] See Bouvier 1968. See also Cameron 1991, pp. 14–16.
[38] Cited in Ollerenshaw 1997, p. 60. Centralization also led to internationalization – the topic of the next chapter.

Access to the center allowed the banks to offer their clientele of investors instruments that were more diverse and that generated higher returns than local banks could. Thanks to their geographic ubiquity, they could use the excess deposits of agrarian districts to discount excess bills in industrial districts. In so doing, they could offer more generous interest rates on deposits in agrarian districts and more advantageous discounts in industrial districts than local banks could.[39] Their branch networks and membership in a clearing association also allowed them to offer efficient payment services to their clienteles throughout the country.

These new lines of business were safer than the investments available to local banks. Acceptances, call loans, and the discount of commercial paper were short-term, liquid investments, of the kind that matched the short-term maturity of the resources that they collected in the form of deposits. In contrast, local banks were excluded from these low-profit, thin-margin operations, but employed their funds in advances to local business. Although advances were better remunerated than discounts, they were also riskier, for they were usually sought by borrowers who had exhausted their access to discounts.

The redistributional effects of branch banking

The disappearance of country banks could only have negative implications for their local environment. It harmed borrowers, the small and medium-sized firms. Banking, until then, had relied on personal connections. Bankers borrowed from and lent to individuals whom they knew well, either because they lived in the same towns or because borrowers and bank shareholders were often the same people – a relation that Lamoreaux (1994) has appropriately dubbed "insider lending."[40] Country bankers also lent long. They were disposed to see the short-term credits granted to firms renewed and consolidated into de facto long-term advances should these firms experience temporary cash-flow problems or have a need for expansion or modernization. Physical presence and long-term relationships made for effective bank monitoring.

---

[39] See Saurel 1901, p. 100.

[40] Pressnell (1956, p. 322) emphasized the "mingling of business and banking" during the British industrial revolution. Cottrell (1992, p. 53) wrote: "Until the 1880s English country banks were products of the localities and regions that they served; customers and shareholders were frequently the same people. The bank's constituencies both owned the banks and did business with them. Directors and managers knew their customers well and with prudence and local knowledge were prepared to go beyond the bounds of short-term lending." Regional bank–industry relations in Sheffield in the middle of the nineteenth century are also examined by Newton (1996).

The trend toward agglomeration made local banking more difficult. Headquarters could not trust local branch directors to enforce the lending preferences of their bank and thus multiplied impersonal criteria.[41] Like French prefects, local agents were rotated for training and promotion purposes, but also to prevent local mores from eroding the bank's corporate culture. Their capacity to tap local information networks – trade suppliers, chambers of commerce – as a result was limited. Moreover, the trend toward amalgamation made monitoring through physical presence at board meetings impractical for small and medium-sized firms, for bankers were able to attend only so many board meetings in a year, preferably those of the largest companies. Further, the joint-stock banks would substitute impersonal relations between the banker and his client.[42] Finally, the liquidity crises experienced by banks made them less willing to immobilize their resources in industry.

A lesser capacity by banks to monitor firms compelled banks to refrain from lending to small and medium-sized firms. Unlike larger firms, small and local enterprises lacked the visibility that would allow them to rely on the equity market for external funding. The centralization of deposit banking threatened to thin the ranks of small and medium-sized firms.[43]

More generally, agglomeration in the center threatened to depress the industrial vitality of regions with a concentration of small and medium-sized firms. Recent research on flexible specialization points to the existence in nineteenth-century Europe of what Alfred Marshall called "industrial districts" – regional production systems, such as those found in Sheffield and Solingen (cutlery), Lyons (silk), Vaud and Neuchâtel (watch-making), and Bologna (metalworking), based exclusively on small and medium-sized firms.[44] Industrial districts were networks of small enterprises working together to serve differentiated and volatile international markets with quality, specialty products. Product flexibility disqualified internal scale economies, thriving instead on the external scale economies

---

[41] See Eugene Nelson White (1998, 21) on the opening of credit departments in US banks.

[42] As an English country banker put it in defense of his trade, "in the intercourse which subsists between a Banker and one of his customers, a degree of confidential honour is necessary, which is entirely inconsistent with the principle of a bank established on the joint stock basis" (cited in Cottrell and Newton 1999, p. 88).

[43] Capie and Collins (1997, p. 168) argue that the demise of local banking in Britain and the centralization of the "Big Five" banking conglomerates in the City, in close proximity to the markets, and far from the provinces, where domestic industry was largely based, contributed to Britain's investment problem. Deeg (1999, ch. 2) argues that in "regions where the Berlin banks had taken over provincial banks . . . [the Berlin banks] generally provided less credit to the *Mittelstand* than the provincial bank had done."

[44] Flexible specialization has attracted a good deal of attention among economic historians, among whom are Piore and Sabel 1984, Sabel and Zeitlin 1985, Herrigel 1996, Deeg 1992, and the contributions to Bagnasco and Sabel 1995 and to Sabel and Zeitlin 1997.

generated by the agglomeration of versatile, low-capitalized firms, spreading risk among one another. Firms in industrial districts used a skilled workforce and relied on local municipalities, guilds, and trade associations to supply them with the necessary externalities – vocational training, price and wage regulation, marketing facilities, quality normalization, and, more importantly to the present study, access to capital. Capital for industrial districts was provided by local banks – private and savings – and credit cooperatives.

All countries had, by 1850, a high density of industrial districts; large, vertically integrated production, serving mass markets, was still embryonic. The growth of the financial core under the two-pronged impact of bank amalgamation and agglomeration threatened to dry up one of the key inputs to production in industrial districts – access to capital. The foreseeable monopolizing of deposit taking by a handful of center-located banks, each at the head of a nationwide network of branch offices, threatened to drain individual savings from local districts and channel them instead into national and foreign government-backed paper. Changes in capital markets caused a tension between center and periphery. Local governments would find it harder to finance infrastructure projects by local investors, while the industrial vitality of regions with a concentration of small and medium-sized firms would be depressed.

Not all peripheral districts would necessarily suffer from the geographic concentration of capital markets. As I mentioned in an earlier chapter, those districts that accommodated firms that were large enough to tap equity markets would not necessarily be harmed by the decline of local, industrial banking. There is hardly any doubt that in an area like the Ruhr – the traditional stronghold of German coal, steel, and other heavy industries – the rise of large industry compensated for the decline in craft-oriented sectors. One would expect these districts and the firms to which they were home to espouse the cause of financial deregulation.

The disappearance of country banks in centralized countries

Local governments, wherever they enjoyed the power to do so, sought to block the penetration of the countryside by joint-stock banks. They had that power in only one country – the United States. The last joint-stock bank to be given the right to open branches in the United States was the Second Bank. In 1832, President Jackson staked his reelection bid on his veto of the bill rechartering the Bank. Legal restrictions prevented state-chartered banks from developing interstate branch networks. It was not until 1927 that the national banks, which had been chartered by the government since 1863, won the right to open branches in the community in which they were located on a par with state banks. Until recently, only private bankers could develop interstate networks of offices or partnerships.[45]

Local economies enjoyed no similar power in other countries. The consequence was the disappearance of country banks and the gradual concentration of for-profit commercial banking in the hands of a few joint-stock banks. They absorbed the country banks and began to attract individual deposits from the local non-profit sector. Evidence of this trend can be gleaned from qualitative country studies and a few countries for which we have data on country banks – Switzerland, Germany, the UK, and the USA (see figure 3.3).[46] Although these various time-series are not directly comparable (see note to figure 3.3), they indicate a swift process of consolidation outside the United States. Although local banks in many cases formed regional combines, buying them another decade of relative independence, the centralizing trend, however, was unmistakable. The country banks that managed to escape outright absorption were forced to acknowledge the pull of the center, often by becoming junior partners in an implicit alliance with a center bank.

The disappearance of the country banks accentuated the specialization of banking. Formerly, during the first half of the century (earlier in Britain), the wealthy banked with the center banks (mostly private then), the poor with the savings banks, and all the middling groups banked with the country banks. As the latter merged or were absorbed, their clienteles parted ways; the industrial sectors that were on the rise logically went to the center banks, whereas agrarians and small business fell back on the non-profit sector. For instance, in the case of Germany, Donaubauer (1988, pp. 206–09) found that, as country banks were taken over by *Kreditbanken*, the small industrial firms, which had raised external finance from country banks, turned to savings banks and credit cooperatives for funds. This fallback strategy on the part of small business, however, presumed the existence of a lively local non-profit sector ready to fill in for the fading country banks. I have already showed that there was no such thing anymore in politically centralized countries such as Britain, France, and Belgium. It existed only in decentralized countries, except in regions of large industry. Whether it would prove able to move into the segment

---

[45] Branching restrictions had negative consequences for the payments system in the short run. They forced the bilateral settlement of net imbalances between each pair of regional exchange centers and the resurgence of specie as an interregional means of payment. Following the National Banking Act, however, country banks held positive balances with New York banking correspondents. See Knodell 1998, 719, and James 1978.

[46] On the disappearance of the country banks in Britain, see Cottrell 1980, p. 194; for Germany, see Riesser 1977, 602ff., and Donaubauer 1988.

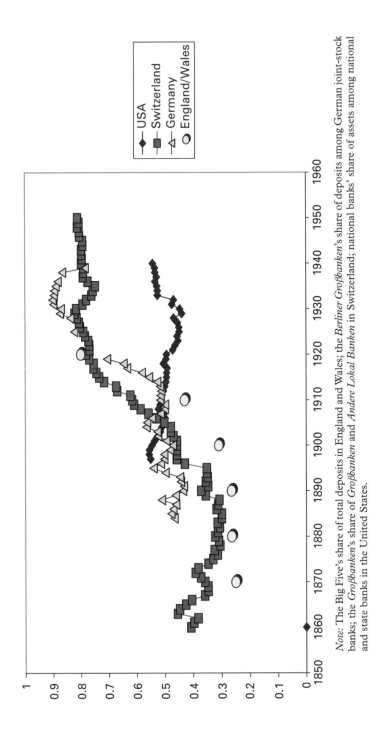

Note: The Big Five's share of total deposits in England and Wales; the *Berliner Großbanken*'s share of deposits among German joint-stock banks; the *Großbanken*'s share of *Großbanken* and *Andere Lokal Banken* in Switzerland; national banks' share of assets among national and state banks in the United States.

Sources: England and Wales: Capie and Rodrik-Bali 1982; Deutsche Bundesbank 1976, p. 16; Ritzmann 1973; Board of Governors of the Federal Reserve System 1959.

Figure 3.3. Center bank assets as a proportion of for-profit assets

vacated by country banks was still undecided. It would depend on the capacity of the local non-profit sector to convince legislators to let them move freely into commercial banking.

The rise of the local non-profit sector

In decentralized countries, local governments wished to preserve the deposit base of savings banks, which they more or less managed. Savings banks were useful on three counts: they were a well of resources, an important and reliable financier of local infrastructure projects, and, often, an investor in municipal bonds. In centralized countries, in contrast, the savings banks were of no use to local governments, investing all their funds in long-term government securities, either directly or via a state-run fund.[47]

European savings banks made no loans to local business, at least not until after 1900.[48] This role was performed by two other categories of institution – local-government-owned banks and independent credit cooperatives. I examine each category successively. Local government chartered their own banks in Switzerland. Each canton government in Switzerland created a fully owned *Kantonal* bank in response to electoral pressure from agrarians and members of the urban petite bourgeoisie voiced by the *Mouvement démocratique*.[49] Until the creation of the central bank in 1905, the cantonal banks financed their investments by issuing notes, a privilege denied to center banks. After 1905, when deposits became the exclusive source of funds, the cantonal banks still enjoyed inordinate advantages such as tax exemption and a local government guarantee on deposits. In exchange, the banks were expected to meet all reasonable local demands for credit and to lend below market rates.[50]

Most of the local credit banks were not public banks but independent cooperatives, set up by small groups of farmers, rural cottage industrialists, and urban craftsmen. These credit cooperatives would lend only to their members, based on the resources contributed by these members and bank loans contracted on the basis of collective liability. They

---

[47] With respect to France, Moster and Vogler (1996, p. 78) write that as a result of the investment policies pursued by the savings banks, "the department and municipalities were not encouraged to make any investments, which plunged France into a state of public infrastructure deficiency until 1945."

[48] The situation was quite different in the United States, notably New England, where the savings banks were important suppliers of long-term finance to the textile industry (see Lance Davis 1960, 9, and Vatter 1961, 216–17). Regulation varied across states.

[49] See Guex 1997, p. 338.

[50] Hartmann 1947, pp. 50, 53, and 56. See also Bänziger 1985.

were particularly active in Germany, where they acquired their own giro system, in competition with the savings banks' own, the Post Office's, and the Reichsbank's (the central bank). Mutual credit societies failed to develop in centralized countries. They were nonexistent in Britain. They were unsuccessful in France, where, like the savings banks almost a century earlier, the *banques populaires* fell under state regulation in 1917. Everywhere else, Italy in particular, credit cooperatives remained local institutions.[51]

Savings banks and credit cooperatives were complementary at first. Savings banks collected deposits and invested them primarily in mortgages, secondarily in public debt, whereas credit cooperatives lent capital to and borrowed money from their members.[52] The two institutions were often local monopolies. Their fates were linked; it was easier for a savings bank to deter a center bank from entering its local market if the market for local credit was already in the portfolio of a credit cooperative and vice versa. In some instances, savings banks and cooperatives collaborated with each other. In his study of Piacenza, Polsi found that their respective directors belonged to the same circle. They shared information. More significantly, Polsi found that the popular banks would take risks, extending one- to three-year loans, while the savings banks acted as lender of last resort, relying on the trust that local people had in them.[53]

By World War I, earlier in Scandinavia, later in Germany and Italy, the savings banks became full-fledged banks, performing standard commercial bank activities, such as operating current accounts, transfer and checking accounts, discounting bills and lending to business firms. Such lending was short at first, and long thereafter. Joint-stock banks would regularly denounce any extension of the sort as unfair in light of the tax and other privileges enjoyed by the savings banks. Such privileges, however, were regularly upheld by legislators and state regulators who were partial to the local non-profit banks, to their clientele of farmers and small business, and to local governments, which, in decentralized regimes, occupied a position of power. The resulting incapacity of branch

---

[51] On the French *banques populaires*, see Gueslin and Lescure 1995, p. 49, and Albert 1995. On the failure of mutual credit societies in Britain and Ireland, see Guinnane 1994 and 1995. For a general introduction, see Born 1983, pp. 110–14.

[52] Mortgage banks were usually not distinct from savings banks, at least not in decentralized countries, where the savings banks invested a majority of their assets in mortgages. It is only in countries where savings banks were prevented from investing in mortgages, in France, Britain, the United States, and the dominions, that the field was opened to specialized mortgage banks – private building societies in Britain, savings and loans associations in the United States, the state-owned Crédit Foncier in France.

[53] Polsi 1997. See also Conti and Ferri 1997.

banks in those countries to gain a toehold in peripheral economies made it unavoidable that savings banks would be left to fill in the gap in the provision of banking services.[54] In countries of Germanic background, savings banks created their respective clearing systems, first at the regional level, then at the national level, separate from the profit sector.[55] These clearing organizations gradually assumed the functions of savings banks' banks, through which locales with an excess of savings would lend to locales with a shortage. In this way, peripheries developed a vertically integrated credit network separate from, and parallel to, the commercial bank network (which was crowned by the central bank), with both networks equally present in the center and the periphery, although in reverse proportions.

In centralized countries joint-stock banks branched out nationwide and dominated the deposit market.[56] In decentralized countries, in contrast, center banks had a more limited territorial coverage. Either the law prevented them from opening branches to compete with savings banks, as was the case in Norway. Or, more simply, entry in the territory of local banks was too hazardous.[57] Instead, the center banked with the periphery through the mediation of correspondent banks. In the United States, correspondent banking was facilitated by the possibility, granted to smaller country banks under the 1864 legislation, of counting their deposits in large city banks as part of their reserves. But there was no central check-clearing system until 1913.[58] There was no bank-based giro system in Germany either. Bank concentration in Germany prior to World War I did not take the form of branch banking as in Britain or France, but of *Konzern* – communities of interest centered on the five Berlin *Kreditbanken*, sanctioned by the exchange of stock among members. *Konzern* were not created to collect deposits – few savings flowed into the banking system – but to keep up with the parallel cartelization of German industry.[59]

[54] On Denmark, see S. A. Hansen 1982, 583, 589. On Germany, see Feldman 1991, p. 69; Deeg 1992, pp. 73–79. On Austria-Hungary, see Michel 1976. On Sweden, see Nygren 1983, 33, 43–44. On Norway, see Nordvik 1993, 69; Egge 1983, 281.

[55] On savings bank clearing organizations, see, on Germany, Deeg 1992, pp. 69, 81, 84, and 94, and Guinnane 1997. On Austria-Hungary, see März 1984 and Michel 1976, p. 37. On various countries, see contributions to Brück et al. 1995, pp. 52, 101, 231, 282.

[56] On Britain, see Pressnell 1956, p. 285; Cottrell 1992; Horne 1947; Guinnane 1994. On France, see Bouvier 1968; Gueslin 1992; Gueslin and Lescure 1995. On Belgium, see Chlepner 1926. On the Netherlands, see Kymmel 1996. On Canada, see Drummond 1991a; Rudin 1990. On Australia, see Wotherspoon 1979; Wallace 1964.

[57] On Norway, see Egge 1983 and Lange 1994. On Austria-Hungary, see Michel 1976, pp. 30–43, Köver 1991, and Albrecht 1990, p. 79. On Denmark, see Per H. Hansen 1991 and S. A. Hansen 1982. On Sweden, see Nygren 1983. On Italy, see Polsi 1993, 1996.

[58] See James 1978.   [59] See Engberg 1981, pp. 45–53, and Riesser 1977, p. 664.

A new competitor: postal savings

The center banks were the most important, yet not sole, potential raider of local resources. A second predator was the state. The state could not pass up the opportunity to capture a segment of these new resources. Deposits were less costly to remunerate than the public debt, and collecting them would entail no fixed cost, for, thanks to its postal system, the state was already present everywhere in the country. Postal savings – a government piggybank piggybacking the post office network – along with the postal giro system, would provide this novel form of seignorage. Bunbury argues that the Canadian federal government used the government postal savings (along with the government savings banks) to finance the construction of the Canadian Pacific Railway.[60] Of course, creating a postal savings system would mean chartering a formidable competitor to the other credit sectors, especially the already existing savings banks. The British and French governments had no difficulty overruling the opposition of the savings banks: in 1861 in Britain, in 1883 in France.[61] The British savings banks never recovered from the blow.[62] The Belgian government too, upon the failure or near-failure in 1848 of the handful of joint-stock banks that had taken over the old savings banks in the 1830s, consolidated all savings banks into one state-owned agency – the Caisse Générale d'Epargne et de Retraite (CGER), founded in 1865.

However, Britain, France, and even Belgium were centralized states. No such overbearing posture could be easily assumed in less centralized countries. There, the savings banks controlled a larger segment of the existing market for savings, and, more importantly, they had the endorsement of the local governments, which, given the decentralized nature of the regime, enjoyed veto power over eventual postal savings legislation.[63] This is why central treasuries refrained from competing for local capital through postal savings in Denmark, Norway, and Switzerland, and did so with little success in Germany, Austria, Sweden, and Spain. Postal

---

[60] Bunbury 1997, 583.

[61] On France, see Duet 1991, p. 40. On Britain, see Horne 1947.

[62] The British savings banks' relative market share (in percentage of all bank assets) dropped from 13 percent in 1860 to 5 percent in 1913, while postal savings grew to representing 12 percent in the same period; life insurance policies are not included in this calculation. The source is Sheppard 1971. Vittas writes that the creation of postal savings in the UK and Ireland narrowed the scope of urban and rural credit cooperatives (1997, p. 172). Gueslin and Lescure (1995) argue that the non-profit sector in France suffered from the competition of the state sector.

[63] In the case of Germany, Deeg (1992, p. 81) reports that the savings banks joined together in defeating the proposal of the imperial government to establish a postal savings bank in 1878.

savings were nonexistent in Switzerland. The only decentralized state to fully exploit postal savings was Italy.[64]

Government savings took resources away from the country banks, which were already doing battle with the center banks. This was probably the case in Canada, where a surge in government savings during the 1880s had the probable effect, according to Bunbury (1997, 597), of exacerbating the decline of regional banks. The fact is that Canada was a rather centralized country at the time. Its southern neighbor, in contrast, was decentralized, with the effect that neither center banks nor postal savings were permitted to interfere with the country banks' (and savings banks') monopolistic capture of local deposits.

Nonetheless, the fight over postal savings was a sideshow in the larger confrontation between center and periphery. Indeed, the French, Belgian, and British savings banks had no great stakes in their respective local economies. Long since despoilt of the means and power to chart their own course, local governments in those countries were indifferent to the choice between private savings and postal savings.

Surely, postal savings and kindred schemes were also in competition with the rising center banks. Although initially justified as providing banking services for the poor, postal savings, like savings banks in an earlier age, soon became successful with the middle class. In most cases, however, the center banks refrained from open recrimination, probably because postal savings preceded branch banking. There was one exception to this, Canada, where the deposit market was from the outset dominated by the private chartered banks (the center banks). The Canadian government incurred their opprobrium in the 1880s, when it helped the postal savings (along with the government savings banks) boost their joint market share of deposits from 11 percent in 1880 to 25 percent in seven years.[65] Although the government determinedly braved the criticism of these banks throughout the 1880s, during the height of railway construction, it gradually gave in to their request of non-competition thereafter.

In sum, in decentralized countries, local and non-profit banking relied on the power of local governments to resist the competition from the joint-stock banks and postal savings. In centralized countries, in contrast, the latter crowded out the former. The evidence that I have so far provided is anecdotal and drawn from secondary sources. The next section contemplates the possibility of an exception – the French case – while the last offers systematic evidence.

---

[64] Note too that all Australasian governments, except that of South Australia, established postal savings before they joined the loosely centralized Australian Commonwealth, which waited for ten years to create a government competitor in 1913.

[65] Bunbury 1997.

A French exception?

The French case points to a paradox of state centralization. Centralization had two inconsistent effects. As elsewhere, it intensified the competition between center and local banks, accelerating the concentration of banking in the core. But in France, it apparently had offsetting effects as well, eliciting allies for and eliminating potential enemies to the country banks, and thus keeping these in business until a later date.

The first of these offsetting effects was the alliance between the Banque de France and the local banks.[66] The very success of the joint-stock banks in attracting deposits and good commercial paper threatened both the central bank and the local banks. Somehow, the two potential losers un-wittingly pulled resources together, the provincial banks making long-term advances to local business, and the central bank refinancing the provincial banks. The local banks generated lower-quality paper on aver-age because their main business was to open current accounts, which were mainly used for overdrafts. When these overdrafts reached threateningly illiquid proportions, the bank would draw a note on the borrower, sell it, repay itself, and renew the loan. Spurned by the large commercial banks, these "accommodation bills," as they were called, found their way into the local branch of the central bank, which, for lack of better business, would rediscount them. This *alliance contre-nature* between Napoleon's bank and the local banks was phased out after 1897, when the central bank ordered its local branches to directly source bills with large industrialists, thereby sidestepping the local private banks.

State centralization may have helped delay banking concentration in Paris in a second way. State centralization curbed the development of non-postal savings banks and mutual cooperatives, thereby eliminating an important rival to the local banks. The geographical dispersion of French industry sustained a local demand for loans that country banks alone were able to meet, provided, of course, that they could finance such loans short of illiquidity – by rediscounting accommodation bills until 1897, and by relying on their own funds and their captive clients' deposits afterward.

The actual extent to which these countering trends allowed local banks to survive is unknown. The consensus among French historians un-til a few decades ago was that the country banks entered a period of crisis at the turn of the century. Recent research suggests, however, that the date of the death of local banking in France must be post-poned to the banking crises of the 1930s. Many local banks imitated

---

[66] See Saurel 1901 and Nishimura 1995.

the Parisian banks by branching out, targeting individual deposits, and shortening their investments, thereby turning into regional deposit banks (for instance, the Crédit du Nord, Société nancéienne de crédit, Société marseillaise de crédit). They managed to survive the competition for liquidity from the local agencies of both the center and the central bank.[67] Relying on disparate studies, Bouvier offers the following sectoral concentration ratio of the top four Parisian banks in deposits: 1891, 60 percent; 1901, 66 percent; 1913, 51 percent; 1929, 37 percent; and 1937, 45 percent.[68] Although these figures should not be interpreted to say that center banks captured only 37 percent of the deposit market in 1929 – many other banks were headquartered in Paris, while all regional banks had an agency there – the trend is startling. The apparent superior resilience of French banks in comparison to English banks is remarkable, more analogous to that of the United States, and yet without any of the regulatory protection characteristic of the latter – a point for which I have no explanation.[69]

The agglomeration hypothesis

I look at the quantitative evidence available in support of the first of two propositions: local banking was a negative function of state centralization. The independent variable is *state centralization*, measured as the proportion of government revenues drained by the central government. The exact measure is a fraction having as numerator the sum of central government receipts and as denominator the sum of all government receipts calculated for 1880. Although this way of operationalizing state centralization is imperfect and subject to many caveats, the rank-ordering of the countries that it produces is in keeping with both existing qualitative historical accounts and more refined partial calculations (see appendix 3 for a discussion). The date was chosen to allay any suspicion about the direction of the causal relationship (I initially wanted data for 1850 but had to give up). At any rate, state centralization is a variable with a long memory, most unlikely in the short run to be endogenous to financial development. The dependent variable – the proportion of deposits captured by the *local banking sectors* – is computed from table 3.1 as the row-sum of the second and fourth columns. Table 3.1 presents the distribution of all deposits among the four sectors – center, local non-profit, state, and country banks.[70]

---

[67] See Lescure 1999, Plessis 1999.   [68] Bouvier 1973, pp. 123–26.

[69] Note that the French exception bears on the idea that the scale of production in France was small in relation to Britain. For a different opinion, see Kinghorn and Nye 1996.

[70] The four banking sectors are defined in table 2.2 and appendix 2.

Table 3.1. *Deposit market shares of the four credit sectors, 1913 (percentages)*

	Center	Local non-profit	State	Country
Canada	92	3	5	0
United Kingdom	80	6	14	0
Spain	67	33	0	0
France	66	23	10	0
Australia	65	34	1	0
Sweden	63	35	2	0
Belgium	59	1	40	0
New Zealand	58	4	38	0
Netherlands	54	22	23	0
Denmark	49	51	0	0
Norway	49	51	0	0
Switzerland	39	61	0	0
Austria-Hungary[a]	37	58	5	0
United States[b]	33	25	0	42
Germany	28	71	1	0
Italy	27	40	33	0

Notes: Categories are defined and sources provided in appendix 2.
Rows may not add to 100 because of rounding.
[a] Austria and the Czech Lands.
[b] 1914.

A casual look at table 3.1 suggests that, by 1913, state decentralization, which, as just described, came along with the political protection of local banking, was associated with a considerable fragmentation of the market for individual deposits. Whereas less than 10 percent of the deposit market went to local savings banks and mutual credit societies in Britain, Belgium, Canada, and New Zealand, equivalent figures were above 50 percent in Denmark, Norway, Austria-Hungary, Germany, and Switzerland, 40 percent in Italy, 35 percent in Sweden, and 22 percent in the Netherlands. Although the equivalent datum for the United States was 25 percent, it came on top of the market share held by the state-chartered banks – evaluated at 42 percent, bringing the United States to a whopping 67 percent. The data for the dominions are misleading, reflecting the strong penetration of London banks. Clearly, Britain, France, and Belgium (and the dominions) had by 1913 a centralized deposit market, whereas the other states did not, instead allowing peripheral governments to split the lion's share.

The direct relation between capital market dispersion and political centralization is plotted in figure 3.4. The negative relation is straightforward, marred only by the two Australasian observations. Australia and New

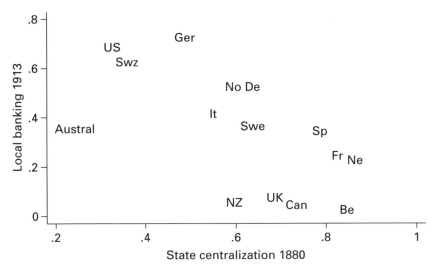

Figure 3.4. Local banking and state centralization

Zealand are, with Canada, outliers; the financial agglomeration hypothesis did not apply to them. The agglomeration of the banking systems found in the dominions had more to do with their previous colonial status than with their respective degrees of political centralization in 1880; market institutions preexisted political institutions rather than stemming from them. Indeed, all dominions showed a high degree of banking concentration despite wide variations in fiscal centralization (high in Canada and New Zealand, low in Australia).

To check the robustness of the findings, I ran a multiple regression in which I controlled for the potential effect of three other variables. The size of the *population*, first; the idea is that a large size made centralization more difficult. *Wealth*, second; Goldsmith argued that the size of the non-profit sector was a function of economic development.[71] *Financial depth*, third; Goldsmith also argued that the size of the non-profit sector was a function of the ratio of financial assets to GNP. The tests have a small number of observations, making the results case sensitive – it takes but a few outliers to make or break a correlation. I compensate for this limitation by duplicating the OLS' estimates of standard errors and confidence intervals with the bootstrapping technique.

The results are reported in table 3.2. Regression 1 controls for population size and wealth and regression 2 for financial depth. Consider regression 1. The coefficient for the political centralization variable ($= -1.18$)

[71] Goldsmith 1975, p. 87.

Table 3.2. *Local banking as a negative function of state centralization*

	Dependent variable: *Local banking 1913*	
	1	2
State centralization 1880	−1.18	−1.03
	(0.26)**	(0.28)***
	[0.49]***	[0.28]**
GNP per capita 1913	−0.0002	
	(0.0002)	
	[0.0003]	
Population 1913 (in millions)	0.0004	
	(0.002)	
	[0.003]	
Financial depth 1913		0.0001
		(0.001)
		[0.001]
Intercept	1.31	1.02
	(0.26)	(0.25)

Notes: Ordinary least squares with standard errors and bias-corrected confidence intervals calculated on 1000 bootstraps. Each cell reports values of observed coefficients and corresponding regular and bootstrapped standard errors in parentheses and brackets respectively. Confidence intervals using bootstrapped standard errors are bias-corrected; *, **, *** indicate coefficients situated in the 90%, 95%, and 99% confidence intervals respectively. The number of observations is twelve: Belgium, Denmark, France, Germany, Italy, Netherlands, Norway, Spain, Sweden, Switzerland, UK, and the USA. *Sources:* Definitions and sources for the dependent variable are supplied in table 3.1 and appendix 2. For state centralization, see appendix 3. GNP per capita in 1913 is from Bairoch and Lévy-Leboyer 1981, p. 10. Population in 1913 is from Maddison 1991, pp. 232–35. Financial depth is the ratio of all assets held by financial institutions to GNP in 1913; it is from Goldsmith 1969, p. 209.

is significantly different from zero, negative, and sizable – a one percentage point increase in state centralization yields a corresponding decrease in the market share of local banks that is greater than one. The findings are also robust to the change in control variables, population size and wealth in regression 1, financial depth in regression 2. The coefficients for the control variables are not statistically different from zero. In sum, the evidence confirms the existence of a systematic relation between the spatial concentration of banking and the centralization of the state.

Table 3.3. *Unit banking ratio, 1929*

Country	Ratio	Country	Ratio
United States	0.47	Belgium	0.06
Italy	0.29	Sweden	0.03
Switzerland	0.24	New Zealand	0.01
Netherlands	0.21	Australia	0.006
Germany	0.21	Canada	0.003
France	0.09	United Kingdom	0.002

Sources: For France, Gueslin 1992, p. 86. For other countries, Société des nations 1931, tab. II, p. 13.
Note: The numerator is the number of commercial banks. The denominator is the number of commercial banks and commercial bank branches. A higher ratio means a higher occurrence of unit banking. In contrast, a lower ratio reflects a greater occurrence of branch banking.

The unit banking hypothesis

A second empirically testable hypothesis is that unit banking was negatively associated with state centralization. Unit banking is a system in which banks are not allowed to establish branches outside the area where they are headquartered – it is the opposite of branch banking. Although legally barred from branching out in only two countries, Norway and the United States, center banks had difficulties penetrating peripheral markets in all other federal and semi-centralized countries as well. Rather than open branches, they relied on correspondents to bank with the periphery. Unit banking was important in the United States, Italy, Switzerland, the Netherlands, Germany, and certainly Norway, for which we have no data. In Britain, France, and the dominions, in contrast, joint-stock banks wove nationwide branch networks. In table 3.3, I offer a 1929 measure of unit banking – a ratio with, as numerator, the number of commercial banks and, as denominator, the number of commercial banks and branches. No earlier data could be found. Although branch banking had considerably advanced in the 1920s, there is no reason to suspect, though, that the country ordering for 1929 would be significantly different from that for 1913.

State centralization, the hypothesis goes, is negatively associated with unit banking. The negative relation is visible in the bivariate scattergram of figure 3.5. The cross-sectional distribution is roughly similar to the one in figure 3.4 (between state centralization and local banking), with Germany, Italy, and the United States at one end and Belgium and the

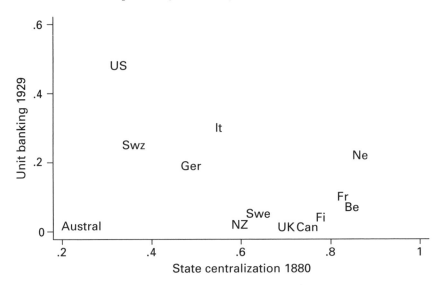

Figure 3.5. Unit banking and state centralization

UK at the other. Also similar is the outlying position of Australia and New Zealand, for the same reasons as given earlier. The only significant difference is the outlying position of the Dutch observation, exhibiting more unit banking than expected in light of its high degree of state centralization. The case of the Netherlands is probably sui generis; as Jonker (1996b) argued, it is a case in which the money market was functioning so well that it stunted the growth of the joint-stock banks. Even in 1929, the largest Dutch banks were poorly branched-out in comparison to their European neighbors. The Dutch case is unique, but no exception to the theoretical claim that state centralization caused financial agglomeration – only to the fact that in all other countries the core–periphery pattern was accomplished by the joint-stock banks and not the financial markets as in the Netherlands. Finally note the moderately outlying position of the French and Belgian observations, probably reflecting the relatively large size of state banking in these two countries – a large postal savings sector may have prevented the joint-stock banks from sweeping the deposit market.

I test the robustness of the statistical association by controlling for the two series of control variables used in the previous test – population and wealth together (regression 1) and financial depth (regression 2). I also include a dummy variable for the *Dutch observation* to control for the historical specificity of the Dutch case. A last control variable is the

Figure 3.6. Unit banking and local banking

relative size of the *state banking* sector. Results are reported in the first two regressions of table 3.4. The coefficient of the state centralization variable is marginally negative in regression 1 and more comfortably so in regression 2. A one-standard-deviation increase in state centralization is associated with a roughly equivalent increase in unit banking in both regressions.

If state centralization negatively affects both local banking and unit banking separately, then one should observe a positive, mutually reinforcing relationship between local and unit banking. I check the data for the existence of a positive relationship (I do not have enough variables to check for mutual reinforcement). The bivariate relation between the two variables is shown in figure 3.6 on the entire population of countries for which we have data. Indeed, there should be no need for the Dutch dummy since, irrespective of the size assumed by financial markets, local banking and center banking should be inversely related. The Australasian observations are also included, for I am testing a relation that is strictly internal to the banking system.

Although the positive relation is visible, the fit is poor. The data are aligned on two parallel lines, an upper one including Belgium, Netherlands, and Italy, and a lower one including Germany, Sweden, and Australia. The interval seems to reflect the negative effect that a high level of state banking (postal savings) might have had on branch banking,

Table 3.4. *Unit banking as a negative function of state centralization and a positive function of local banking, 1913*

	Dependent variable: *Unit banking ratio 1929*			
	1	2	3	4
State centralization	−0.71	−0.80		
	(0.24)*	(0.20)***		
	[0.78]*	[0.47]**		
Local banking			0.57	0.63
			(0.18)**	(0.15)***
			[0.57]**	[0.21]**
Population (in millions)	0.002		0.0008	
	(0.001)		(0.001)	
	[0.008]		[0.007]	
GNP per capita	−0.00003		0.0002	
	(0.0002)		(0.0002)	
	[0.0007]		[0.0002]	
Financial depth		−0.001		−0.00065
		(0.0006)		(0.0006)
		[0.004]		[0.0016]
State banking	0.40		0.71	0.40
	(0.30)		(0.31)*	(0.23)
	[1.14]		[0.92]*	[0.22]**
Netherlands (dummy)	0.25	0.20		
	(0.12)	(0.11)		
	[0.21]***	[0.15]***		
Intercept	0.50	0.78	−0.32	−0.04
	(0.21)	(0.17)***	(0.19)	(0.09)
Number obs.	9[a]	9[a]	11[b]	12[c]

Notes: Ordinary least squares with standard errors and bias-corrected confidence intervals calculated on 1000 bootstraps. Each cell reports values of observed coefficients and corresponding regular and bootstrapped standard errors in parentheses and brackets respectively. Confidence intervals using bootstrapped standard errors are bias-corrected; *, **, *** indicate coefficients situated in the 90%, 95%, and 99% confidence intervals respectively.

Sources: The dependent variable is the unit banking ratio of table 3.3. All variables are calculated for 1913, except for unit banking, which is for 1929, and state centralization (see appendix 3) which is circa 1880. State banking and local banking are from table 3.1. Population, GNP per capita, and financial depth are presented in table 3.2.

[a] Belgium, France, Germany, Italy, Netherlands, Sweden, Switzerland, UK, USA.

[b] Australia, Belgium, Canada, France, Germany, Italy, Netherlands, Sweden, Switzerland, UK, USA.

[c] Australia, Belgium, Canada, France, Germany, Italy, Netherlands, New Zealand, Sweden, Switzerland, UK, USA.

with the former crowding out the latter and thus allowing unit branching to emerge at lower levels of local banking than it would in the presence of a lower or non-existent level of state banking.[72]

I probe this conjecture according to the protocol followed so far. The dependent variable is unit banking, the independent variable is the relative size of the local banking sector, and the control variables are the relative size of state banking, wealth, and population in regression 3 and financial depth in regression 4 (table 3.4). The results confirm the positive association between local and unit banking; the coefficient of the local banking variable is significantly positive. State banking is also positively associated with unit banking.

Omitted variables

Several cases fit the argument in part only. The dominions, Belgium, France, and the Netherlands are outliers with respect to this or that aspect of the theory. I focus on these cases to infer the variables that are omitted from the model and that one would want to introduce in an ideal world of large n's and quantifiable variables.

The dominions

A condition of application of the present theory, the endogenous development of the financial market, is not realized in the case of the dominions. The theory assumes that state institutions were established before market institutions. In the dominions' case, however, both state and financial structures reflected British interference. All three countries had the same odd financial market structure – centralized, yet without a central bank – reflecting London's persisting centrality to dominions' finance. The fact that Canada and New Zealand were politically centralized, but Australia decentralized, seems to have made no difference. Note that the omitted variable is not late state formation – the Italian and German states were formed late as well. What seems to matter here is foreign interference in the domestic (market) affairs of a nation.

Belgium

The theory is blind in part to a second important variable – liberalism. I already explained that state centralization had two inconsistent effects: it worked against one source of market segmentation – local banking – but promoted another – state banking. In the event that the two effects

---

[72] The explanation does not do justice to the US observation, which should be aligned with the decentralized rather than the centralized countries.

were equally strong, they would have canceled each other out and no correlation between state structure and local banking would have been discernible. This did not obtain because the period under scrutiny was dominated by liberalism. Had the deposit revolution, instead, occurred in an era dominated by state interventionism of the kind that followed World War I, when many governments conceded borrowing privileges to specialized banks – mostly to supply long-term investment to small business – no correlation between state structure and market fragmentation would be observable. This was not yet the case in the prewar era, although such tendencies were already discernible in Belgium. In Belgium, commercial banks were crowded out from deposit banking when the state savings bank (CGER) was founded in 1865. The validity of the conjectures, to reiterate, is contingent on the era of liberalism.

The Netherlands

A last omitted variable is the financial market. The existence of a large market, as was the case in the Netherlands, along with the presence of a large savings bank sector, squeezed out all modern forms of banking – joint-stock, branch, and deposit. The Dutch case is unique, however. In all other countries, I will show in chapter 5, financial markets and center banking were symbiotic, growing simultaneously and not at the expense of each other. A possible explanation for the Dutch exception may place the emphasis on a delayed industrialization. It is not until after the turn of the century that firms called on the banks to finance long-term investment, a demand to which Dutch banks responded in the first stage by obliging the growing demand for loans, and in the second stage by liquidating their losses and retrenching from industry – an evolution not dissimilar to that of the Crédit Lyonnais, albeit forty years behind schedule.

Conclusion

This chapter related two closely associated stories. The first is the story of a technical trend. Deposit banking was the result of two simultaneous innovations: a legal innovation in the form of the liberalization of joint-stock banking around the first half of the nineteenth century; and an economic innovation, in the form of the spread of the benefits of industrialization to a large section of the population, occurring earlier in Britain, later on the continent. Deposit banking led to the substitution of the check (or wire transfer) and the overdraft for the trade bill. Deposit and overdraft threatened the banks with illiquidity, a problem to which they responded by curtailing loans to industry and shortening the maturity of their assets.

Weaving diversity into this general trend is the political story. The generalization of the deposit account around the middle of the nineteenth century unleashed competition between banking sectors for the control of individuals' savings. The outcome of this competition depended on the degree of spatial concentration of the financial market, which in turn was a reflection of the degree of centralization of the state. In centralized countries, such as Britain, France, Belgium, Canada, and to some extent New Zealand and the other Australasian states prior to 1901, the local non-profit sector, hindered in its growth by the central treasury, lost the competition to the profit and state sectors. Instead of promoting a network of locally run savings banks, central state treasuries pinned them down to their early nineteenth-century philanthropic ends, preferring instead to promote their own deposit-collection system in the form of postal savings. In centralized countries as well, with perhaps the exception of France, most local banks within the profit sector lost the competition to, or were absorbed by, the largest commercial banks.

In contrast, in decentralized countries, the local non-profit banks and country banks were promoted and protected respectively against the competition of both center banks and state treasury. Local governments saw the maintenance of a vigorous indigenous banking structure, linking local savings to local investment, as a prerequisite for local welfare and a warrant for fiscal independence. In countries where local governments both enjoyed political power and had a tradition of intervening in the local economy, their representatives used the political power that the decentralized institutions conferred upon them to protect local banks against the competition of center banks and postal savings. This was the case in Switzerland, the United States, Germany, Austria-Hungary, and Scandinavia. In Italy, although the central government was able to develop a powerful postal savings system, it did not prevent the savings and popular banks from becoming dominant, especially in the north of the country.

I conclude by pointing to two paradoxical effects of state centralization. Rather than weakening local banks, as it usually did elsewhere, state centralization may have also strengthened them in France and the Netherlands. The contradiction derives from two secondary effects of state centralization. In France, state centralization turned the central bank into the liquidity provider of the local banks for a while and, by strengthening postal savings, eliminated the credit cooperatives – two effects that helped the provincial banks survive for another twenty years. In the Netherlands, state centralization had the effect of strengthening the money market to the point of making redundant bank intermediation for the middle class, leaving the lower end of the market to the savings banks.

4   The internationalization of finance

The previous chapter established that centralized countries registered relatively high levels of financial agglomeration. Without regulatory and legislative power, local governments in centralized countries could not – nor did they want to – stop center banks from opening a branch on every local "Main Street." The reasoning, however, rested on an autarkic model – one without an international dimension. This chapter brings the international dimension into the picture, asking whether it ran parallel to or mitigated the process of agglomeration at work in the domestic economy. Theory and historical evidence both suggest that internationalization happened simultaneously with agglomeration, and more markedly in centralized than in decentralized countries.

Consider a country with two regions – the basic model of chapter 2. Graft onto it another country with a similar structure. Allow capital to flow freely between regions of a same country but not across countries. Burden the exchange of financial products with information asymmetry so that the losses incurred are lower between two financial cores than between a given core and a foreign periphery. The rationale for this differential in asymmetric information is that nineteenth-century foreign investors had an overwhelming preference for large, central, visible assets in foreign countries – mostly government bonds – over small, peripheral, and unfamiliar ones. It is reasonable to expect from such a model that the core–periphery pattern within a country and the degree of internationalization of the financial sector in that country would be mutually reinforcing.

Such is what the historical record showed. On the one hand, internationalization reinforced the domestic power of large center banks, because it provided them with access to a larger pool of "good" assets, and thus a greater ability to match their deposits with appropriate assets. Financial internationalization was a large-bank policy designed to meet the liquidity problem caused by deposit banking. On the other hand, the existence of a large financial center, draining the savings of the whole country and serving the needs of industry everywhere in that country, provided the basis for the internationalization of the financial center. The degree of openness of the financial system was a function of its degree of liberalization at the national level. I show in this chapter that the degree to which a country depended on international finance, whether as a creditor or a debtor, was a function of the spatial concentration of its financial system which was, in turn, a reflection of the centralization of the state.

A first section presents the contribution of the gold standard to the supply of short financial assets. A second section stresses the redistributional consequences of the surge in global finance that occurred under the gold standard. The third section offers systematic evidence for the existence of a relation between political centralization and the degree of dependence on cross-border capital flows.

The gold standard and the supply of short financial assets

An alternative source of good paper, besides the domestic payments system, was the international payments system, in which the largest banks were able to source part of the coveted short instruments. Coincidental with the revolution of payments systems at the domestic level, the international payments system boomed, spurred by the advent of the gold standard. The gold standard gave a boost to the international payments system directly by assisting the market for acceptances.[1] It did so by reducing the currency risk. We do not know to what extent. Surely, the currency risk was already low under the bimetallism that preceded the gold standard. Moreover, the market for international acceptances was, from 1870 on, monopolized by London; international acceptances substituted for vanishing bills of exchange in Britain, but not elsewhere. The greatest contribution to the uniform supply of short assets across financial centers, I believe, was more indirect; it was a spinoff of the boom in long-term foreign investment. I first develop the impact of the gold standard on long-term foreign investment and then its related effects on banks' short assets.

The gold standard stimulated the long-term financial market. The gold standard operated as a commitment rule, according to which gold countries pledged to maintain a fixed parity between one unit of their currency and a given quantity of gold. The gold standard is viewed by Bordo and Kydland (1995) as a solution to the time-inconsistency problem analyzed by Kydland and Prescott (1977). In the initial story, a government with discretion over the formulation of monetary policy has an incentive

---

[1] An acceptance is an international bill of exchange. See the section entitled "The rise of branch banking" in chapter 3 for a minimally technical description of its working.

to engineer an unexpected burst of inflation to stimulate employment. Absent a binding commitment, the public comes to anticipate the outcome, leading to an inflationary equilibrium. A solution to the dilemma is for the government to waive discretion and pledge to abide by a binding rule. A variation on that story, one that makes time inconsistency relevant to the gold standard, runs like this. A government with discretion over its monetary and fiscal policy has an incentive to borrow and then default on its debt via inflation or suspension of payments. Anticipating default, bond holders either ask for a higher interest rate or do not purchase government debt. A solution to the dilemma is for the government to commit to gold convertibility at a fixed rate – a transparent and simple rule (Bordo and Kydland 1995). Bordo and Schwartz (1994) found that the countries that adhered to the gold standard rule generally had lower fiscal deficits, more stable money growth, and lower inflation rates than those that did not.

Operating as a commitment rule, the gold standard made possible the systematic transfer of capital from capital-rich or slow-growing economies to capital-poor or fast-growing economies. Countries seeking long-term foreign capital paid lower interest rates on loans contracted in London, Paris, Berlin, and other financial centers if they adhered to the gold standard.[2] In the Russian and Austrian empires, partisans of industrialization thought that industrialization could be a speedy process if foreign capital intervened to stimulate it; going onto the gold standard would lead to the investment of foreign capital.[3] Reflecting on the experience of Spain, which suspended gold convertibility in 1883, Martin-Aceña argued that, by staying out of the gold standard, "Spain missed out on growth." Not only did imports of foreign capital cease from 1883 until 1906, when a new administration finally opted for a return to gold, but yields on the public debt were "consistently maintained above British, French, and even Italian yields."[4]

The generalization of the gold standard coincided with a rise in international capital outflows to levels never before approached. Bairoch's (1976, p. 103) estimates for capital flows for all net creditor countries show a slowdown in the depression decades of the gold standard, followed by an unprecedented surge after 1900:

> 1840–70: 2.5–3.5% GNP,
> 1870–1900: 1.5–2.0% GNP,
> 1900–13: 5.5% GNP.

---

[2] See Bordo and Rockoff 1995, p. 18.   [3] De Cecco 1974, p. 52.
[4] Martin-Aceña 1994, pp. 144 and 160.

Comparable data for the 1920s, 1960s, and 1970s were below 1 percent. It is only since the mid-1980s that international investment has surged again.[5]

Most of this investment, about three-quarters, came from three countries (the UK, France, and Germany) which were running persistent current account surpluses by generating savings in excess of domestic investment. Relative to total domestic savings, net capital outflows in 1910 represented 52 percent for the UK and 15 percent for France.[6] The rest was contributed by the Netherlands, Belgium, Switzerland, and, toward the end of the period, Sweden. Most of this investment went to a few countries – the United States, Canada, Australasia, Argentina, Brazil, Mexico, Russia, Spain, Portugal, Italy, Austria-Hungary, and the Scandinavian countries.[7]

What made foreign investment so popular among savers in Britain, France, Germany, and other creditor countries was its greater safety, at equivalent yield, than domestic paper. In the case of Britain, Edelstein (1982, p. 138) found that overseas returns exceeded home returns over the years 1870–1913; he also found that overseas returns were not significantly riskier than domestic returns, but in fact tended to be less so. The greater safety of foreign investments relative to home investments is easily explained; it derived from the nature of these investments, which, according to Arthur Bloomfield (1968, p. 4), "depended directly or indirectly on government action." Either loans went to foreign governments (Russia and countries in central and southern Europe), or, even when they went to private companies, as in the case of railroad construction and other public investments (utilities, roads, bridges, harbors, telegraph and telephone networks), they were made possible by government assistance in the form of guarantees, land loans, and cash grants. Finally, the bulk of this investment was portfolio; a generous estimate places the relative share of direct investment of the total long-term international debt in 1914 at only 35 percent.[8]

The higher yield of foreign over domestic investments holding risk constant, albeit empirically established, is more difficult to explain. Edelstein (1982, p. 140) offered two interesting hypotheses. A first hypothesis, which the author thought to be valid in the case of the United States, views foreign returns constantly running ahead of expectations:

---

[5] Bordo et al. (1998, p. 26) argue that for a relatively narrow range of homogeneous assets (government securities, railroad bonds) the pre-1914 markets were as tightly integrated as in the present day.

[6] See Green and Urquhart 1976, 241 and 244.   [7] See Cameron 1991, p. 13.

[8] See Dunning 1992, p. 116.

Overseas regions had a tendency to generate greater amounts of profitable innovations and new market opportunities, periodically fostering greater disequilibria,
which in turn left their mark on realized returns.

A second hypothesis looks for higher returns in market imperfection.

Overseas areas evinced a tendency to generate more circumstances involving
imperfect competition and, possibly, greater monopoly rents. (Edelstein 1982,
p. 140.)

The active role played by host governments in attracting foreign capital,
predictably, was a consequential source of monopoly rents.

A third hypothesis, I venture, was the relative backwardness of receiving countries. With the exception of the Netherlands, creditor countries
(Britain, France, Germany, Belgium, Switzerland) were generally more
advanced industrially than debtor countries. The differential timing of
industrialization triggered a product-cycle effect: high-growth sectors in
debtor countries already were stable-growth sectors in creditor countries.
Although yields on new ventures may have been the same, risks were lower
in newly industrializing economies. In contrast, investing in an advanced
economy meant putting one's money into new ventures with untested
rates of return.

The boom in long-term flows would supply banks with the short assets
they were so desperately seeking in two ways. First, the joint-stock commercial banks on the continent earlier, and in Britain later, took over the
floating and placement of long-term bonds. Although these bonds were
nominally long-term and a standard practice for banks was to hold such
bonds no longer than it should take to place them among their clienteles, the safety and trading volume of these instruments made them easily
disposable assets, easily convertible into cash, and thus de facto substitutes for short-term paper. Michie (1998) argues that US railroad bonds,
among others, were akin to an international medium of exchange, being
actively traded in New York, London, Paris, Amsterdam, and Berlin.
Banks would transfer cash from their London account to their Paris account by simultaneously selling and buying equivalent amounts of US
railroad bonds in London and Paris respectively.

Second, commercial banks would float a government or government-
guaranteed long-term bond issue provided that they be given a share in the
more lucrative short-term debt issued by these same governments. The
volume of a short-term government paper depended a lot, in the end, on
the popularity of its equivalent long-term debt, since the usual way of repaying the short-term debt was to consolidate it into long-term debt. The
more savers purchased bonds issued by foreign governments, the more
bankers would consent to short-term advances to foreign governments.

Short-term government debt was usually safer than its long-term equivalent, as no treasury, even if compelled to default on its long-term debt, could afford to default on its short-term debt, lest it be forced to shut down immediately.

By taking part in long-term foreign government investment, joint-stock banks gained access in proportional amount to a supply of short-term government debt, which, unlike the market for acceptances, could not be monopolized by London. It could not be monopolized by the City because of the implicit links just mentioned between long and short government debt imposed by bankers, and also because long-term debt, unlike short-term debt, exhibited fewer scale economies. London bankers largely financed world short-term transactions by the positive current accounts held by traders in London, with the result that any increase in world trade spontaneously yielded an equivalent increase in bank resources. Long-term lending, in contrast, was financed by savings, making the size of domestic savings accumulated in any specific country a constraint on how much the banks in that country could lend.

The reasoning applies to both creditor and debtor countries. Loans were floated by international syndicates of bankers, including banks from both debtor and creditor countries. The bonds were issued both in the lending and in the borrowing country. Moreover, there was a tendency over time for government bonds and good railway securities issued in Berlin, Paris, or London to return to domestic investors, who held them as chief long-term savings instruments, earning interest in Deutschmarks, French francs, or pounds sterling. As a result, British, French, German, Dutch, Belgian, and Danish government securities were entirely held at home by the mid-1870s; Austrian and Hungarian investors owned two-thirds of their own state debt; US government securities were almost entirely taken and held at home.[9]

In sum, the gold standard enabled the expansion of a global market for short government paper. The international supply of short instruments coincided with a domestic demand for "shorter" assets. This mutually reinforcing dynamic upset established ways of banking.

The redistributional effects of internationalization

The surge in capital flows across borders worsened the center–periphery cleavage within each country. We saw in the previous chapter that deposit branch banking threatened a concentration of domestic capital markets through the concentration of banking around a handful of gigantic,

[9] See Platt 1984, pp. 84, 92, 165, 176.

tentacular banks, draining local savings to the financial center. The presence of a burgeoning capital international market reinforced this process of concentration in two ways. First, by supplying large banks with a readymade supply of good paper, internationalization relieved the liquidity problems caused by the banks' increasing reliance on individual deposits, thus favoring an even larger reliance on deposits. Second, internationalization supplied eventual depositors with new investment opportunities, thereby increasing the attractiveness of the banks for depositors, and allowing the banks to drain more savings to the center. Globalization, where it occurred, usually strengthened the center at the expense of the periphery.[10]

While the reasoning so far has borne on creditor countries, that is, countries with spare money to invest abroad, the draining of peripheral capital was as likely to affect debtor countries, countries with an investment demand in excess of domestic savings. Not all local borrowers in debtor countries could benefit from the infusion of foreign capital. As already mentioned, foreign capital had a preference for safety. Foreign capital also had a preference, all else being equal, for large, visible investments, easier to monitor from afar than small, unreported ones. The preference for safety and the steeper monitoring costs faced by foreign savers, therefore, tended to divide local investors into two groups: the state-sponsored, large investors, who would get access to the foreign manna, and the small, unsponsored investors, who would be bypassed.

Not only would small and medium-sized firms in debtor countries be unlikely to receive foreign investment, but they were in danger of losing their privileged access to local capital as well. Foreign capital had a seeding effect; the effect of an initial infusion, in Platt's words, was "to stimulate domestic finance, to supply domestic savings with the confidence and familiarity that capitalists required for new forms of investment."[11] Since this demonstration effect operated exclusively in favor of concentrated sectors, it might exert a centripetal attraction on peripheral capital until then invested in local projects. Local, decentralized districts might lose from local savers' greater awareness of new investment opportunities in

---

[10] The surge in capital flows across countries had a second effect. In accordance with standard Heckscher–Ohlin premises, it pitted borrowers against savers. Domestic savers in creditor countries were better off, for they were offered a wider and better array of investment opportunities. In contrast, local borrowers of capital, who were dependent on external finance, were relatively worse off, for they were in competition with foreign borrowers to attract capital and thus pressed to remunerate it better. The situation was the exact reverse in debtor countries. The switch to the gold standard hurt local savers, as they were competing with foreign savers for a given demand for capital, whereas local borrowers benefited from it.

[11] See Platt 1984, p. 6.

their own country. The joint-stock banks threatened to drain peripheral capital irrespective of the debtor or creditor status of the country.

However, the degree to which a financial system became internationalized was a reflection of the previous degree of spatial concentration of the deposit market. Dependence on cross-border capital flows was inversely correlated with the fragmentation of the domestic capital market. In creditor countries, fragmentation meant that a smaller share of the pool of national savings was available for foreign investment. The existence of vigorous local banking facilities had the effect of "localizing" – and thus "nationalizing" – local savings. Conversely, concentration made the entire savings pool available for investment abroad.

In debtor countries fragmentation meant that a smaller share of investment opportunities was open to foreign investment. Most investments in the periphery, those that were financed by savings banks, credit cooperatives, or local commercial banks, were off limits, because the presence of local capital reduced the need for foreign capital, and also because these local banks and firms were unable to attract foreign capital. Concentration, in contrast, opened the entire capital market to foreign investment. Therefore, in both creditor and debtor countries, fragmentation implied that a smaller share of the economy was to be internationalized. Fragmentation hindered global interdependence, whereas concentration made it easier.

Since market concentration reflected the degree of centralization of the state, then internationalization also reflected the degree of centralization of the state. The surge in cross-border foreign investments would never have reached these unprecedented levels had it not found fertile ground in domestic institutions. The existence of a handful of countries with centralized political institutions, in which the government could ignore the pleas of the potential losers – local districts of small farms and firms – without incurring political retribution, provided the international financial system with its largest suppliers (Britain, France, Belgium, the Netherlands) and demanders (Canada, Australasia) of foreign capital. In contrast, states with powerful subnational entities were the least able to take part in the global market.

The impact of state institutions on internationalization was mostly indirect, ministered via the mediation of domestic market concentration. The sectors that were expected to lose from concentration and internationalization – agriculture and small and medium-sized firms – checked internationalization by checking financial concentration at the domestic level. In contrast, those that were expected to benefit from openness – large commercial banks in alliance with savers in creditor countries, and large firms in debtor countries – promoted internationalization as a byproduct of promoting deregulation and competition at the domestic level.

In some cases, expected losers and winners from financial internationalization directly confronted each other on the issue. Debates between coalitions of financial internationalists and nationalists crystallized around the relative merits of gold and silver. Agrarians in Germany under Bismarck in the 1880s as well as in the United States in the 1880s and 1890s resisted gold, fearing its deflationary consequences for agricultural prices; they called, instead, for bimetallism.[12] Small business would join the fray in the 1920s, arguing that foreign investment depleted the domestic pool of capital available for domestic business. Rather than campaigning for silver or exchange controls, however, they asked for – and obtained – the funding of state banks specializing in long-term lending to small business.[13]

Systematic evidence for the relation between state centralization and internationalization

This section tests the hypothesis introduced in the previous section: the idea that internationalization was a function of state centralization. The key to cross-national variations in levels of dependence on foreign capital flows – whether in or out – reached by each country, I claim, should be sought in the degree of concentration of the domestic capital market – and thus of political centralization. Britain, France, the Netherlands, and Belgium should score high as centralized creditors; Canada and New Zealand should score high as centralized debtors. All other countries should score low relatively.

Table 4.1 provides two values of long-term foreign investment stocks, the first, weighted per capita, the second, by unit of GNP. Data are listed in the order of their absolute value, from the highest to the lowest. The absolute value measures the relative dependence of the economy on foreign investment inwards and outwards without distinction between debtor and creditor status. Capital flows were not evenly distributed across economies. British, Swiss, French, and Dutch savers held a greater proportion of foreign assets than their German and Belgian counterparts, while Canadian and Australian borrowers were more leveraged abroad than their Austrian, Italian, and US equivalents. I checked the data against Goldsmith's estimates of net foreign asset holdings for

---

[12] On the silver movement in Germany, see Gallarotti 1995, p. 153. For the United States, see Ritter 1997.

[13] On state banks, see Verdier 2000.

Table 4.1. *Long-term foreign investment stock, 1914*

	Outflows (+), inflows (−)	
	Per capita (in 1914 US $)	Divided by GNP
Switzerland	375	1.96
Netherlands	333	1.77
United Kingdom	413	1.66
Canada	−463	−1.44
Belgium	186	1.20
France	236	0.99
Australia	−340	−0.93
Spain	−95	−0.79
Sweden	−95	−0.57
Norway	−52	−0.56
Germany	97	0.52
Austria-Hungary	−52	−0.38
Italy	−27	−0.20
United States	−37	−0.09

Sources: Foreign investment stock in 1914 US dollars are from Cameron 1991, p. 13, except for Sweden and Norway, for which the data are from Arthur Bloomfield (1968, pp. 43–44) and converted to US dollars at the old gold parity of 0.2680 krone to the dollar (Svennilson 1954, p. 318). Data used in the computation of stocks for Sweden and Norway start only in 1861 and 1871 respectively, with the effect of slightly underestimating Swedish liability while slightly overestimating Norwegian liability. Population data are from Maddison 1991, pp. 232–35. GNP data are for 1913: 1913 GNP data in current prices (Mitchell 1983, 1992; for Austria-Hungary, Komlos 1990b, p. 126) were converted to US dollars using 1913 exchange rates (Svennilson 1954, 318–19).
Note: All data are gross foreign investments as of 1914, except in the case of the United States, the only country with known significant two-way flows, for which data are net.

seven countries in 1912/1914.[14] The correlation coefficient between the two series of data for six observations is a comfortable 0.86.

The relation between internationalization and state centralization is shown in figure 4.1. The positive relation suffers the usual exception

[14] For this comparison to be possible, it is necessary to assume that all foreign assets were transferable securities as opposed to foreign direct investments, an assumption that was broadly true for the prewar period. Goldsmith's figures for net foreign assets as a proportion of national assets are, in percentages, Belgium: 7.7, Denmark: 0.6, France: 8.5, Germany: 3.1, Switzerland: 11.2, the UK: 17.8, and the USA: 1.7. The source is Goldsmith 1985, appendix A.

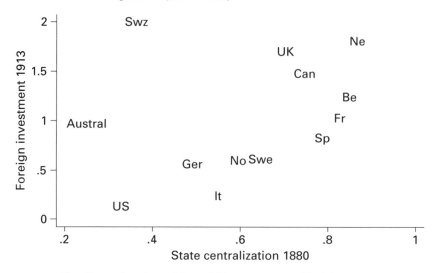

Note: For explanations of the variables, see note to table 4.2.

Figure 4.1. Foreign investment and state centralization

of Australia – a dominion to which the centralization hypothesis is not applicable (see chapter 3).[15] The second exception is Switzerland. The Swiss observation is an outlier across specifications – its degree of internationalization (a total creditor position of $1.5 billion in 1914, the second-highest capital-export-per-capita figure behind Britain) is over-blown relative to its very low degree of state centralization, its well-developed local and non-profit banking sectors, and its high incidence of unit banking. It could be that the data on foreign investment stocks over-state the creditor position of the Swiss place. Cameron (1991, pp. 12–13) warns that

By the beginning of the twentieth century Switzerland had apparently recovered its position as a capital exporter, but that is by no means certain; because of its geographical and political position, Switzerland became a favorite site for the location of international holding companies, especially in the electrical industry, resulting in myriad inflows and outflows of capital.

[15] Endogenous relations between state structures and banking concentration were upset and concealed by two series of events: first, a collection of colonies enjoying limited autonomy joined in a federation in 1901, moving state structures from centralization to decentralization; second, the financial sector was from the outset dominated by London banks and thus highly concentrated.

Note: For explanations of the variables, see note to table 4.2.

Figure 4.2. Foreign investment and local banking, 1913

Or it could be that Switzerland is an exception, a country with an unusual share of international banking owing to factors that are left out of the present argument (see next section).[16]

Excluding the dominions and neutralizing the Swiss outlier by means of a dummy variable, I test the robustness of the relation between internationalization and state centralization by controlling for population size and wealth together, and financial depth separately. A plausible alternative hypothesis is that internationalization is a negative function of size.[17] Another is that internationalization is a positive function of wealth and financial depth. The results are reported in table 4.2. In both regressions 1 and 2, the coefficient for the state centralization variable is significantly positive, while its impact measured in standard deviation change is equivalent to 100 percent in regression 1 and 60 percent in regression 2.

If state centralization causes internationalization, then market segmentation should work against internationalization. The bivariate scattergram of the two variables is shown in figure 4.2. The negative relationship is

[16] The high figure reported by Goldsmith for Swiss foreign asset holdings (see n. 14) would seem to confirm the latter interpretation.
[17] For an argument that small economies are more dependent on world markets, see Katzenstein 1985.

Table 4.2. *Cross-border capital investments, state centralization, and local banking*

	Dependent variable: *Absolute value of foreign investment stock divided by GNP as of 1913–14*			
	1	2	3	4
State centralization 1880	3.13	2.60		
	(0.82)***	(0.81)**		
	[1.51]***	[1.13]*		
Local banking 1913			−1.68	−1.92
			(0.67)**	(0.62)**
			[2.12]**	[0.69]**
Population (in millions) 1913	−0.001		−0.004	
	(0.005)		(0.007)	
	[0.08]		[0.02]	
GNP per capita 1913	0.001		0.0005	
	(0.0005)*		(0.0007)	
	[0.001]		[0.007]	
Financial depth 1913		0.0008		0.0005
		(0.004)		(0.004)
		[0.006]		[0.009]
Switzerland (dummy)	1.89	1.77	1.37	1.53
	(0.50)***	(0.74)**	(0.56)**	(0.76)*
	[1.17]***	[1.18]***	[1.95]***	[1.81]***
Intercept	−2.00	−0.98	1.14	1.45
	(0.71)**	(0.74)	(0.49)**	(0.41)***
Number obs.	11[a]	11[a]	12[b]	11[a]

Methodology: Ordinary least squares with standard errors and bias-corrected confidence intervals calculated on 1000 bootstraps. Each cell reports values of observed coefficients and corresponding regular and bootstrapped standard errors in parentheses and brackets respectively. Confidence intervals using bootstrapped standard errors are bias-corrected; *, **, *** indicate coefficients situated in the 90%, 95%, and 99% confidence intervals respectively.

Notes: The dependent variable is the absolute value of foreign investment stock divided by GNP as of 1913–14; see table 4.1. All the other variables were defined in table 3.2.

[a] Belgium, France, Germany, Italy, Netherlands, Norway, Spain, Sweden, Switzerland, UK, USA.

[b] Austria, Belgium, France, Germany, Italy, Netherlands, Norway, Spain, Sweden, Switzerland, UK, USA.

tight, with the expected exception of Switzerland, a case with an over-blown international financial sector. The negative relationship is robust to the usual control variables (see table 4.2, regressions 3 and 4). The coefficient for the local banking variable in regression 3 (–1.68) reflects an impact equivalent to 62 percent measured in equivalent changes in standard deviations.

Omitted variables: the Swiss exception

In all countries but Switzerland, internationalization was the reward for the presence of a regulatory comparative advantage – a money market unshackled by protective regulation, and thus well supplied in the case of creditor countries or wide open to foreign investment in debtor countries. The Swiss money market, in contrast, was segmented and a priori unfit for internationalization. Its success with international investors, however, suggests that the existence of an unregulated money market, though an important condition for internationalization, was not a necessary condition; comparative advantages of another nature, such as conservatism, political stability, neutrality in foreign affairs, and, most importantly, ter-ritorial inviolability were sufficient to overcome regulatory impediments. Surely, the harsh competition between the local (*Kantonal*) banks and the center banks, as Guex (1997, p. 342) argued, led the latter to turn their attention toward international affairs. Benz (1987, 185) wrote that Swiss banks were "more inclined to work at the local and international than national level."[18] Yet, they would not have been successful in attracting foreign business if their resources had been limited to their share of the domestic market. In other words, internationalization as a response to crowding out of the domestic deposit market worked only in the case of Switzerland, the money sanctuary of Europe. Similar crowding out in Germany, Austria-Hungary, Scandinavia, and Italy failed to produce a comparable effect.[19]

Conclusion

The gold standard brought financial centers closer to one another, while taking each financial center farther away from its own periphery. The elimination of the currency risk brought to life an international market

---

[18] Swiss banks were "plus portées à travailler sur un plan local ou international que na-tional." The international success of the Swiss place was even more remarkable because it occurred in spite of the weakness of the Swiss currency until the centralization of note issuing in 1905.

[19] For an opposing view with respect to Sweden, see Schön n.d.

for government paper which banks, all over the world, were eager to hold as a first-line defense against illiquidity. It allowed these banks to extricate themselves from less liquid industrial and peripherally located assets and increase their reliance on deposits. Globalization, where it occurred, strengthened the national level at the expense of the local.

The centralizing effect of financial internationalization did not happen uniformly, however, but exhibited clear symptoms of self-selection. It was mostly encountered in countries where the financial core had already triumphed – or was in the process of triumphing – over the periphery. Decentralized countries, in which the potential losers could avail themselves of the regulatory and political power enjoyed by local governments, did not embrace global finance, at least not to the same extent. In those countries, governments passed policies that had the effect of fragmenting the domestic capital market and preventing the drain of local savings from peripheries. In a sense, the gold standard merely amplified the redistributional effects of extant domestic transformations – it did not initiate them.

The gold standard experiment in global finance points to a negative relation between local power and globalization. States with powerful subnational entities were the least able to take part in the global market. The existence of a handful of countries with centralized political institutions, in which the government could ignore the pleas of the potential losers without incurring political retribution, provided the international financial system with its largest suppliers and demanders of foreign capital.

5   The origins of corporate securities markets

The second industrial revolution, based upon electricity, chemicals, and the internal combustion engine, and characterized by capital intensity and large initial investments, was made possible by the emergence of corporate securities markets. Markets allowed banks to transform long-term loans to industry into securities, recoup their liquidity, and lend anew. The development of securities markets in general was made possible by the agglomeration of savings in the core. Secondary securities markets needed a lot of liquid assets to function well. Yet, most securities markets did not find the cash they needed to grow and, as a result, stagnated. Securities markets were starved of cash in countries where local credit sectors carved up a sizable portion of the deposit market. Stock markets in the second half of the nineteenth century constituted, along with large commercial banks, a new "corporate finance," geared to the financial needs of the new industrial sectors. Land and other traditional sectors, in contrast, had no use for "corporate finance," but, instead, were banking with the non-profit sector (savings banks, credit cooperatives, and mortgage banks). The two financial sectors were in competition for resources, mainly deposits. The competition was adjudicated politically, through regulation. Since the size of the local non-profit sector was a negative function of the degree of centralization of the state, the development of corporate securities markets conversely was a positive function of state centralization.

Existing accounts approach the issue of the origins of modern capital markets from an angle that is radically different from the one adopted here. Some argue that markets develop if embedded in a congenial legal or institutional context, whether it is common law (La Porta et al. 1997a, Rajan and Zingales 1999) or a well-developed public debt (North and Weingast 1989, Sylla 1997, 1999). Others view markets as engaged in a zero-sum game with universal banks (Sylla and Smith 1995, Sylla 1997, Tilly 1966). Third, historians generally hold the level of economic development to be the prime suspect accounting for cross-national variation in financial market development.[1] A larger pool of savings made for more cash available for investment in stocks and bonds. A last variable is the quality of investment information (Sylla and Smith 1995). A moderate level of information asymmetry between lender and borrower is a requisite for anonymous markets in corporate finance to emerge. Insiders alone can successfully cope with high asymmetry, through personal information on the borrower.[2] All these hypotheses are plausible a priori and are tested along with the for-profit-sector dominance hypothesis in this chapter.[3]

Corporate versus non-corporate finance

Corporate securities markets were a functional response to the second industrial revolution. The banks could not finance the large immobilization of capital in steel, chemicals, electrical machinery, and communications (telegraph, telephone) by means of loans, which would have been too large and would have undermined the banks' liquidity (their capacity to call in loans to face eventual deposit withdrawals). To reiterate, markets allowed banks to transform long-term loans to industry into securities, recoup their liquidity, and lend anew.[4] Still, few individuals were willing to merely take over corporate financing from the banks and immobilize their savings in the form of securities in risky private ventures. They could get an honest return at no risk by buying public debt. The creation of a secondary market for corporate securities, allowing the owner of a security to sell it at any time, is what earned stock markets their mass appeal.

Secondary securities markets, however, needed – and still need – a lot of liquid assets to function well. Stable, reliable pricing requires thick trading and constant short-term buying and selling by brokers, market makers, and leveraged speculators, in constant need of vast sums of short funds. To function well, the securities market had to be leveraged by the second component of corporate finance – an equally well-working money (short-term) market. The long and short markets were linked through call loans: securities brokers would pledge securities as collateral on callable loans from the banks.[5]

[1] See Rybczynski 1988, 6, and Sylla and Smith 1995, p. 182.
[2] For a more extensive review of the literature, consult Verdier 2002.
[3] The hypothesis that posits an incompatibility between market and universal banking will be addressed in the following chapter.
[4] Markets were cyclical, each cycle lasting about ten years. Banks would renew advances to their good clients in bear periods in the hope of transforming them into securities at the next bull market.
[5] See Powell 1966, p. 594.

Initially, the money market utilized the idle cash found in traders' current accounts, which the banks would use to extend standardized overnight or fortnight loans to brokers. By the middle of the century, a new source of liquidity emerged in the form of individuals' checking accounts. Individual deposits, we saw in chapter 3, became the single most important source of funding for banks from the middle of the nineteenth century onward. The collection of small deposits from millions of geographically dispersed individuals required the development of the third component of corporate finance in the form of large, joint-stock banks, headquartered in the financial center, draining deposits from the periphery through networks of local branches. The point to appreciate is that the corporate financial revolution rested on individuals' bank deposits leveraging the stock market as much as on individuals directly purchasing stocks. The two aspects were mutually reinforcing: the more deposits were channeled to the financial center, the more liquid the stock market, the lower the risk of holding corporate stocks, and the more attractive corporate stocks in relation to public debt.

A requisite for the development of capital markets, therefore, was that financial capital was geographically mobile; it had to flow from the periphery to the financial center, in a centripetal way. Had all producer groups found their interest in corporate finance, mobility would have automatically ensued. However, corporate finance had redistributional effects. As I have argued in previous chapters, corporate finance benefited modern industry at the expense of traditional sectors – agrarians, artisans, shopkeepers, the self-employed, workers skilled in traditional crafts, and, more generally, sectors characterized by small enterprises.

Traditional sectors had little to gain from incorporation and stock markets. Consider the case of the agrarians. Koning argues that the agricultural depression destroyed any prospect for agrarian capitalism in the world.[6] Large farms closed, and with them ended early agrarian support for corporate finance. Small farmers, who could work harder and accept lower profits, became the dominant force in agriculture. Even Dutch and Danish farms, which managed a conversion away from traditional grains to animal husbandry, thereby becoming the number one supplier of bacon and eggs for the English breakfast table, remained small. Even in the United States, where mechanization allowed farms to be larger than in Europe, farms were family-owned, with no prospect for incorporation. Other traditional sectors had no hope for incorporation either. Too small to enable market investors to evaluate their earning potential with a

---

[6] Koning 1994, p. 26.

modicum of confidence, small and medium-sized firms relied exclusively on bank loans.

Traditional sectors had no use for the newly established joint-stock banks either. The center banks could not accommodate farmers' demand for long-term finance, needed for land purchase, mechanization, or land improvement.[7] Nor could they help farmers issue debt directly on the market in the form of securitized land mortgages. Private mortgage securitization, by which a bank would finance mortgage loans by issuing bonds, was too risky to be left to the private sector. It was attempted several times in the United States and British dominions, to little avail. It was unstable, rarely managing to outlast more than one – two at best – business cycles.[8]

Not only had traditional sectors nothing to gain from corporate finance; they also had everything to lose from banking concentration. The center banks threatened to absorb the country banks and to enter the market for savings deposits, until then the *chasse gardée* of local government-chartered savings banks.

Confronted with the challenge of corporate finance, the traditional sectors faced four options: first, they could try to hinder the development of stock markets by having government pass regulation damaging to the markets. Volatility – markets crashed about every ten years – provided their enemies with an easy battle cry: markets were speculative and amoral, like casinos. Second, traditional sectors could try to defend the local monopolies of local banks by raising center banks' costs of entry in local markets. Denying center banks access to local cash would starve the money market and indirectly contain the growth of the capital market. Alternatively, third, they could try to ask for compensation in the form of subsidized credit. In those days of slim government budgets, this meant having the market work for them. The government would charter special credit banks, with the mission to channel loans in specific traditional sectors, financed through issues of attractive, default-free bonds, enjoying state guarantee. Although state banks would crowd out for-profit market participants in the short term, they would also help diffuse the practice of holding bonds among the population, thereby contributing to the enlargement of the market over time. Fourth, the traditional sectors

---

[7] Prudential rules were thrown to the wind, however, in periods of – and countries subject to – land speculation. The most famous instance is the Australian financial panic of 1896.

[8] Snowden (1995) chronicles four successive attempts in the United States to develop private mortgage securitization, first in the 1870s, another in the 1880s, still another with the federal (yet private) joint-stock mortgage banks in the 1920s, and last with the private issuing of mortgage-backed securities since the 1970s (although the latter is mostly about housing and commercial real estate). Of the four, only the last has not ended up in collective bankruptcy. Congress also established a successful system of central mortgage banking enjoying federal guarantee, the Federal Land Bank System, in 1916.

Table 5.1. *The impact of politics on corporate securities market growth in 1913, ceteris paribus*

	Political power of traditional sectors	
	High	Low
State Institutions		
Centralized	well-developed market, with state credit banks	well-developed market
Decentralized	underdeveloped market	Ø

could accept the verdict of the markets and seek no redress through political action.

Whether the traditional sectors chose to confront, piggyback on, or adjust to market pressures depended on two parameters: their political power and the degree of centralization of the state. Where traditional sectors enjoyed no political power, the political route was closed to them. This was verified irrespective of the nature of state institutions, albeit decentralization seems to have always empowered traditional sectors – the weak political power–decentralization cell was empty (see table 5.1).

Where the traditional sectors did enjoy political power, the critical factor determining their choice of a course of action was the degree of centralization of the state. In centralized states, traditional sectors sought compensation in the form of special credit banks. No other option was open to them. Defending local banking would have been problematic or inefficient. For-profit local banks were indefensible short of nationalizing them or suspending market competition outright – a much too radical option for the time. Defending non-profit banks (savings and cooperatives) was inefficient in the absence of fiscally responsible local governments. The state administered the deposits collected by savings banks, in conformity with state treasury priorities. Furthermore, regulatory wrenches thrown into the wheels of the securities markets might ricochet in the saboteur's face, for special credit banks financed themselves on that market. In sum, the conflict between new and old finance in centralized states where traditional sectors enjoyed political power could be fought only along sectoral lines, and had to be contained; in the end, it was successfully contained to a debate on the relative size of the debt issued by state-guaranteed entities.

In decentralized states, in contrast, traditional sectors had something to defend – the local banks, whether for- or non-profit. Being well represented in the board rooms of the local banks and, in the case of the savings banks, in the local governments monitoring these banks, traditional sectors could make the banks work for themselves. They also enjoyed power at the central government level to block any attempt at dispossessing local governments of their financial powers, as such a decision would have had to pass the high chamber or be acceptable to agriculture ministers, two institutions in which local governments were traditionally overrepresented. Finally, not needing corporate finance and being strong in the lower chamber, as well, allowed traditional sectors to adopt a systematically negative attitude toward financial markets and seek to regulate them out of existence. The financial conflict was geographic, pitting financial center against periphery, and all-out – center banks, the money market, and the capital market, both public and private, were at stake.

From this political dynamic it is easy to predict that corporate securities markets developed mostly in countries either where traditional sectors, agrarians especially, were weak politically, or, if such sectors were strong, where state institutions were centralized. In contrast, markets were least likely to develop in countries where traditional sectors were strong and where state institutions were decentralized.

Three paradigmatic cases

A somewhat detailed presentation of the British, French, and German cases will help flesh out the argument. These three cases were chosen for their closeness of fit with the argument. Britain epitomizes the case in which politically weak traditional sectors adjusted to market forces. France and Germany are two cases in which traditional sectors, agrarians especially, were politically strong. But France was centralized, and traditional sectors played the card of the special credit bank, whereas Germany was decentralized, and agrarians sought to strangle the markets. In the end, the French and British markets boomed, whereas the German one stagnated.

Traditional sectors in Britain were politically weak. Their main component, the agrarians, lost the tariff battle in 1846 and became a spent electoral force afterward. They were a captive constituency of the Conservative party and, in the British majoritarian system, powerless. Even when the party embraced tariff reform in 1907, a program with something for almost everyone, not much was in it for the agrarians.[9] As for the other traditional sectors, it was not until the 1920s that their strategic location – at the center of a partisan system polarized into two class

---

[9] See Verdier 1994, p. 142.

blocs – brought them some visibility.[10] Britain was also a centralized country. Local governments impotently witnessed the absorption of local banks by the London banks.[11] The London Stock Exchange was, behind New York, the second largest worldwide. Corporate bonds and stocks represented 9 and 30 percent respectively of all financial assets in England and Wales in 1913, adding up to 132 percent of GNP.[12] The last regulatory attempt at curbing the growth of the exchange, the Bubble Act, was repealed in 1825. The exchange exhibited the most advanced rules of information disclosure.[13] Its development occurred at the expense of local communities and small business.

In France traditional sectors were strong, thanks mostly to the electoral strength of agriculture, credited for backing the Second Empire and forming a 300-member-strong farm bloc in the Chamber of Deputies in 1890.[14] Agrarians were instrumental in extricating France from the free-trade-oriented bilateral treaty system launched by Cobden and Chevalier in 1860; they formed an iron-and-wheat alliance with industry for a protectionist tariff.[15] Although French agrarians were unhappy with Parisian finance, few local banks lent to farms anyway. The savings banks controlled 23 percent of total deposits, but, like their British counterparts, they placed all their resources in a central state agency. Mutual credit cooperatives failed to take root.

As a result, French agrarians did not try to hinder the spatial concentration of banking or the draining of savings from the provinces, but sought instead to have a part of these savings return to the provinces in the form of state-subsidized credit, both direct and intermediate. In 1852, the year he was elected emperor by a plebiscite, thanks to the rural vote, Louis Napoléon chartered the Crédit Foncier, a private bank financing mortgage loans by issuing bonds enjoying state guarantee.[16] It represented 7 percent of French securities capitalization in 1902. Then, in the 1890s, Parliament laid out the bases for what became the Crédit Agricole – a system of mutual credit societies that were guaranteed, partially run, and subsidized by the state. The republican majority squeezed the required subsidies out of the privately chartered Bank of France, as a condition for the renewal of its fiduciary privilege in 1897.

French agrarians never tried to curb the development of the Paris bourse. They had no credible local non-profit alternative to the displaced

---

[10] This is when the Macmillan Committee discovered the eponymous "gap" in bank funding of small business. See chapter 7, n. 2.
[11] See chapter 3.   [12] According to Goldsmith 1985, p. 233.
[13] According to Sylla 1997, p. 210.   [14] Golob 1944, p. 170.   [15] See Lebovics 1988.
[16] According to Karl Born, "Napoléon was returning a favour to his supporters among the rural population" (1983, p. 104).

local for-profit banks. They also had a stake in the development of the public component of the market in the form of the Crédit Foncier. Corporate stocks and bonds represented 13 and 14 percent of financial assets respectively; the two combined made for 135 percent of GNP (against 132 for England/Wales).[17]

The situation was radically different in Germany, where the decentralization of the state made it possible for local governments, overwhelmingly controlled by agrarians and small business interests, to protect local banking.[18] Strong because of this secure outpost in the countryside, the agrarians pursued a two-pronged strategy; they vetoed any attempt by the imperial government to centralize bank regulation; and they pursued a policy of verbal and regulatory harassment of the securities markets. The German Agrarian Party (it was not a party proper but a lobby), whose support was essential to the survival of almost all imperial governments from 1878 until World War I, launched a crusade against "speculation."[19] The new company laws of 1884 restricted the liberal incorporation law of 1870, raising the minimum size of shares, lengthening the time lag between incorporation and listing, and strengthening the position of the supervisory board.[20]

Then they turned their guns against short selling, a sale involving a future delivery of goods or stocks, claiming that it fueled bearish speculation, depressing the price of farm products. As a result of their pressure, the law of 1896 prohibited futures in grain and flour as well as dealings for the account in the shares of mining and industrial companies, and requested that all parties to deals in industrial futures enter their names in a register, denigrated as the "gambling register." The law increased cash transactions, demoralized the money market, increased costs and legal uncertainty, and led to the migration of business to London.[21] The upshot was a rather depressed stock market. Corporate stock and bonds represented 8 and 2 percent respectively of total financial assets, adding

---

[17] According to Goldsmith 1985, p. 217.

[18] According to Borchardt (1971, p. 117), agricultural mortgages represented half of all mortgages issued by savings banks in 1890, and about a quarter in 1914.

[19] Only under the Caprivi government in the early 1890s did agrarians suffer serious policy setbacks.

[20] On company laws, see Tilly 1986, 126. The German land aristocracy also had a mortgage bank issuing bonds, the Preußische Landschaften, founded in the eighteenth century, but its functioning needed no market, as all the bank did was to bestow a solidary liability on its members' bonds, facilitating their sale by each landowner through local notaries or other informal networks; see Borchardt 1971.

[21] According to a contemporary account (Emery 1908). Also nervous about speculation was the American public. For technical examples of legal prohibitions based on popular suspicion, see Parker 1920, p. 10.

up to about 44 percent of GDP (against 132 and 135 in England/Wales and France).[22]

Evidence from a nine-country dataset

My purpose so far has been to illustrate the argument. I now try to assess its generalizability to the six other cases for which we have data – Belgium, Denmark, Italy, Norway, Switzerland, and the United States. Stock holdings data are taken from Goldsmith's study of national balance sheets, which he established for various countries and benchmark years.[23] Goldsmith's tables provide us with the relative percentage of financial assets held in the form of corporate equity, listed or not. Admittedly, not all stocks were listed on exchanges, let alone actively traded. But since exchanges promoted incorporation and incorporation fed exchanges, the country rank-ordering across the two variables should not differ. Measures of corporate stock holdings are available for at least one of the three years preceding World War I. Figure 5.1 displays the relative size of the corporate stock markets in relation to bonds (corporate and government), bank loans, mortgages, and other financial assets. Foreign financial assets are not included in financial assets.

The small number of observations, nine, recommends saving degrees of freedom. To that effect, I eliminate unnecessary control variables. The earlier survey of the literature suggested four plausible explanations of the origins of corporate securities markets: economic development (GNP per capita), government debt (government bonds divided by total assets), asymmetric information (proxied by the proportion of corporate bonds among corporate instruments),[24] and legal origins (dummy for common law). A look at the bivariate scatterplots between each control variable and the ratio of corporate stocks to financial assets reveals two relations: a first between market development and economic development (GNP per capita), filling in for the demand for securities (see figure 5.2). This finding confirms the historians' hunch that the size of corporate securities markets in 1913 reflected levels of development.

A second relation is also observable between market development and common law origins – this can be seen in figure 5.2 as well, where the

[22] According to Goldsmith 1985, pp. 225–26.

[23] Goldsmith (1985) also provided data for India, Russia, and South Africa, which I did not include for lack of data on the other variables.

[24] I proxied asymmetric information by the proportion of bonds among securities in accordance with Baskin and Miranti's (1997) finding that poor information led investors to choose bonds over stocks.

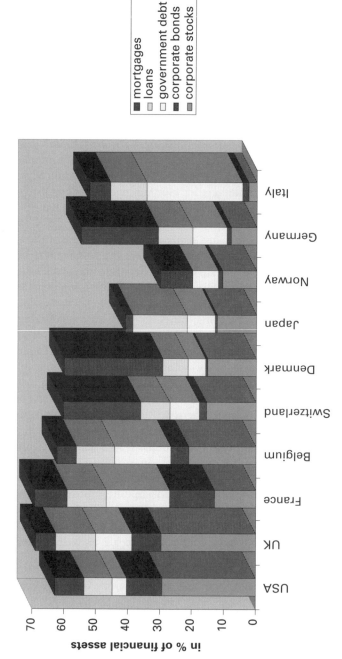

Data description and sources: Countries are ranked by the proportion of corporate instruments (stocks and bonds). Each type of asset is calculated as percentage of all financial assets circa 1913. The source is Goldsmith 1985, appendix A.

Figure 5.1. Selected financial assets in percentage of total financial assets, 1912–14

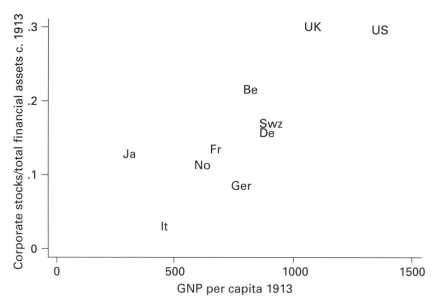

Figure 5.2. Stock holdings and wealth, 1913

common law countries, Britain and the United States, are both located at the top of the graph. Although two countries do not make a rule, qualitative evidence indicates that Australia, Canada, and South Africa also had very well-developed stock markets. And they also were among the wealthiest countries in the world, confirming the potential problem of multicolinearity between common law origins and wealth exhibited in figure 5.2. The other two control variables, government debt and information asymmetry, show no relation with corporate securities markets (results unreported).[25] This preliminary analysis suggests the need to control for one variable in all subsequent experiments – GNP per capita – proxying both for demand for securities and common law origins.

I then plot the bivariate relation between stock market development and the local non-profit banking sector in figure 5.3. The relation is negative, confirming the crowding-out hypothesis, according to which capital locked into local networks was unavailable for redeployment toward the financial markets. Visual observation further suggests that most of the observations are aligned on two parallel lines according to wealth – the United States, UK, Denmark, and Switzerland, the wealthier countries, are on the higher line, whereas Belgium, France, and Italy, the countries with lower GNP per capita, are on the lower one. I check the robustness

[25] Even when controlling for GNP per capita.

Figure 5.3. Stock holdings and local non-profit banks, 1913

of this clue by using multivariate regression (OLS), with bootstrapped standard errors and confidence intervals. The dependent variable is the relative size of stock holdings in the financial system, the independent variable is the relative size of the local non-profit banking sector, and the control variable is GNP per capita, all for 1913.

Statistical results for the crowding-out hypothesis are reported in regression 1, table 5.2. The strongest impact is that of wealth: a one-standard-deviation increase in GNP per capita ($262) yields an increase in the dependent variable of almost one (79 percent) standard deviation ($[262*0.00027]/0.09 = 0.79$). The coefficient for the local non-profit banking variable is statistically significant (at the 1 percent level); a one-standard-deviation increase in that variable corresponds to a decrease of less than half ($[0.24^* - 0.15]/0.09 = -0.40$) a standard deviation in the dependent variable. Therefore, the 1913 data indicate that the share of corporate stock holdings among financial assets was a function of the level of economic development, primarily, and of the size of the local non-profit banking sector, secondarily. The poorer the economy and the stronger the savings banks, the smaller the market.

I use a similar model to estimate the relationship between stock market size and state centralization (the state-centralization hypothesis). Results are reported in regression 2, table 5.2. Both coefficients are significantly

Table 5.2. *The origins of stock markets*

	Dependent variable: Corporate stocks, c. 1913	
	1	2
Local non-profit banks 1913	−0.15 (0.06)*** [0.04]***	
State centralization c. 1880		0.19 (0.06)** [0.17]***
GNP per capita 1913	0.0003 (0.00003)*** [0.00005]***	0.0004 (0.00004)*** [0.00007]***
Intercept	−0.005 (0.05)	−0.25 (0.06)***

Methodology: Ordinary least squares with standard errors and bias-corrected confidence intervals calculated on 1000 bootstraps. Each cell reports values of observed coefficients and corresponding regular and bootstrapped standard errors in parentheses and brackets respectively. Confidence intervals using bootstrapped standard errors are bias-corrected; *, **, *** indicate coefficients situated in the 90%, 95%, and 99% confidence intervals respectively. The number of observations is nine: Belgium, Denmark, France, Germany, Italy, Norway, Switzerland, UK, and the USA.
Data description and sources: Corporate stocks is calculated as a percentage of all financial assets circa 1913; Goldsmith 1985. *GNP per capita* is from Bairoch and Lévy-Leboyer 1981, p. 10. *Local non-profit banks* is the market share of that category calculated in deposits, but assets in the Swiss case (see appendix 2). *State centralization* measures central government revenues as a percentage of general government revenues circa 1880 (see appendix 3).

different from zero with 99 percent confidence. Once again, the strongest impact is that of wealth – about 100 percent calculated in standard deviation change ([262*0.00036]/0.09 = 1.05). The equivalent impact of state centralization is around 40 percent ([0.18*0.19]/0.09 = 0.38). In order to get a sense of each country's relative position, I plot the partial regression plots of regression 2 (figure 5.4).[26] Holding wealth constant,

---

[26] Each plot generates a coefficient and a fit that are equal to the coefficient and fit of the dependent variable against the chosen right-hand-side variable, while simultaneously controlling for the effect of the other right-hand-side variables on both variables. See Bollen and Jackman 1990.

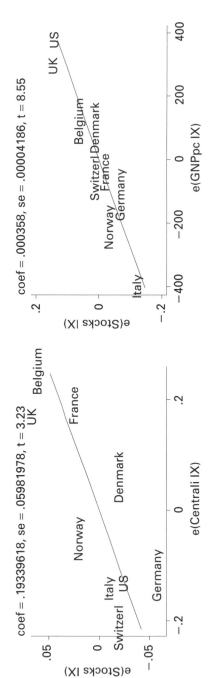

coef = .19339618, se = .05981978, t = 3.23

coef = .000358, se = .00004186, t = 8.55

Note: X stands for right-hand-side variable(s) other than the one reported on the horizontal axis; e(VARIABLE|X) stands for residuals of VARIABLE regressed against X. It is a property of partial regression plots that the coefficients, standard errors, and *t* statistics for each plotted independent variable should be the same as in the corresponding regression.

Figure 5.4. Partial regression plots for regression 2, table 5.2

stock markets were most developed in Belgium, the UK, and France –
the centralized countries – and least developed in Germany, Switzerland,
Italy, and the United States – the decentralized countries. It is theoret-
ically gratifying to observe the proximity between the German and US
observations on the left-hand graph of figure 5.4. Despite hosting the
largest corporate securities market in the world, the United States was no
exception to the fact that decentralization had a negative influence on the
development of financial markets. This negative influence was hidden by
the contrary influence of wealth. It so happened that the United States
also had one of the richest economies on earth.

Conclusion

The industrial revolution touched off a concomitant process of banking
agglomeration and market securitization (corporate finance) that threatened to divert capital from traditional sectors. Mobilized and integrated
markets flourished in the absence of blocking coalitions that had an interest in keeping finance local. The power of blocking coalitions was a
reverse function of the degree of centralization of state institutions.

The evidence confirms the positive role of wealth. The ubiquity of
the wealth variable points to the relevance of an entirely different family
of explanations, stressing economic as opposed to political constraints.
Although the present evidence is compatible with the legal origins argument, it would take a different historical reality, one in which wealth and
common law did not coincide, to separate its effect from that of wealth.

6   The origins of universal banking

> The business of banking ought to be simple; if it is hard it is wrong. The only securities which a banker, using money that he may be asked at short notice to repay, ought to touch, are those which are easily saleable and easily intelligible.   Bagehot 1991, p. 119.

Commercial banks varied between extreme specialization – as in Britain, where merchant banks, colonial banks, clearing banks, issuing banks, trustee banks, discounters, jobbers, stockbrokers, and savings banks each engaged in distinct financial activities – and universality – as in Germany, where all these activities were indifferently handled by large banks. More generally, a universal banking system is defined as a system in which banks engage in both lending and the underwriting of securities. In contrast, a specialized banking system keeps the two activities under separate roofs. Before 1913, universal banking is commonly held to have existed in Belgium, Germany, Austria, and Italy, whereas specialized banking was mostly encountered in France and the Anglo-Saxon countries.

Gerschenkron argued that universal banking reflected a median intensity in firms' capital needs – higher than in England, but lower than in Russia.[1] From the perspective of the information asymmetry literature, universal banking is the most advanced form of delegated monitoring in conditions of acute information asymmetry.[2]

The present account stresses the effect of capital spatial concentration. The size of the financial center determined the degree of specialization of bank assets in that center. Wherever the financial market was allowed to develop unshackled, banks tended to specialize. The hypothesis builds on Adam Smith's (1976, p. 21) famous quotation that the division of labor is limited only by the extent of the market:

As it is the power of exchanging that gives the occasion to the division of labour, so the extent of this division must always be limited by the extent of that power, or, in other words, by the extent of the market.

---

[1] See chapter 1 above.
[2] See Calomiris 1995 for an argument along these lines.

In contrast, legal protection of local and non-profit banks reduced the expected returns of specialization. Universal banking was a rational response to market segmentation.

Market segmentation was a necessary but not sufficient cause for universal banking. A second condition had to be met in the form of the existence of a lender of last resort. Universal banking was less liquid than specialized banking. The absence of developed corporate securities markets in most segmented credit systems meant that center banks could not solve their liquidity problems by unloading illiquid loans on the securities market. Their liquidity, instead, required a lender of last resort in the form of a modern central bank.

These two conditions (segmentation and central banking) in turn were two consequences of one single cause – the degree of centralization of the state. Financial segmentation was found along with decentralized state institutions (see chapter 3), whereas central banking first appeared in centralized states. As a result, universal banking was most likely to emerge in states that were neither so centralized that local banks were displaced by center banks, nor so decentralized that there was no central bank.

I claim that market segmentation and central banking were two necessary and sufficient conditions for the emergence of universal banking. I devote a section to the correlation between universal banking and an undeveloped corporate securities market. I survey the unexplained residual in a penultimate section, before summarizing the main findings.

The first requisite for universal banking: market segmentation

Following the payments system revolution, the joint-stock banks moved along a secular trajectory from investment banking, in which they had catered exclusively to new and concentrated industries, toward modern deposit banking, in which they would mostly cater to individual depositors. When allowed to capture the market of individuals' deposits unhindered, joint-stock banks became deposit banks, leaving the business of investment banking to institutions especially created for that purpose – investment funds, investment banks, and the stock market. They abandoned the field of investment banking altogether in order to match the maturity of their assets with that of their newly gained short liabilities. The outcome was specialized banking.

However, if frozen in mid-course, because local commercial or non-profit banks cornered the market for smaller depositors, the center banks were left to cater to a clientele of large, industrial depositors, with whom they found both their most profitable lending opportunities and, as "every loan creates a deposit," their most abundant sources of deposits.[3] Unable to fully capture the field of deposit banking, joint-stock banks were forced to rely on their own resources to a greater extent than did pure deposit banks. Their liabilities showed a greater share of "own resources" relative to individual deposits (I will use this ratio below to measure universal banking). The greater cost of "own resources" – shares earned more than deposits – was an additional reason to stick to investment banking, a more profitable, because riskier, line of business. Consequently, unlike joint-stock banks in concentrated capital markets, joint-stock banks in segmented markets could not completely vacate the field of investment banking. Segmentation of the deposit market was the first requisite for universal banking.

Because geographic segmentation was a cause for universality, banks in universal banking systems were quite "specialized" in terms of whom they lent to. Center banks lent to large national firms, and local banks lent to small local firms. The banks were also "specialized" in terms of whom they borrowed from. The bourgeoisie banked with center, branched banks, whereas peasants and artisans banked with local banks, savings banks, and mutual credit societies. Capital mobility was territorially and socially bound; Siemens, for example, could not raise capital from the lower classes to finance its heavy immobilization. In contrast, joint-stock banks in Britain and France would lend short to any firm, irrespective of size, and draw resources from all depositors without regard for social strata and area of residence.

Cash-starved center banks could not make up for the deficient domestic money market by tapping the international money market because segmented credit markets were also the least open toward international banking with one exception – Switzerland (see chapter 4).

The second requisite for universal banking: liquidity guarantee

Fragmentation of the deposit market was a necessary, but not sufficient, condition for the stabilization of universal banking. For this to happen, a second condition had to be met as well: the existence of a liquidity guarantor.

Mixing long- with short-term assets, universal banks had difficulties matching the maturity profile of their assets with that of their liabilities. The source of the problem was not so much that assets were systematically

---

[3] See Riesser 1977. The citation is generally attributed to Reginald McKenna.

longer than liabilities; all banks took advantage of the information and collective action costs faced by their creditors to engage in maturity transformation. Rather, the issue was one of cyclicality. Cyclical business downturns typically froze assets (the bank couldn't sell except at an unacceptable loss) while melting liabilities (actual terms of deposit grew shorter), thereby worsening the mismatch in maturity profiles between the two sides of the balance sheet. The extent of the problem depended, of course, on the intensity of the crisis, but also (and this is why universality presented a higher risk than specialization) on the range of maturity between the most and least liquid assets. Mixing one-day-long with one-year-long assets made the bank more vulnerable to an illiquidity crisis than mixing one-day-long with three-month-long assets or six-month-long with one-year-long assets.

The situation grew worse with the product diversification in which banks engaged toward the end of the nineteenth century. To attract new business, banks developed new instruments with variable liquidity. The discounting of commercial paper, we saw earlier, was progressively replaced by advances on current accounts, substituting for a rigid ninety-day loan one that was flexible and that could effortlessly be prolonged. New as well, advances against stock exchange securities could be temporarily or indefinitely renewed, depending on the health of the stock market. Individual deposits with all kinds of terms could all be withdrawn at a moment's notice against a penalty the amount of which reflected the length of the otherwise-due advance notice. The new instruments – current accounts, advances, and deposits – were elastic and subject to the vicissitudes of the business cycle.

The appearance of elastic instruments made balance sheets uninformative. They would not reveal the actual solvency of a bank, all the more so as they were regularly window-dressed to hide profits from shareholders. Outsiders could tell only post facto, after crises weeded out insolvent banks. The impenetrability of balance sheets diluted a means for bankers to elicit depositors' trust – the capacity to commit to certain liquidity targets. Absent such a commitment, depositors would invariably suspect that mixed banks were placing the needs of the industries in which bank directors had vested interests above those of the banks' depositors. The accepted way out of this dilemma was to establish a rule of thumb, which could signal liquidity in a way that was, in Bagehot's terms, "simple" and "intelligible." The London clearers professed to touch only short assets, while the French bankers, following Heny Germain, professed to stay out of industry at all costs.

Universal banking was therefore unstable. The unpredictability of crises, combined with the cyclicality of most assets and liabilities, made universal banks either unprofitable during booms (they were in a sense financing a greater proportion of very liquid assets with highly stable liabilities) or insolvent during slumps (they were financing less liquid assets with more volatile liabilities). This uncertainty plus the high monitoring costs faced by depositors made universal banking an unlikely occurrence. Without a lender of last resort committed to tiding them over periods of economic slowdown, the universal banks had difficulties eliciting depositors' confidence.

The decisive step toward the institution of a liquidity guarantor to joint-stock banks in times of financial crises was the creation of a central bank.[4] Historically, a central bank is a private note-issuing monopoly – a rent the ruler would concede in exchange for emergency cash and the underwriting of treasury paper.[5] Central banking helped promote universal banking in two ways. Its first and more basic contribution was to monopolize note issuing, taking it away from commercial banks. Banks that finance a sizable part of their business by issuing notes must hold many liquid assets (bills of exchange bearing more than one signature) in order to be able to redeem their notes in cash when they are presented for payment. Systems of free banking (only four were left by the turn of the century: Canada, Australia, New Zealand, and Switzerland), in which commercial banks were banks of issue, could not afford the illiquidity of universal banking. The few attempts to mix the two, in Belgium before 1850 and in Switzerland before 1905, were unsuccessful, ending in a crash in the Belgian case and fueling recurring crises and depressing the exchange in the Swiss case.[6] Second, central banks helped stabilize universal banking by assuming the role of lender of last resort in the event of a depositor run. Though less volatile than notes, deposits were not predictable enough to serve as a basis for underwriting or for building durable relationships with firms.

Unfortunately, the extension of a liquidity guarantee to commercial banks is not an event that one can easily observe and precisely time. As Ziegler (1990) reminded us in his study of the Bank of England, a note-issuing monopoly is not necessarily a liquidity guarantor. But it can

---

[4] Central banking is not the only mechanism that can help banks overcome the liquidity and commitment problems present in universal banking systems; a state regulator, armed with inspection rights, along with treasury support, is an equally valid alternative. Although more common today, the regulatory option was found only in Sweden during the nineteenth century. Self-regulation by a corporatist association of bankers, along with ad hoc treasury support, was found in Canada.

[5] On the historical origins of central banks, see North and Weingast 1989 and Broz 1998.

[6] On Belgium, see Chlepner 1926, p. 317; on Switzerland, see Guex 1993, pp. 20–38. Like Chlepner (1943, p. 35) with respect to Belgium, Tilly (1986, 122) argues that the creation of the Prussian State Bank in 1846, well before the deposit revolution, helped promote investment banking in Prussia.

become one at the government's request, usually in the wake of a serious banking panic; the central bank, after all, owes its rent to the government. Complicating the matter is that central banks are deterred from extending any automatic guarantee, lest they invite moral hazard. Central banks typically tailored the guarantee to the needs of their banking system (limited in Britain and France, greater elsewhere).

Nevertheless, it is possible to identify a relation between state centralization, the early creation of the central bank, and the early extension of the liquidity guarantee. First, the timing of central-bank creation was related to the timing and depth of state formation. Note-issuing monopolies were granted earlier in centralized countries (Britain 1684, France 1800) than in decentralized countries (Switzerland 1905, Australia 1911, United States 1913, and Canada 1934).[7] It usually took a strong political center (or, as in Denmark and Norway, a military and financial debacle) to impose an English-type central bank on its unwilling periphery. Indeed, the centralization of note issuing would sometimes diminish the amount of short-term capital available for commerce and industry located at the periphery. Having to make its notes as good as gold, a central bank typically invested in commercial paper of high quality – issued by a reputable merchant or industrialist and endorsed by a reputable banker, mostly based in the center. Governments in Britain and France would in vain press their central bank to open branches in the countryside; either the bank would refuse to create regional branches or, when it did, it would discriminate against them.[8] Toward the end of the century, however, the severe competition with joint-stock banks for good paper led central banks in many countries to rediscount larger quantities of country paper.[9] Another negative distributional consequence of central banking for the periphery stemmed from what is called nowadays the "too big to fail" doctrine, according to which the beneficiaries of the liquidity guarantee tend to be the largest banks, mostly based in the center. Last, with its deeper involvement in foreign business, the financial center had a lower tolerance for monetary slack than the agrarian periphery.[10]

As a result, wherever agrarian peripheries had the power to do so, they blocked the creation of a private central bank. It took fifteen years (1891– 1905) of trials and a couple of referenda on the Swiss *Großbanken* to overcome the opposition of local interests in alliance with Left politicians, who

---

[7] For a similar argument, see Broz 1998, 242.

[8] On Britain, see Ziegler 1990, pp. 131–34; on France, see Plessis 1985, pp. 158, 279, and Bouvier 1988, p. 80.

[9] More on this can be found in chapter 3 in the section "A French exception?"

[10] See National Monetary Commission 1911, p. 506.

supported nationalization.[11] Likewise, it took three attempts for central banking to take root in the United States, and the final outcome fell short of a central bank, as money-center banks conceded a plurality of reserve banks to the local states.[12] In Sweden, where the periphery was strong, though not decisively so, the agrarians pressed for a government-run central bank and successfully managed to gain control over it against the opposition of the money-center banks, whose own objective was a privately owned central bank, independent from the state.[13] In Germany, where state building was too advanced for the periphery to oppose the creation of a privately owned central bank, the agrarians kept pushing for ever tighter *Reich* regulations.

Second, the timing of the liquidity guarantee was also related to state centralization. For instance, although Scandinavian countries had early national banks (Sweden in 1688, Norway and Denmark in 1816 and 1818 respectively), the pull of the agrarian periphery was such that it was not until the end of the century (slightly earlier in Denmark) that each state could force its bank to take on the function of liquidity guarantor of the for-profit banking sector.[14] In the case of Spain, a country torn by political and territorial rivalries, the liquidity guarantor came in 1924, long after the national bank was created in 1874.

The relation between the timing of the liquidity guarantee and state centralization is quite systematic. To show this, I built a dependent variable, using Broz's timing of the advent of last-resort lending for ten early central banks (UK 1860, Netherlands and Portugal 1870, Austria-Hungary 1878, France, Germany, Denmark 1880, Finland, Sweden, Norway 1890). I postponed the Norwegian date by a decade (setting it to 1900), to reflect the fact that relations between the central bank and the commercial banks escalated into an open conflict in the 1890s, with some banks creating their own central bank – hardly a propitious climate for last-resort lending.[15] I supplemented Broz's list with a second one, including central banks that were expressly created to extend a liquidity guarantee to unstable banking systems. In the latter case, the advent of last-resort lending corresponds with the creation of the note-issuing monopoly, making its timing interpretation-free (Belgium 1850, Italy 1893, Switzerland 1905, Australia 1911, the United States 1913, New Zealand 1930, and Canada 1934). The date used for Spain was 1924.[16]

---

[11] See Zimmerman 1987.   [12] See Broz 1997.   [13] See Nygren 1983, 34.

[14] On Denmark, see Johansen 1992, p. 165; Per Hansen 1991, 25; on Sweden, see Nygren 1983, 34; on Norway, see Egge 1983, 273–75. For a comparative treatment, see Goodhart 1988.

[15] See Egge 1983, 278.   [16] According to Martin-Aceña 1995, p. 504.

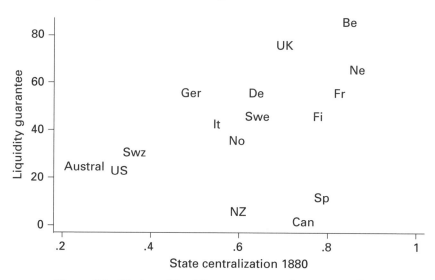

Figure 6.1. Timing of liquidity guarantee and state centralization

I then inverted the scale so that higher values correspond with earlier (and stronger) liquidity guarantee. The resulting measure of liquidity guarantee is given by the formula:

1934 – year of initiation of last-resort lending,

with 1934 being the year of creation of the Canadian central bank, the maximum value taken by the variable.

I plot the bivariate relation between the thus-inverted measure of liquidity guarantee and the tax proxy for state centralization in figure 6.1. The plot reveals a rather strong linear correlation, spoiled by three potential outliers – Canada, New Zealand, and Spain. The first two, to which one should add Australia, are real outliers. In all three cases, as I explained in an earlier chapter, the lateness of the central bank did not reflect domestic state institutions, but the international status of these countries as British dominions. They should not be included in any test featuring state centralization among the regressors.[17] The Spanish observation is more difficult to account for and will be the object of a special discussion in the penultimate section.

I have argued in this section that universal banking needed a liquidity guarantor to remove note issuing from commercial banking and stabilize

[17] See remarks to that effect in the introduction, in the section "Case selection and methodology," and in chapter 3, in the section "The agglomeration hypothesis."

deposits. I have argued and shown that the existence of a liquidity guarantor, in turn, reflected the existence of a strong political center, able to impose its preference against the opposition of the agrarian periphery; the more centralized were state structures, the easier it was for the center to overcome the opposition of the periphery.

Universal banking as an inverted-U function of state centralization

We can now bring the two necessary conditions for universal banking together. Segmentation of the capital market and the existence of a central bank extending a liquidity guarantee together yielded universal banking. But if one of these conditions was not met, specialized banking obtained. The segmentation condition was not met in fully centralized polities in which the agrarian periphery was very weak; the liquidity-guarantee condition was not met in very decentralized polities in which the agrarian periphery was very strong. Only in the intermediate category of semi-centralized states, in which center and periphery were balanced, were the two conditions jointly met and universal banking thus made possible. Universal banking was an inverted-U function of the degree of state formation.

The predicted inverted-U function can be represented in the form of a graph, with the horizontal axis representing the centralization of the state and the vertical axis measuring the likelihood of universal banking (figure 6.2). The segmentation effect is captured by a negative linear function; a more centralized state generates a lesser need for universal banking. In contrast, the liquidity guarantee effect is captured by a positive linear function; a more centralized state favors the provision of the liquidity guarantee (without which universal banking is unsustainable). The product of the two linear functions generates an inverted-U function.

The joint-product hypothesis

The present argument yields two distinctly testable hypotheses about the origins of universal banking. A first hypothesis (the *joint-product hypothesis*) bears on the immediate origins: universal banking was the joint product of market fragmentation and liquidity guarantee. A second hypothesis (the *inverted-U curve hypothesis*) bears on the indirect, distant origins: universal banking is an inverted-U function of state centralization. The two hypotheses are tested successively.

In both cases, the first order of business is to measure the dependent variable – universality v. specialization. Ideally, one would want to

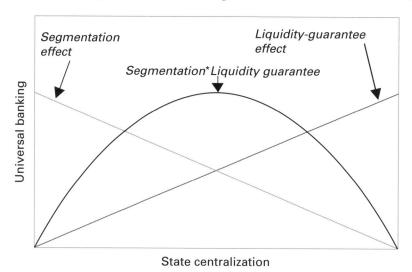

Figure 6.2. The inverted-U curve model

measure the average maturity of bank assets for a sample of banks in each country. In practice, this is not easy to accomplish, for banks grouped assets with little respect for maturity and in ways that were not comparable across banks and countries. Furthermore, limited availability of bank accounts in many countries disqualifies random sampling. The measure of banking specialization must instead be proxied.

I used the equity-to-deposit ratio. It is the ratio of a bank's least liquid resources (capital plus reserves) to the most liquid ones (individual deposits, savings, and notes, when any). The idea behind the measure is straightforward: commercial banks that specialize in short-term lending usually have little need for long-term equity, but finance most of their activity with cheaper short-term deposits and savings (and notes for banks possessing note-issuing rights), without risk of illiquidity. In contrast, commercial banks with long-term positions in industry must employ dear long-term resources. The ratio is bounded upward, for too high a value would indicate a specialization in investment banking.[18]

---

[18] Surely, the existence of a central bank proffering a liquidity guarantee to the commercial banks relaxes the extent to which universal banks have to cover long-term loans with equity. But it does not eliminate it altogether, for this guarantee is never complete. The supply of liquidity to the banking system is constrained by the central bank's obligation to stabilize the currency. Furthermore, wary of moral hazard, the central bank exercises discretion in extending its guarantee to each individual bank, and thus can induce commercial banks to maintain what are considered in national banking milieus as safe levels of equity.

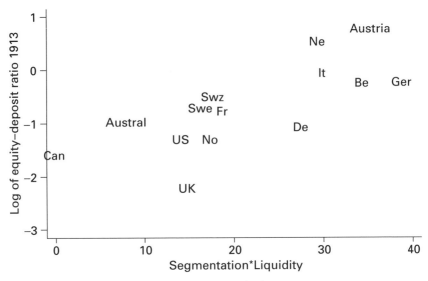

Figure 6.3. The joint-product hypothesis

The data for the year 1913, shown in appendix 4, track the overall sense of historians: at the lower extreme, the specialized Anglo-Saxon banks (UK, Canada, and the USA), at the other the universal type (Germany, Italy, and Austria-Hungary). Spain is definitely an outlier; it has a 5-to-1 equity–deposit ratio, reflecting an investment banking specialization. I dropped the Spanish observation from the present analysis and will come back to it in the next section. The only real surprise is the Netherlands, a country with no documented consistent long-term banking up until World War I, and yet for which the ratio is inexplicably high.[19] I will come back to this case in the next section.

I first consider the joint-product hypothesis. The hypothesized independent variable is the product of market segmentation and liquidity guarantee. The first term (segmentation) is the aggregate market shares of local non-profit, state, and, whenever available, country banking. The logic is that center banks are competing for deposits with sheltered banks. The second term (liquidity guarantee) is proxied by the timing of liquidity-guarantee variable (used above in figure 6.1). I multiply the two terms because they are both necessary to produce universal banking. The bivariate

---

[19] Although most historical accounts point to the emergence of universal banking in 1910–11, that alone cannot account for the 1913 datum. Vanthemsche (1991, p. 107) and Jonker (1991) date the Dutch move toward universal banking to 1910, Van Gor and Koelewijn (1995, p. 158) to World War I.

Table 6.1. *The joint-product hypothesis*

	Dependent variable: Log of equity–deposit ratio, 1913		
	1	2	3
Segmentation Liquidity guarantee*	0.07 (0.02)** [0.02]***	0.05 (0.02)*** [0.01]**	0.10 (0.04)** [0.06]*
GNP per capita 1860	0.0007 (0.001) [0.001]		
Growth 1890–1913	−0.004 (0.02) [0.03]		
Financial depth 1913		−0.0005 (0.003) [0.005]	
Segmentation			−1.15 (1.55) [2.57]
Liquidity guarantee			−0.02 (0.01) [0.03]
Intercept	−2.25 (1.18)*	−1.75 (0.50)***	−1.33 (0.62)*
Number of obs.	14[a]	13[b]	14[a]

Methodology: Ordinary least squares with standard errors and bias-corrected confidence intervals calculated on 1000 bootstraps. Each cell reports values of observed coefficients and corresponding regular and bootstrapped standard errors in parentheses and brackets respectively. Confidence intervals using bootstrapped standard errors are bias-corrected; *, **, *** indicate coefficients situated in the 90%, 95%, and 99% confidence intervals respectively.

Sources: The dependent variable is the equity–deposit ratio, 1913, of appendix 4. For *GNP per capita 1860*, Bairoch and Lévy-Leboyer 1981, p. 10. For *growth 1890–1913*, I used the difference between the 1913 index (=100) and the 1890 index, Maddison 1991, p. 209. This difference is then subtracted from 100 so that a higher value corresponds with a higher growth rate. For *financial depth*, see table 3.2. *Segmentation* is the aggregation of the country, local non-profit, and state banking sectors in table 3.1. For *liquidity guarantee*, see text.

[a] Australia, Austria-Hungary, Belgium, Canada, Denmark, France, Germany, Italy, Netherlands, Norway, Sweden, Switzerland, UK, USA.
[b] Australia, Belgium, Canada, Denmark, France, Germany, Italy, Netherlands, Norway, Sweden, Switzerland, UK, USA.

scattergram of this variable and the equity-to-deposit ratio, shown in figure 6.3, provides visual evidence of the strength of the findings (Spain is excluded). Note the presence of Austria, a country that we had to exclude from most tests for lack of data, as a country with high segmentation, early liquidity guarantee, and much universal banking. Note also the extreme location of Canada to the left, reflecting a low value on *both* fragmentation and last resort lending – an anomaly reflecting previous English colonization.

I check the robustness of the joint-product hypothesis displayed in figure 6.3 by controlling for financial depth and for two measures of Gerschenkron's timing-of-industrialization hypothesis – relative backwardness (measured by the GNP per capita in 1860) and speed of late industrialization (measured by the growth of GNP in the 1890–1913 period). I use OLSs with bootstrapped standard errors and confidence intervals. Findings are reported in table 6.1. The first finding is the lack of association between the economic control variables and the universal banking variable. The coefficients for the variables relative wealth in 1860 and the speed of growth in the 1890–1913 period are not significantly different from zero (regression 1), even when tested alone (results unreported). I do not claim to have falsified Gerschenkron's hypothesis about relative backwardness and the impact of growth spurts, as it is first and foremost a longitudinal hypothesis, for which the present methodology is not the most appropriate. The financial-depth ratio also fails to exhibit any impact (regression 2). The second finding concerns the joint-product variable. Its coefficient is significantly different from zero across specifications, although its impact is difficult to interpret given the interactive nature of the variable. In regression 3, I falsify the null hypothesis that it is not the product but the joint presence of the segmentation and liquidity guarantee variables that are responsible for universal banking.

The inverted-U curve hypothesis

The second hypothesis, that universalism is an inverted-U function of state centralization, is plotted in figure 6.4. The inverted-U is observable, except in the cases of the Netherlands, Belgium, and France. I explore these cases in the penultimate section. There are finally smaller anomalies that lessen the fit of the expected relation with the measured reality. The level of universal banking in Norway is lower than expected. Being a further step remote from the dependent variable, the inverted-U curve hypothesis suffers more exceptions than the joint-product hypothesis. Note last that the dominions, Australia and Canada, fit the curve for the wrong reason.

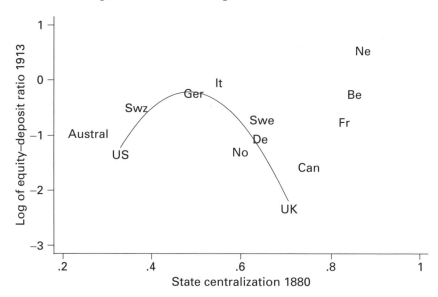

Figure 6.4. The inverted-U curve hypothesis

Universal banking and the stock market

Many financial historians have pointed to a correlation between universal banking and the existence of a poorly developed stock market. Figure 6.5 evidences this fact by graphing universal banking against corporate securities market size. The two Anglo-Saxon countries in the sample, the UK and the USA, have specialized commercial banks and large markets, whereas Italy and Germany have universal banks and small markets. France, Japan, Denmark, and Switzerland score in the median. I will ignore for the moment the two outliers – Belgium and Norway.

Historians differ as to how to explain this stylized fact. Some make market development endogenous to banking specialization, arguing that universal banks choked financial markets, locking in resources that would otherwise have flown into the markets.[20] Others argued, instead, that the causation ran the other way. In the absence of a well-functioning securities market, banks were forced to develop an internal financial market, holding some of the equity themselves and placing the rest through each bank's retail placement network. Michie (n.d., p. 10) argues that the taxation and overregulation of the German stock market may account for the growth of universal banking in Germany, "which shielded activity in securities

[20] See Riesser 1977, p. 772, Tilly 1966, p. 120, Sylla 1997, p. 211.

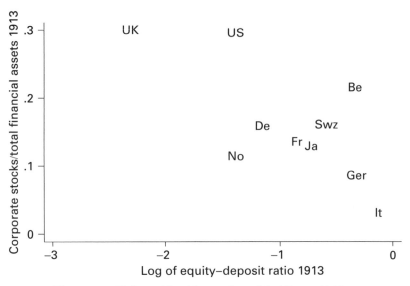

Figure 6.5. Universal banking and stock holdings, 1913

from both taxation and external scrutiny." In a similar vein, Fohlin (1997, 218) argues that the regulatory constraints imposed by German law on firms seeking access to the market account for the long-term bank–firm relations that were typical of universal banking in Germany.

I make a different argument. I do not believe that center banks and ex-changes were in competition, except perhaps in the very short run. In the long run, however, markets and center banks were complementary in two ways: commercial banks supplied markets with daily operating liquidity, whereas investment banks unloaded illiquid loans onto the market in ex-change for cash. This is the way banks operated in countries of specialized banking, France and Britain. There is no logical reason why the location of commercial and investment banking under the same roof in Germany, Italy, and Austria should have lessened the mutual dependence between banks and markets. Rather, universal banking, in these countries, was a pathological development of center banking, one that, like thin trading in financial markets, had its root in insufficient access to liquidity. Being both symptoms of crowding out, universal banking and market atrophy thus coexisted.

Consider the German case. The large local non-profit sector limited the center banks' access to the deposit market. Consequently, these banks could not lend these deposits to the stock market. Trading in Frankfurt was thin. The banks could not easily securitize loans, or had to do it themselves – issuing equity, placing it among their clients through their retail networks, holding the residual that found no taker. This residual was in turn used as a *marge de manoeuvre* which the banks used to make the market for the stock. Keeping the stock at a desirable level insured the bank's customers against losses that could have negative consequences for the other business that these customers might have had with the bank. The banks did not diversify their risk but, absent an independent securities market, ended up carrying it all. As a result, German banking was recurrently threatened with crises of illiquidity, which could be avoided only through the presence of a high-minded central bank.

The US case is also paradigmatic. Although the deposit market was fragmented, preventing center banks from branching out freely and becoming full-fledged deposit banks, the pyramiding of reserves in New York banks, though no substitute for branch banking, provided enough cash to fuel trading in the securities market. Until 1913, in the absence of a central bank, New York bankers were forced to specialize; the center banks focused their activity around short, commercial loans, whereas a handful of private houses monopolized investment banking. Combining both activities would have made the center banks vulnerable to the seasonal jolts that shook up the money market during each crop season. Once the Fed was created, whether the banks would remain specialized or expand their product mix then depended on the relative size represented by current and checking accounts in a bank's balance sheet. There is evidence that, after 1913, some of the largest New York banks developed investment banking units.[21]

The Swiss case was similar to the US case, though for a different reason. Market fragmentation would probably have stunted the growth of the stock market, had not Swiss bankers, like their New York equivalents, found alternative sources of funds. These alternative sources of funds consisted, first, of the balances held by country banks (which held about a tenth of the deposit market). The Swiss case resembled the US case in that respect, although the Swiss country bank sector was much smaller than its US equivalent. The second source of funds consisted of foreign investment. For reasons wholly exogenous to the present analysis, Swiss bankers were able to capture a large segment of international banking. Fueled from abroad, the Swiss stock market was rather active, despite its limited attraction of domestic savings. The reliance on foreign business had the further advantage of allowing the banks to diversify their portfolio. It also had the drawback, though, of making the banks vulnerable to currency risk. Hence, they needed a central

---

[21] See Cleveland and Huertas 1985.

bank to stabilize the currency, in addition to serving as a lender of last resort.

The next section systematically goes over the unexplained residual.

Omitted variables

Several cases fit the argument in part only. The dominions, Belgium, France, Switzerland, Norway, and the Netherlands are outliers with respect to the inverted-U curve hypothesis, but not with respect to the joint-product hypothesis. The Spanish case does not fit the argument at all. I go over these cases, with an eye for omitted variables. Two of these variables were already flagged in previous chapters – the international environment and liberalism. One additional variable is specific to the present chapter – backwardness.

Dominions

The present theory leaves out the international dimension, even though it played a role in several ways. First, it interfered with the domestic logic of interest representation. I covered the case of the dominions in chapter 3. Their financial structure did not reflect the distribution of power between central and local governments, but both state and financial structures reflected British influence. The link with the British empire is responsible for the establishment of a concentrated banking and market system, yet one without a head – the Bank of England served as de facto central bank until a later date. In contrast, imperialism had no consistent impact on state structure, which could be centralized as in Canada and New Zealand or decentralized as in Australia.

Switzerland

Second, the international dimension plays tricks with the present theory by offering a way around cash-starved domestic markets. I showed in chapter 4 that Switzerland was more internationalized than the decentralized structure of its political institutions would lead one to expect. I argued then, in accordance with Swiss historiographers, that the Swiss banks were able to sidestep the liquidity constraint by accessing international financial markets. Yet, I found in this chapter, still in accordance with standard accounts of Swiss banking, that Swiss banks exhibited a degree of universalism very much in line with the degree of decentralization of the domestic political institutions. Since the Swiss banks had managed to transcend the domestic liquidity constraint by tapping international markets, the latter finding has to be something of a coincidence, at least in part. More plausible is that the Swiss Monaco-like strategy was insufficient to overcome the comparative advantage enjoyed by financial places with large, unregulated money markets. Zürich, Basel, and Geneva could not directly compete with London and Paris, but specialized rather in what the others did not want to touch – long-term international industrial investment. Hence the universality of large Swiss banks.

Norway

Like Switzerland, Norway offers a case in which the link with the international economy interfered with the domestic logic at the core of the present theory. Norway is a case where the fragmentation of the deposit market was such that universal banking would have been the only option left to the profit sector, had not it been for the fact that underwriting was controlled by foreign bankers. Norwegian banks exhibited little universal banking. A possible reason for this anomaly stems from the dualism of Norwegian industrialization, with small workshops producing for the national economy existing side by side with a concentrated, export-oriented primary sector, with financial needs that were out of proportion with the domestic money market. While community banks lent to the workshops and foreign banks underwrote the securities of the giant concerns, domestic commercial banks were left with nothing else but the traditional financing of commerce. The Norwegian case suggests that the theory offered here would also fail to apply to most backward countries, whose comparative advantage lies in the production of primary products.

Another variable to which the model does not do justice is liberalism. The discrepancy between figures 6.3 and 6.4 with respect to the position of the "statist" countries (Belgium and France) calls for an explanation. We saw in chapter 3 that state centralization had two contradictory effects: it worked against one source of market segmentation – local banking – but promoted another – state banking. In the event that the second effect was somewhat developed, as it was in France and Belgium, it spoiled the relation between state structure and universal banking. French and Belgian banks were pushed to universality by state competition.

Belgium

The Belgian case was prototypical of this development. State banking preempted the development of deposit banking. Early nineteenth-century

Belgian banks were universal banks *avant la lettre*, in that both the Société Générale and the Banque de Belgique combined investment banking with note issuing and deposit taking. These banks opened savings banks in the 1830s and early 1840s to attract capital from a conservative pool of savers, unwilling to risk their money in stocks, and for whom state bonds were an alternative. Those savings were pooled with all the other liabilities of the for-profit banks. They were as large as the capital held by shareholders in the case of the Société Générale.[22] Absent a central bank extending a liquidity guarantee, this early form of universal banking did not withstand the 1848 financial crisis. But rather than letting the banks adjust by curtailing industrial lending, the state, instead, crowded them out of the collection of short-term resources, forcing them out of note issuing when the central bank was created in 1850 and out of deposit banking when the state savings bank (CGER) was founded in 1865.[23] Van der Wee (1982, 612) argues that, following these reforms, the Société Générale lost its mixed banking character to become a "portfolio company," like the dozens of *crédits mobiliers* that sprouted all over Europe. Although the Belgian banks sought to revive their deposit-collection capacities as the century came to a close, they could not loosen the grip of the Belgian state over domestic savings. The Belgian state controlled about 40 percent of the deposit market in 1913, the highest figure in our sample (table 3.1).

The Netherlands

Still another omitted variable is delayed industrialization. The high Dutch value for universal banking is spurious. The high equity-to-deposit ratio does not reflect universal banking but mere overcapitalization of the large banks. Dutch historians argued that the existence of a large securities market, along with the presence of a large savings bank sector, crowded out deposit banking – commercial banks could not tap individual deposits to finance part of their activities, but remained overcapitalized.[24] The delayed development of heavy industry in the Netherlands allowed this equilibrium to last until the turn of the century. As soon as the second industrialization started, however, Dutch banks went through the same roller coaster ride that French and British banks had been on half a century earlier. They extended loans to industry and opened branches nationwide to finance these loans with deposits, then became threateningly

---

[22] See Witte 1991, p. 181.   [23] Chlepner 1926, pp. 101, 228.
[24] See Eisfeld 1916, Jonker 1995, p. 190 and Kymmel 1996, p. 122. Overcapitalization would suggest that bank shares in the Netherlands were not more remunerated than deposits, as was generally the case elsewhere.

illiquid when the business cycle soured right after the war, and last beat a hasty retreat to short-term lending after the war.

Spain

Delayed industrialization also helps to make sense of the Spanish case at least in part; another important omitted variable in this case is central bank competition. Prewar Spain throws us back to the France of the brothers Péreires, when banking was specialized, divided between a note-issuing monopoly specialized in short instruments and private bankers (or *crédits mobiliers*) supplying long-term instruments financed by equity. The Bank of Spain was the sole institution with extensive national coverage, weighing heavily in the banking system – 68 percent of all assets belonged to it in 1913.[25] Note, however, that economic backwardness supplied only part of the explanation, for, in Spain as on most of the continent, industrialization was sufficiently felt for deposits to displace notes as short-term resources. The explanation would not be complete without mentioning the pervasive political instability that characterized Spanish politics throughout the nineteenth century. A century of political instability, topped in 1897 by the disastrous war with the United States, made for a sizable public debt, which the central bank financed by expanding its share of the market for cash. To that effect, it obtained a note-issuing monopoly in 1874, but, more importantly, it crowded commercial banks out of the deposit market. The financing of debt through the collection of deposits had a significant advantage over note issuing – it did not negatively affect the exchange rate, in care of the Bank. As a result, deposits were not drained by the center banks, but by the central bank, which ended up controlling 58 percent of all bank deposits in 1900. Added to notes, these deposits gave the Bank of Spain control over 82 percent of all short-term bank liabilities in the country.[26] Its share of bank deposits was still 28 percent in 1913, a figure more than three standard deviations away from the European mean. Moreover, unlike the French and English early nineteenth-century central banks, which shunned outlying areas, the Bank of Spain opened branches all over Spain. It is not until after World War I that the Bank assumed the functions of liquidity guarantor and that commercial banks branched out of their regions of origins.[27]

Clearly, there are many other variables that mattered and that are better captured by country studies. My purpose was to identify a cross-sectional pattern, not to account for singular cases.

[25] Martin-Aceña 1995, pp. 504–05.   [26] Ibid., pp. 522–23.   [27] Ibid., p. 504.

Conclusion

This chapter has presented evidence for two general propositions. The first proposition is that universal banking was the product of two conditions – market segmentation and the presence of a liquidity guarantor. This is a strong finding, the only exception to this pattern among the fourteen countries present in the sample being Spain. The second proposition is that universal banking was (through the mediation of the two aforementioned requisites) related to state centralization. Universal banking required an intermediate dose of state formation, insufficient to overcome the agrarian peripheries' claims to maintain local control over local capital, yet enough to impose a central bank on these peripheries. This condition was met in Germany, Italy, and Sweden. In contrast, specialized banking obtained in both very centralized (UK, France) and very decentralized countries (USA). More ambitious than the first, this second proposition is also less robust. There were clear exceptions to this general trend reflecting omitted variables, such as the international environment (the dominions, Switzerland, Norway), state intervention (Belgium), backwardness (the Netherlands, Spain), and political instability (Spain). State centralization was not the only factor shaping banking structures; nor was state centralization the decisive factor in all cases. My sole ambition is to have identified a cause as general as Gerschenkron's timing of industrialization, yet better grounded in reality.

Alexander Gerschenkron gave an assets-side account of universal banking, in which universal banking reflects firms' capital needs. The present account, instead, stresses the liabilities side, in which competition for deposits constrains forms of lending. Although a full account should emphasize both sides of the balance sheet, I suspect that little cross-national variation is likely to come out of the assets side. Industrialization was more or less happening simultaneously among the so-called late industrializers (that is, all countries with the exception of Britain and Switzerland, the early industrializers, and perhaps Spain, the Netherlands, and Russia, the very late industrializers), making it difficult to use that variable to account for the differences in banking structures that obtained between most European countries.

Epilogue

Universal banking systems maintained a relative balance between small and large business and between local and center banks. Less concentrated, less securitized, and less internationalized than specialized banking systems at an equivalent level of development, universal banking systems were more respectful of local and small industry than specialized banking systems. Yet, this was so at the price of making the financial center vulnerable to liquidity shocks. Universal banking systems were more dependent on the support of the central bank for their existence than were specialized banking systems. The withdrawal of this support during the monetary contraction of the 1920s, at a time when central banks around the world were concerned about curbing the inflationary spiral fueled by the war, made universal banking systems more vulnerable to an illiquidity crisis than specialized banking systems. The banking systems of Sweden, Denmark, the Netherlands, and Spain registered failures in the 1920s. Those of Austria, Germany, Norway, Belgium, and Italy, all universal banking countries, were gravely affected by the 1931 crisis. In contrast, British, Canadian, Australian, New Zealand, and French banking systems suffered least. In France, not only were all failing banks local and regional banks with heavy commitments in industry, but their failure also actually strengthened the big deposit banks, to the branches of which local depositors transferred their assets.[28] The country with the lowest occurrence of universal banking, Canada, reported one bank failure for the entire interwar period, in 1923.[29] A memorandum from the League of Nations read:

The experience of the first post-war crisis and that of 1931 demonstrated the undesirability of commercial banks performing "mixed" functions in the existing banking structure. (League of Nations 1939a, p. 93)

---

[28] Laufenburger 1940, pp. 237–40.   [29] See Drummond 1991b, p. 233.

Part III

The second expansion (1960–2000)

Following forty years of stagnation, financial centers started to grow again in the wake of a long and hesitant process of deregulation. The movement began in earnest in the 1960s, was set back by the currency and monetary turmoil of the 1970s, and resumed its course in the 1980s. Deregulation opened up an era of thorough reorganization in all financial systems, marked by sectoral concentration, the acquisition of foreign banks and opening of branches abroad, the development of deep international money markets with the Euromarkets, and the displacement of bank loans by bonds, stocks, and market instruments of varying time lengths. Many banks took advantage of the new freedom to try their hand at new products, especially market-related ones. This initial shakeup was followed by the present period of consolidation, in which banks are now seeking to improve profitability by focusing on what they do best.

The present part reviews the deepening of core–periphery patterns in OECD countries by taking up in the following order the four issues of spatial concentration, internationalization, securitization, and specialization. Like the preceding one, the present part emphasizes the reluctance of decentralized countries to submit to global changes. In it, I argue that concentration has increased across countries, but that it has taken place only within banking sectors, not across sectors. Deregulation has merely restored the degree of competition that existed in the pre-Depression days (chapter 7). Foreign banks have thronged to financial centers that were popular before World War I, with the result that centralized countries are once again at the forefront of internationalization (chapter 8). Corporate securities markets are recovering faster from forty years of stagnation in centralized than in decentralized countries, though, in many cases, such a pattern is hidden by remnants of state intervention in finance and industry (chapter 9). Only the cross-country pattern behind the ongoing process of respecialization is at this point still indeterminate, because of the novelty of that process (chapter 10).

7 Sectoral realignment

The period from 1960 until the present is characterized by a strengthening of core–periphery tensions in finance. Deregulators are removing the protective measures that were established in the wake of the Great Depression; they are also scaling back the state credit sector, which in many countries reached unprecedented proportions in the immediate postwar period.

However thorough and ubiquitous, the present trend is unlikely to bring about the convergence of OECD banking systems on the money-center bank model; it is of a more limited character. Deregulation has merely restored the degree of competition that existed in pre-Depression days. The center banks have managed to regain a sectoral dominance in countries where they were dominant before World War I – in centralized countries. In contrast, center banks have remained a junior partner in countries where the savings and cooperative banks constituted the dominant sector – in decentralized countries. Certainly, concentration has increased across countries, but concentration has taken place only within sectors, not across them.

The interwar and early postwar decades

Ongoing financial deregulation has consisted in the removal of four decades of regulatory layers. These layers took two forms: (1) the promotion of state credit and (2) the regulation of banking competition.

State credit

State credit is the allocation of credit by the central government through so-called specialized credit banks or state credit banks, which finance their needs by issuing state-guaranteed bonds. State credit banks are different from postal (and other state-run) savings banks. Nor should they be confused with nationalized banks, which formerly were publicly traded commercial banks. Because nationalization merely aims at appropriating bank profits, nationalized banks have traditionally been run like any other.[1] State credit, in contrast, aims at reallocating bank credit. Last, a state credit bank is not a central bank either, in that the central bank enjoys a monopoly on note issuing, while a state credit bank enjoys a bond-borrowing privilege.

State credit banks were founded to meet a strongly felt need for credit by a category of borrowers whose relative borrowing power from the capital market did not match their political power. State credit came in three waves: the first wave targeted farmers, the second small firms, and the third traditional sectors. The first state credit banks were built on the model of the French Crédit Foncier, a special agricultural credit institution, created by Louis Napoléon in 1852, the year he was elected emperor by a plebiscite, thanks to the rural vote. Similar state credit banks were created in Sweden and Norway. By the turn of the century, governments created systems of credit to agriculture, notably in New Zealand, the United States, and France, of course, with the Crédit Agricole. The nineteenth century also saw the creation of municipal credit banks to finance urbanization in small towns; the first instance was the Belgian Crédit Communal, founded in 1860.

Whereas the first wave of state credit essentially targeted agriculture and local urbanization, the second wave was aimed at small firms. Small firms were diagnosed as suffering from the famous "Macmillan Committee gap" in the provision of finance over the medium term.[2] The Japanese government created a Relief Fund for Small Farmers and Manufacturers in 1912. Other examples include the French Crédit National (1919) and Crédit Hôtelier, Commercial et Industriel (1923), the Dutch Middenstandsbank (1927), the Swedish AB Industrikredit (1934), the Manufacturing Bank of Norway (1936), and the Belgian Caisse Nationale de Crédit aux Classes Moyennes (1937). The second wave swelled after World War II with the addition of the Canadian Industrial Development Bank (1944), the Industrial Finance Department of the Commonwealth Bank (1945) in Australia, the British Industrial and Commercial Finance Corporation (1945), the Dutch Herstelbank and Nederlandse Participatie (1945), the German Kreditanstalt für Wiederaufbau (1948) and Industriekreditbank AG–Deutsche Industriebank (1949), the Italian Cassa

---

[1] On the French nationalizations, Born (1983, p. 310) writes: "In essence, the business activity of the big nationalized banks remained unchanged. In this sense, it may be said that the French case has demonstrated the pointlessness of nationalizing big banks." On public ownership of banks in Italy, Ceriani (1962, p. 128) writes: "[It] has not led to interferences by the organs of government with the conduct of banking business. Nor has it affected the extent or forms of competition between the various banks."

[2] After the name of the chair of an interwar British committee that diagnosed small firms to suffer from an underprovision of medium-term finance.

per il Credito all'imprese Artigiane (1947) and Mediocredito (1952), the Spanish *Credito Oficial* (a generic term referring to all state credit banks), and the Belgian Société Nationale d'Investissement (1962). Specialized banks were also created in the 1920s to finance international trade. These banks mostly served the needs of large business, and their share of state credit was relatively small.

Many of these banks, along with specially created ones, participated in the postwar financing of the third wave of state credit. Patterned on the Italian fascist model, its purpose was to relieve the failed (and, from then on, tightly regulated) banks of the burden of financing fixed assets in some sectors of heavy industry (steel, shipbuilding). The most important instances were the Istituto Mobiliare Italiano (1931) and the Belgian Société Nationale de Crédit à l'Industrie (1935). This third wave was most developed in Belgium, France, Japan, and Italy, all countries that separated deposit from investment banking after World War II. During the 1960s in Spain, the Instituto Nacional de Industria took over the financing of money-losing sectors such as coal, steel, and shipbuilding, which were deserted by banks.

Although state credit banks emerged in all countries, the relative importance of state credit varied considerably across countries and through time. A perusal of the country graphs exhibited in appendix 2 reveals the following information. Cross-nationally, first, countries fall into three distinct groups. At one extreme are the countries in which state credit reached a high level at some point in history – Belgium, France, New Zealand, the Netherlands, and perhaps Italy. At the other extreme are the countries for which state credit was either nonexistent – Austria, Canada, Denmark, the UK, Ireland, Finland, Sweden, Switzerland – or little developed – Germany, the United States. The residual (Spain, Portugal, Japan, Norway, Australia) falls somewhere in between.

Longitudinally, second, countries also fall into three groups. A first group of countries shows a traditionally high level of state credit – Belgium, France, Norway, New Zealand, and Italy. A second group of countries acquired state credit in the course of the twentieth century, either in the wake of World War I – Spain, Australia, Japan, and the United States – or World War II – Denmark, Germany, Austria, Portugal, and the Netherlands. A third, residual group never acquired state credit. Note finally that state credit has been declining since the 1950s in Australia, the 1960s in France, Belgium, the Netherlands, and New Zealand, and the 1980s in Spain, Portugal, Norway, and Japan.

I have argued elsewhere that the surge in state credit reflected the new political power of farmers and small capitalists.[3] The class cleavage, which

---

[3] See Verdier 2000.

emerged in the late nineteenth century and peaked in the postwar years, placed farmers and small capitalists in the enviable position of arbitrating the conflict between the capitalist Right and the working-class Left. Farmers and small capitalists took advantage of their position to extract regulation favoring local banks or, where local banks were nonexistent, state credit banks. Although general, the rise of the class cleavage made the demand for state credit particularly strong in centralized states, where local banking was traditionally repressed. Such a demand was weaker in countries with decentralized states, where the local non-profit sector already satisfied most of the farmers' and small capitalists' demand for credit.

The appearance of state credit split the centralized countries into two groups, a first with a substantial state credit banking sector (Belgium, France, New Zealand, Greece) and another without (UK, Ireland, Portugal, Netherlands), thereby creating three paradigms: financial systems dominated by center banks, financial systems with a large share of state banks, and financial systems dominated by local banks. The typology overlaps with Zysman's (1983) trinity of market-based, state-based, and bank-based systems, even though the underlying logic is different.

The regulation of bank competition

From the banking instability of the 1920s and 1930s, governments drew the lesson that universal banking systems had fared worse than specialized ones. They sought to remedy the problem through the generalization of the liquidity guarantee to all banks, balanced by stiff liquidity rules to guard banks against moral hazard. The state stepped in as the lender of last resort, extending an informal (formal in the United States) guarantee to depositors of all stripes, while relegating central banks to the daily management of monetary aggregates and the exchange. Moreover, the pursuit of reflationary policies in many countries after 1931, and in all countries during and after World War II, automatically relieved the banking system of its liquidity shortage.

But to prevent banks from investing state-guaranteed deposits into risky assets, governments tried to pull banks away from universality through artificial requirements of liquidity rules, reserve requirements, and the separation of deposits from investment banking. Two series of rules were put in place in the 1930s and consolidated in the 1950s. A first series of rules *delinked* various sections of the credit market from one another, so that deflation in one would not spread to another. Most countries separated deposit taking from securities underwriting, formally in the United

States, France, Belgium, and Japan in the 1950s, and also Spain in 1960, while informally nearly everywhere else. The imposition of high liquidity ratios on commercial banks in all countries, the center bank's approval for issuing securities in Sweden and Norway, and a tax legislation unfavorable to securities in Germany also had the effect of keeping commercial banks out of underwriting.

Post-Depression reformers in some countries also sought to specialize deposits according to maturity, commercial banks offering demand deposits and savings banks and the postal savings system receiving term deposits. To that effect, center banks in Britain, France, Australia, Germany, and Italy were discouraged from opening new branches; center banks in Australia and New Zealand could not open savings banks. In return, except in countries of universal banking, savings banks and building societies were not allowed to offer current accounts or extend loans to business. Medium- and long-term lending was discouraged for center banks, and was explicitly reserved for special credit banks in France, Belgium, and Italy. Mortgage lending was reserved to building societies in Britain, Ireland, and Canada, special subsidiaries of center banks in Italy, and a special state credit bank in Portugal.

A second set of tools enabled bank regulators to maintain bank stability through a series of *price-fixing* mechanisms (liquidity and other ratios, compulsory reserve requirements, interest-rate controls, credit rationing, and so forth). Initially adopted for prudential purposes, price-fixing mechanisms were turned into vehicles for the provision of cheap credit to the postwar economy and then as a means of containing inflation during the oil shocks. Price fixing varied in scope and intensity depending on the country. It was relatively mild in the United States, where returns on demand deposits were set to zero and returns on term deposits could be capped by the Fed (the so-called Regulation Q). In Britain, Canada, Australia, Denmark, and Germany, price fixing encompassed interest rates on both loans and deposits; center banks coordinated rates on the central bank's discount rate. Price fixing was more encompassing in most other countries, where the absence of a money market on which the banks could satisfy their temporary needs for liquidity forced the central bank to ration credit. The Bank of France, for instance, imposed rediscount ceilings on each bank.[4]

---

[4] The present and following paragraphs draw from Bingham 1985 and Bröker 1989. I also consulted the contributions to the following edited volumes: Beckhart 1954, Sayers 1962, de Cecco 1987a, Frowen and Kath 1992, Kaufman 1992, and articles or monographs by Pringle 1975, Francke and Hudson 1984, de Boissieu 1990, Gardener and Molyneux 1990, Ackland and Harper 1992, Olsson 1997, Knutsen 1997, Pérez 1997a, Kregel 1997, and Deeg 1999.

Financial deregulation

Inherited from the banking reforms of the 1930s, the regulatory kit was designed to enable regulators to prevent a recurrence of the deflationary spiral that threw the world into depression between the wars. It did not allow bank regulators to adequately check inflation in the postwar era. The policies presented two flaws. First, they invited circumvention among financial institutions.[5] An example of an innovative dodge was the creation in the United States of non-deposit instruments such as money-market (NOW) accounts, allowing US banks to thwart ceilings on interest rates paid on deposits. Controls on retail deposit rates triggered growth in the wholesale deposit market by means of certificates of deposit (CDs). When controls prevented center banks from innovating, other financial intermediaries, spared from controls, stepped in, taking business away from the banks. In Britain, Australia, and New Zealand, finance companies purchased wholesale deposits and developed leasing as an alternative to regular bank credit. Savings and cooperative banks, in most countries, offered interest rates on deposits higher than those of commercial banks, and developed the personal loan business. In France, the center banks lost business to the Crédit Agricole and the Crédit National, which were not subject to credit ceilings. In Britain and the United States, center banks also lost to brokers and securities firms, which attracted individuals' savings by issuing short-term instruments, such as money-market mutual funds.

Discrimination and segmentation cut into the market share held by center banks. As can be seen in appendix 2, center banks lost market share to other banking institutions from World War I until the 1960s in Belgium, Britain, the Netherlands, and New Zealand, until the 1970s in Denmark, France, Germany, Greece, and Italy, and until the 1980s in Japan and the United States. The market share of Spanish and Portuguese center banks exhibited the same pattern with a delay; the slide began in 1960 and the recovery intervened after 1980, reflecting both economic and political backwardness. Center banks initially viewed the loss in market share with equanimity, enjoying the high level of profitability that price fixing allowed them to extract from depositors and creditors.[6]

In addition to inviting evasion, regulatory controls also made monetary and credit policy (the two were closely tied up) vulnerable to rent seeking. The policy of segmentation of the credit market had the effect of creating entitlements among those borrowers who benefited from credit

---

[5] For a similar argument, see Kane 1981 and de Cecco 1987b.

[6] Pringle (1975, p. 115) reports that the cartel of clearing banks in the UK decided against bidding for deposits throughout the 1960s, lest they increase their costs – a certain proportion would have had to be held in the form of interest-free balances.

subsidies. This was the case with farmers and small business, who were given their own credit state bank. It was also the case in the housing industry, in countries where the granting of mortgages was reserved to building societies or state credit banks. Credit rationing was easily turned into rent seeking, because, absent a money market, it could not be applied bluntly, lest whole categories of borrowers go bankrupt. Instead, it called for multiple exceptions in favor of politically powerful sectors – housing in all countries, agriculture, exports, and small business in most countries, and shipbuilding, steel, coal, textiles, and any sector imperiled by foreign trade in some countries. Credit rationing even offered the base for so-called industrial policy in France, Spain, and Norway. The largest beneficiary of selective credit policy almost everywhere was the treasury, thanks to the obligation imposed on banks to invest part of their portfolio in government bonds.

With the main conduit for monetary policy – the center banks – either losing ground to uncontrolled banks or circumventing controls, while controls became a source of entitlements for well-organized borrowers, the central bank could no longer contain inflation. There was a need for a reform of the institutions. It took two complementary forms. At first, governments and regulators in all countries sought to extend the *coverage* of the controls to offset the circumvention that resulted from innovation. They widened the circle of financial institutions to which monetary tools applied, spreading the constraint among banks and non-banks.[7] They broadened the definition of the monetary aggregate to include time deposits and other close substitutes. A few countries adopted the US open-market technique; the central bank in Australia, Canada, Italy, and the United Kingdom began intervening in secondary money markets to influence the monetary aggregate in the 1970s. The shift to flexible exchange rates in 1973 made the market for foreign exchange a convenient alternative to nonexistent domestic secondary markets.

In a second step, central banks and governments moved to moderate the use of administrative restrictions to reduce the incentive to innovate. They restored market mediation. Market mediation offered the advantage of affecting all participants evenly. It also allowed the bank to make the rediscount rate effective, as a change in the bank rate had repercussions on all financial instruments simultaneously.[8] The abolition of

---

[7] Liquidity ratios were extended to all banks in 1953 except state banks in the Netherlands, in 1984 in France, and 1990 in Switzerland. Lending ceilings were extended to non-banks in 1965 in the UK, 1973 in Denmark, 1980 in Sweden, and 1983 in Norway. Reserve requirements were extended to other banks in 1958 in Italy, 1967 in France, 1973 in Japan, 1975 and 1982 in Sweden, 1980 in the United States, 1981 in the UK, and 1984 in Spain, Germany, Norway, and Finland.

[8] Interest-rate controls were liberalized in part or in toto in Germany (1967), Canada (1967 for lending rates), UK (1971), the United States (1971 for wholesale rates and 1980 for

interest-rate controls was supplemented with three ancillary measures, destined to make market clearing a feasible alternative. The money market was open to all financial institutions enjoying a surplus of liquidity – savings banks, postal savings, money-market brokers, large companies issuing their own short-term paper – and to all large demanders of liquidity – the treasury and center banks.[9] Moreover, because creating a real money market exposed the treasury to rate volatility, it was necessary to delegalize seigniorage; central banks were freed from political control.

Promoting market clearing also implied creating a so-called level playing field between various banking sectors through the elimination of tax and borrowing privileges enjoyed by non-profit sector banks. Fiscal equality between public and private sectors was reached in Belgium in 1962. In France, the Crédit Agricole and the Crédit Mutuel started paying the professional tax in 1971 and corporate taxes in 1981, while savings banks became liable to the former in 1992. In many cases, state banks lost their status as state agencies and were privatized, either as mutual societies (in France, the Crédit Agricole in 1988, the Caisses d'Epargne in 2000), or stock companies (state credit and savings banks in Italy). Some countries went as far as transforming the financial services of the post office system into full-service commercial banks, state-owned in New Zealand, Finland, and the UK, privately owned in Sweden and the Netherlands.[10]

The restoration of market mediation further implied allowing rival sectors to compete with each other. Commercial banks were allowed to compete with savings banks by expanding branches to tap household savings,[11] opening savings banks,[12] and offering the same savings rates

retail deposit rates), Spain (1977 and 1981 for retail deposits), Norway (1980), and Australia (1980). Most countries abolished credit ceilings and mandatory requirements in the 1980s. For a systematic account ending in 1986, see Bröker 1989, pp. 153–62 and 197–99.

[9] In Britain, the central organization of the savings banks was admitted to the London Clearing House in 1976. Note, though, that the appearance of a money market is gradual and difficult to date. Taking the introduction of certificates of deposit by commercial banks as a benchmark, the distribution across countries is: before 1960 (Canada), 1960s (USA, UK, Spain), 1970s (Australia, Greece, New Zealand, Japan, Sweden), 1980–87 (Turkey, Finland, Italy, France, Norway, Germany, the Netherlands, Portugal), and after 1987 (Denmark, Ireland, Switzerland). See Bröker 1989, pp. 162–66 and p. 53 for a summary table also applying to treasury bonds and commercial paper.

[10] Sweden's post office savings bank merged in 1975 with the state-owned Sveriges Kreditbank, to form PK Banken, the largest commercial bank in the country.

[11] Center banks were authorized (or encouraged) to open new branches in rural areas in Germany (1958), France (1967), Sweden (1960s and 1981), Britain (1971), Italy (1974), Spain (1974 and 1985), Austria (1979), Norway (1983), Portugal (1990), and the United States (officially since 1994, earlier in practice).

[12] Commercial banks were allowed to open savings banks in Australia in 1955 and New Zealand in 1964.

as state savings banks.[13] Commercial banks were also allowed to compete with state credit banks by extending long-term credit to business;[14] with building societies by selling mortgages;[15] with investment banks and brokers by underwriting certificates of deposit; and with financial companies by selling hire-purchase instruments.[16] In turn, savings banks were allowed to compete with commercial banks by opening current accounts and lending to business;[17] building societies were allowed to offer a full range of accounts in Britain in 1986. A European Commission directive brought banking regulation for all sectors – whether commercial or savings banks or public sector credit institutions – under the same heading. Savings banks, like commercial banks, were allowed to merge with insurance companies. Pioneered in the Netherlands, Britain, and Belgium, the link between banking and insurance, known in Europe as "bancassurance" or "Allfinanz," was legalized by a European Commission directive effective as of January 1994.[18]

A final feature of desegmentation was the legalization of mergers across categories. Because of their legal character, savings banks cannot be freely purchased by other banks nor can they be listed on stock exchanges, unless they are turned into public corporations. In Britain, Australia, New Zealand, and the United States, many building societies (thrifts in the USA), often in the wake of failure, adopted the joint-stock bank format. In Belgium, the three largest savings banks became commercial banks in 1993–94. In Italy, following the Amato Law of 1992, all savings banks were converted to stock status, the stock of each bank being given to a parent foundation. Spanish savings banks were also readied for demutualization, enabling takeovers by banks.[19]

Deregulation had several consequences. First, market mediation removed an opportunity for rent seeking. Absent credit controls,

---

[13] In France, savings banks alone could offer tax-free savings accounts until 1983, when the tax exemption was extended to commercial banks. Tax exemptions given to holders of savings accounts were phased out in 1979 in Britain, and in 1987 in Japan with respect to postal savings.

[14] The key dates are 1961 for Belgium, 1967 for France, 1969 for Spain, 1971 in Britain, 1972 for Turkey, and 1986 for Portugal.

[15] France 1966, Spain 1969, USA 1971, Britain 1973, Japan 1981, Québec 1983.

[16] France 1967.

[17] Savings banks were already allowed to open current accounts in countries of universal banking such as Austria, Germany, Denmark, and Finland. They were granted that right in 1956 in Sweden, in 1969 in the Netherlands, in the 1970s in Italy, in 1975 in Belgium for private savings banks, in 1977 in Spain, in 1980 in the USA and Belgium for the state savings bank, and in 1984 in Australia and France. Savings banks were freed from territorial restrictions in Spain and Austria in 1979.

[18] The new monetary policy also had consequences for capital markets and foreign banks, two dimensions that are addressed in the following chapters.

[19] *The Banker* December 1997.

well-connected groups could no longer allege impending bankruptcy to extract exemptions. The French system of *encadrement du crédit*, probably the most advanced of its generation, through which the government gave itself the means to allocate credit sector by sector, region by region, and financial institution by financial institution, was dismantled. Not all special programs were terminated; those that remained, however, either had to be financed from the government budget, or were administered by state credit banks no longer benefiting from borrowing privileges or a monopoly over the distribution of medium- and long-term credit to industry.[20] With credit no longer serviceable for rent seeking, rent seekers vacated the lobbies. Central banks could stabilize prices at last. Second, center banks were able to reclaim the ground lost to their competitors. I develop this point in the next section.

Sectoral realignment: evidence

As a consequence of monetary reform, center banks reclaimed the market share that had long been lost to state banks. State banks declined the most after the 1960s in countries where they had gained the most before the 1960s. This convergence effect appears with clarity in figure 7.1 (left-hand graph), in which the change in state credit banking over the 1963–90 period is plotted against its initial 1963 value. A negative linear relation is observable, indicating that countries with a large state banking sector in 1963 lost most of it afterward. In contrast to state banks, local banks experienced no convergence effect. The plot of the change in local banking against its initial value shows no discernible pattern (figure 7.1, right-hand graph).

Second, state banks lost market share to center banks. I computed the average change in market shares for twenty-one countries over the 1963–90 period.[21] Consider the last row of table 7.1. On average, state banks lost 8.8 percentage points, 8.3 of which were captured by the center banks. Only half a point went to local banks.

In contrast to state banks, local banks on average held their ground against the center banks. Their market share did not decline over the 1963–90 period, but increased by a meager 0.5 percentage point as mentioned. The reason is that local banks, in the countries in which they were

---

[20] Since 1981 in Norway, the cost of subsidizing credit to eight state banks has been covered by appropriations in the government budget. Since 1986 in France, batches of subsidized loans to agriculture and housing among others are auctioned off to all banks, thus forcing special credit banks, which once enjoyed a monopoly over the allocation of such subsidies, to compete on a par with center banks.

[21] The countries are the twenty-one used in figure 7.1.

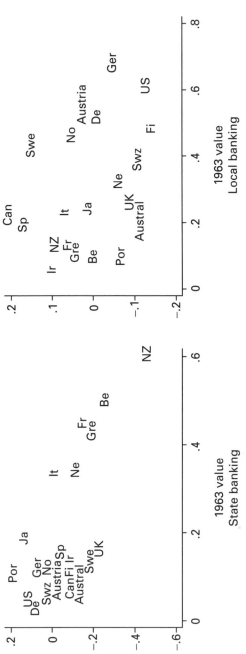

Data description and sources: The vertical axes feature the difference between the 1990 and 1963 asset market shares of the state (credit and postal) banking sector and local banking sector respectively. See appendix 2 for sources for the dependent variables and other market share variables.

Figure 7.1. Convergence tests, 1963–90

Table 7.1. *Average change in market share by degree of state centralization, 1963–90*

	Obs.	Average change in market share of:		
		State banking %	*Local banking* %	*Center banking* %
Decentralized countries	11	−4	−1	5
Centralized countries	10	−14	2	12
All countries	21	−8.8	0.5	8.3

Data description and sources: For market shares, see appendix 2. Centralized countries are those with a state centralization (see appendix 3 for a definition) average of the 1963 and 1990 values above or equal to the mean calculated for twenty-one observations; decentralized countries are the others.

strongly implanted, were so before the Depression era. Unlike state banks, their presence was not predicated upon the regulatory framework of the post-Depression era. Nor did they generally benefit from it, except perhaps in three cases – the British building societies, US savings and loans, and Japanese cooperatives. Deregulation, consequently, did not cut into their market shares. Although on average, there are exceptions to this statement. The market share of local banks dropped below its historical level in Australia, where most building societies transformed themselves into commercial banks,[22] and in Switzerland, where the retreat of the local banking sector reflected the expansion of the Swiss center banks in international markets rather than the decline of local banks in the domestic market. Conversely, the market share of local banks rose above its historical level in Canada on account of political decentralization, in Spain on account of democratization,[23] and New Zealand for no known reason.

More or less concentration?

The above evidence that the periphery is withstanding the competition from the center is at odds with the common perception of all-out consolidation and growing sectoral concentration in banking. This perception is notably fueled by the US experience. According to a recent study, the

---

[22] See Ackland and Harper 1992.
[23] The upward trend of Spanish savings banks, according to Pérez (1997a), reflected the exceptional political status assumed by large banks under the Franco regime, which they lost with democracy.

number of independent commercial banks in the United States fell from 12,463 to 7,234 in less than twenty years (between 1979 and 1997).[24] Almost all of the reduction involved small banks, merging with a larger bank in the wake of the deregulation of interstate banking. Concentration levels in US banking increased over the period. The top eight banks held 35.5 percent of total domestic assets in 1997, against 22.3 in 1988.[25] Contrary to what I argue here, local banking in the United States did not buck the trend toward concentration, but gave up ground to center banks.[26]

Moreover, a similar reduction in the number of banks is observable in countries other than the United States. Using OECD data, I built an index of change in the number of banks over the 1960s. This index shows that, of the fifteen national banking systems included, nine registered a speed in consolidation that was superior or very close to that of the United States – France, Italy, New Zealand, Iceland, three Scandinavian countries, Germany, and Austria (see figure 7.2). If consolidation trends in these countries are steeper or equal to that in the United States, why believe that local banking is not a victim of deregulation?

Complete desegmentation may be the regulators' stated goal. However, in decentralized countries, with perhaps the exception of the United States, desegmentation exists only on paper. In reality, the market is still segmented, at least in countries where this segmentation was pronounced in the past – i.e., in all decentralized countries. Local non-profit banking sectors in these countries are still entrenched; banking concentration at the local level either is untouched by the consolidations taking place at the national level, or is, in effect, reinforced. Indeed, segmentation channels bank mergers within, rather than across, banking sectors. If a bank enjoys a monopolistic position at the local level, as most savings banks and cooperatives do, consolidation within the sector is unlikely to bring in competition at the local level.

US local banks were in a different situation. Once interstate banking was allowed, New York center banks merged with local state-chartered banks. Some of them even bought savings and loans during the fire-sale held in the wake of the S&Ls' crisis that virtually bankrupted federal and state deposit insurance companies. Nevertheless, even in the

---

[24] Berger et al. 1995 and 1998a.   [25] Berger et al. 1998b.

[26] This trend is visible in the long-term evolution of market shares in the United States reproduced in appendix 2. From 1978 on, center banks increased their share at the expense of state-chartered banks and savings banks. Then, following the crisis of the S&Ls in the mid-1980s, the share of the savings banks dropped, being parceled out among center, state-chartered, and federal credit banks.

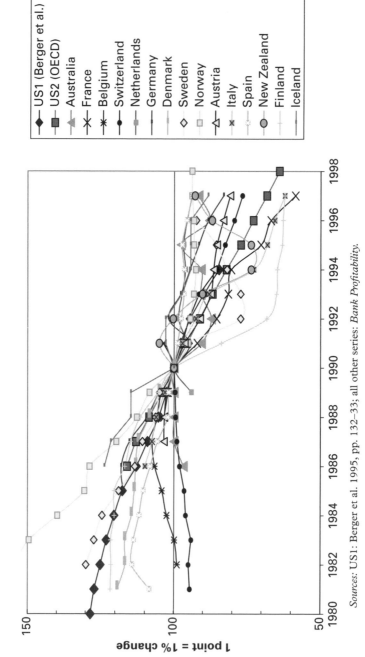

Legend (right to left reading of figure):
- ◆ US1 (Berger et al.)
- ■ US2 (OECD)
- ▲ Australia
- ✕ France
- ✳ Belgium
- ● Switzerland
- ▪ Netherlands
- | Germany
- | Denmark
- ◇ Sweden
- ▢ Norway
- ◁ Austria
- ✕ Italy
- ✳ Spain
- ● New Zealand
- | Finland
- | Iceland

Sources: US1: Berger et al. 1995, pp. 132–33; all other series: *Bank Profitability.*

Figure 7.2. Change in the number of all banks (1990 = 100)

United States the announced death of local banks may be premature. A simulation by Berger et al. (1995, pp. 114–17) found that the spread of interstate banking in the wake of deregulation lagged substantially behind what could have been foreseen. Unit banking legislation was not the only obstacle; federal deposit insurance equalized deposit safety across banks of all sizes.

I mentioned earlier the existence of an emerging trend toward the incorporation of non-profit banks, a trend that should facilitate mergers between the profit and non-profit sectors. This trend is specific to some centralized countries, where savings banks and cooperatives have found it impossible to compete with other financial institutions without incorporating and becoming part of all-purpose banking conglomerates. In Britain, the trustee savings banks merged into one bank and were eventually bought by an insurer – Lloyds. The larger British, Australian, and New Zealand building societies merged with, or became, banks. In Belgium, savings banks have become the retailing component of all-purpose banking groups. The Dutch savings banks have maintained their non-profit status, but their market share has plummeted. Only Rabobank, the bank of Dutch local cooperatives, has successfully maintained its mutual status.

The situation is different in decentralized countries. In Germany, nothing has been done so far to alter the separate legal status enjoyed by savings banks and cooperatives, and only one public–private merger – the 1994 Bankgesellschaft Berlin – had proceeded by the year 2000. In Germany, savings banks are generally guaranteed by the local municipalities and cannot open branches outside the municipal jurisdiction. In Italy, the transformation of all savings banks into joint-stock companies following the Amato Act of 1992 did not lead to privatization. The non-profit foundations owning the banks – one per bank – refused to sell their controlling positions. The privatization of savings banks is not proceeding seriously in Austria either, where four out of the five largest banks are controlled directly or indirectly by public sector banks. The last large center bank – the Creditanstalt – was initially sold to Bank Austria, a savings bank, before eventually being acquired by a foreign bank.

The rationale for the survival of the non-profit sector in Germany, Italy, and Austria is politics. "For many public-sector bankers," writes Covill (1998, 53), "privatisation is the greatest fear of all." Covill argues that privatization would mean the loss of the government guarantee, without which German *Landesbanken* would lose their "A" credit rating, which enables them to refinance more cheaply than the private banks despite making riskier loans.[27] Privatization, Covill also argues, would also mean a loss of personal influence for local politicians, a lesser ability to promote local industry, and a loss of hard cash: "Small-town mayors earn some 10,000 every year for belonging to the supervisory board of the local Sparkasse."[28]

Similar fears lie behind the failure of the Amato Act to privatize savings banks in Italy. Rather than selling the bank shares and using the revenues to build diversified investment portfolios, as the government had hoped, the owning foundations, each an emanation of the local business and financial community, held on to the shares. They feared that new owners would weaken their bank's local ties.[29] Bank mergers would also consolidate management jobs, an arduous assignment in Italy's deep-rooted political patronage system.

The case of Austria is different. Being the last large center bank around, Creditanstalt could not be sold to another private bank without falling under foreign control, but had to go to a savings bank. Still, it took almost a decade for the Austrian government to resolve the matter, due to the local identity and thus partisan bent of each savings bank. Bank Austria, the bank that eventually won the prize, is controlled by a foundation linked to the City of Vienna, a city traditionally governed by the social democrats. Bank Austria owes its investment-grade borrower status from Standard & Poor's to the guarantee of the City of Vienna.[30] The autonomy of savings banks in Germany and Italy and their dominance in Austria reflect the decentralized nature of state institutions.

In sum, the current trend toward banking sectoral concentration is not seriously threatening the market shares of local non-profit banks in decentralized countries. Bank concentration is mostly felt in centralized countries. In what follows, I supply systematic evidence of the existence of a relation between bank concentration and state centralization. I first construct measures of bank concentration.

[27] In a study of German *Landesbanken*, Sinn (1999, p. 34) reports actual credit ratings and hypothetical ratings that would be given to these banks on the strength of their balance sheet structure if they had no government protection. The resulting downgrading is equivalent to the step from triple-A to double-A, or from double-A to a single A, allowing banks to get five-year money on the Eurobonds market for 20 base points less than comparable private competitors who do not have the protection of the formal government guarantees.

[28] The currency is Deutschmarks; *Sparkasse* are savings banks.

[29] *The Banker* August 1995, 27.

[30] *The Banker* February 1997, 38. The City of Vienna eventually divested itself of Bank Austria, trading its shares for HypoVereinsbank shares, Germany's second biggest bank and, from now on, full owner of Bank Austria (*International Herald Tribune* July 24, 2000, 13).

Measuring banking concentration

Extant measures of sectoral concentration fail to reveal the actual state of concentration. Herfindahl indices, measures of the market share of the top five or ten banks, and tallies of the number of institutions controlling half the market all assume that the banking system is homogeneous – that all financial organizations compete equally with one another. The fact that this is not the case makes the interpretation of those measures intricate. Concentration measures are sensitive to the sector of reference and curiously so. High concentration in the commercial banking sector may correlate with low concentration overall. For instance, in 1996 the top five banks represented 66 percent of commercial banking in Germany against 60 percent in France, making German banking look more concentrated than French (see table 7.2). But the top five banks of the for-profit and non-profit sectors combined represented 21 percent in Germany against 37 in France, reversing the rank order between the two countries. Relying merely on concentration ratios calculated for the commercial banking sector would lead us to the fallacy that banking is more concentrated in Germany than in France.

Generally, the larger the local non-profit banking sector, the bigger the discrepancy between concentration in the commercial banking sector and concentration in all banking sectors. This is easily shown by regressing the *commercial* top-five index against the *overall* top-five index and the relative size of the local non-profit sector. If the two indices were identical, their correlation coefficient should be unity. If not, there is a discrepancy, and if this discrepancy is a function of the size of the local non-profit sector, as I argue it is, then the coefficient on the local non-profit sector variable should be positive and significant – the larger the local non-profit sector, the more concentrated the commercial sector. Results for this simple regression (table 7.3, regression 1) confirm the existence of a discrepancy between the two indices and its association with the non-profit sector.[31] Correcting for potential outliers in regression 2 does not modify the results. The interpretation of the commercial top-five ratio as a measure of banking concentration is thus quite problematic.

Calculating concentration using the entire banking system may guard us against the reductionist fallacy, but its significance is limited. Combining banks that operate in different sectors (for-profit and non-profit), that serve a different market (national versus local), and that are

[31] Though far from negligible, the impact is moderate: a one-standard-deviation increase in the local non-profit market share corresponds to a 45 percent of a standard-deviation increase in the commercial top-five concentration index.

Table 7.2. *Concentration ratios, 1996*

	Top five banks' market share of the commercial banking sector, in %	Top five banks' market share of all banking sectors, in %
Iceland	100	93
Finland	100	96
Sweden	94	63
New Zealand	92	80
Canada	89	78
Denmark	89	70
Norway	88	59
Belgium	85	62
Greece	83	74
Switzerland	83	63
Austria	78	66
Netherlands	76	66
Australia	73	62
Ireland	72	54
UK	69	40
Germany	66	21
Spain	62	47
France	60	37
Italy	56	34
Portugal	55	53
Japan	41	27
USA	30	17

Data description and sources: Both ratios were calculated using data from Fitch-IBCA 2001.

in competition only at the margin, the ratio has no readymade interpretation. Consider, for instance, the value scored by Dutch and Austrian banks (table 7.2). The same value, 66, hides two radically different realities. Among the top five banks, four are commercial in the Netherlands, only one in Austria – the others are non-profit. Private banks dominate non-profit banks in the Netherlands while non-profit banks dominate private banks in Austria. Given that the private sector is more open to competition than the non-profit sector, especially at the local level, competition is actually greater overall in the Netherlands than in Austria.

A crude way of approximating the degree of banking concentration existing at the local level is to calculate the relative size of the local banking sector. The larger the local banking sector, the more monopolistic banking is at the local level. A more refined way is to calculate the extent to which commercial banks are branched out – or its opposite, the unit banking ratio introduced in chapter 3. Local competition is a function of the degree of entry of center banks in local credit markets. If entry

Table 7.3. *Explaining the difference between concentration indices, 1996*

Independent and control variables		Dependent variable Commercial top-five index, 1996	
		1	2 (1 without outliers)
Local non-profit banking sector, 1990		29.18 (9.95)***	21.68 (10.21)*
Overall top-five index, 1996		0.77 (0.08)***	0.76 (0.10)***
Intercept		21.67 (5.85)***	24.62 (6.23)***
Adj. R-sq.		0.82	0.80
Num. of obs.		21[a]	19[b]
Potential outliers	Strong[c] Mild[d]	None USA, Germany	Not calculated Not calculated

Notes: Values of standard errors are given in parentheses; *, **, *** indicate coefficients situated in the 90%, 95%, and 99% confidence intervals respectively.
Data description and sources: The indices are from table 7.2. The market share variable is from appendix 2.
[a] Australia, Austria, Belgium, Canada, Denmark, Finland, France, Germany, Greece, Ireland, Italy, Japan, Netherlands, New Zealand, Norway, Portugal, Spain, Sweden, Switzerland, UK, USA.
[b] Same as [a] without Germany and the USA.
[c] With a DFITS absolute value > sqrt(p), with p the number of right-hand-side variables plus one.
[d] With a DFITS absolute value between sqrt(p) and 2*sqrt(p/n), with n the number of observations.

in local markets is easy, center banks build wide branch networks. If, in contrast, entry is difficult, the scope of these networks is much more limited. We do not have systematic data on center banks' branching networks, but we have data on the number of commercial banks and the number of commercial bank offices. Dividing the number of commercial banks by the total number of commercial bank offices (headquarters plus branches) yields an approximation of the scope of branch networks, and thus of the degree of penetration of the local credit market. Since the ratio increases in reverse proportion with the scope of the branch networks, I called it the unit banking ratio. I calculated this measure for the year 1990 (see table 7.4).

The two above measures of local banking concentration – local banking market share and unit banking ratio – should be correlated. The Pearson correlation coefficient between the two variables, using the log value of the unit banking ratio, calculated on seventeen observations, indeed is 0.57.

Table 7.4. *Unit banking ratio, 1990*

	Number of commercial banks	Number of commercial banks' branches	Unit banking ratio %	Note and sources
United States	5047	31764	13.7	Fed member banks; *Statistical Abstract of the United States.*
Austria	55	826	6.2	*Statistisches Handbuch für die Republik Österreich.*
Germany	332	6289	5.0	Deutsche Bundesbank, *Monatsberiche der Deutschen Bundesbank.*
Norway	22	602	3.5	*Bank Profitability.*
Denmark	69	1907	3.5	Commercial banks and savings banks in 1989; *Statistisk Årbog.*
Netherlands	83	2338	3.4	1987; BIS 1989.
France	332	10056	3.2	Banque de France a.
Switzerland	29	1133	2.5	Large and other Swiss commercial banks; *Statistisches Jahrbuch der Schweiz.*
Greece	18	1062	1.7	*Bank Profitability.*
Sweden	21	1345	1.5	*Sveriges officiella statistik Bankinspektionen.*
Italy	115	7889	1.4	Banca d'Italia a.
Canada	8	7414	1.0	1987; BIS 1989.
Japan	144	14324	1.0	*Bank Profitability.*
Portugal	11	1253	0.9	1989; Mexia and Nogueira Leite 1992.
Belgium	25	3533	0.7	Banks under Belgian control; Commission Bancaire et Financière 1990.
Spain	67	14961	0.4	1989.
UK	45	12547	0.4	*Bank Profitability.*

Note: The unit banking ratio is the number of commercial banks divided by the number of commercial bank offices (headquarters plus branches).

Cross-national patterns show resilience over time; local banks have maintained their past strength. The Pearson correlation coefficient between the 1929 and 1990 values of the unit banking ratio is a remarkably high 0.80.[32] It is 0.65 for the 1913 and 1990 values of local banking market share.[33] Of course, this is no evidence that nothing has changed, only that countries have changed in step.

State centralization and sectoral competition

State institutions have shaped present banking structures in two ways. First, not all countries experienced the realignment of market shares to the same extent – the action was essentially concentrated in centralized countries. Centralized states were more affected by the market realignment than decentralized countries because the main victim of deregulation was state banking, which only developed in centralized states (though not in all of them). Table 7.1 (p. 140) breaks down the aggregate data into two roughly equal country groups according to state centralization. State banks lost an average of 14 points in centralized countries against only 4 in decentralized countries. Center banks gained 12 points on average in centralized countries, against only 5 in decentralized countries. Local banks gained 2 points in centralized countries, and lost a point in decentralized countries.

Second, concentration varies across countries according to state centralization. I plotted the 1990 values of the variables "local banking market share" and "unit banking ratio" against the contemporary value of state centralization. Local banking market share is negatively associated with state centralization (figure 7.3). The one potential outlier is a familiar one – the unique degree of internationalization of Swiss banking inflates the market share of center banks, which are international, at the expense of local banks, which have strictly domestic business.

The unit banking variable is not as plainly associated with state centralization. A look at the plot (figure 7.4) suggests that the relation would be stronger in the absence of Canada – the other country, besides Switzerland, with the worst outlying record in this study. Canada is a country with changing state structures, and thus with changing financial structures as well, although with a lag.

It is hard not to feel a sense of *déjà vu* (from chapter 3) at the sight of these results. Not only are the same variables associated across the span of a century, but the associations show the same outliers today as before: Canada because of its still unsettled federal structure, Switzerland

---

[32] For ten observations.   [33] For seventeen observations.

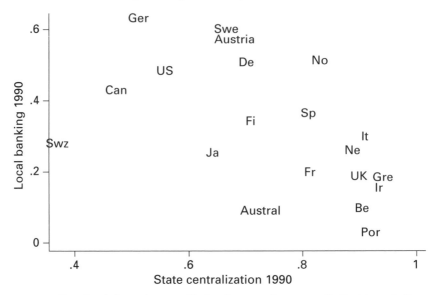

Data description and sources: Market shares are from appendix 2; state centralization from appendix 3.

Figure 7.3. Local banking and state centralization, 1990

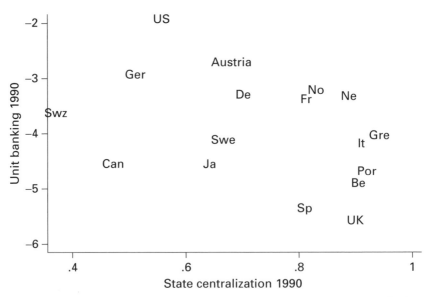

Data description and sources: Unit banking is from table 7.4; state centralization
from appendix 3.

Figure 7.4. Unit banking and state centralization, 1990

Table 7.5. *Non-financial firms' dependence on equity and bank debt according to size, 1995–96 average*

Firm size	Own funds in % of liabilities	Bank debt in % of liabilities	Interest paid on financial debt in % of turnover
Small	28.6	24.1	3.09
Medium	33.8	20.1	2.00
Large	39.7	12.5	2.16
No. of countries included in the averaging	12[a]	8[b]	9[c]

Data description and sources: The data are from the BACH dataset (European Commission, DGII 1998). The dataset contains aggregate and harmonized information on the annual accounts of non-financial enterprises. Small enterprises are those with a turnover of less than ECU 7 million; medium-sized enterprises are those with a turnover of between ECU 7 million and ECU 40 million; large enterprises are those with a turnover of over ECU 40 million. Data are for the manufacturing industries. *Own funds* includes capital and reserves; *bank debt* includes amounts owed to credit institutions within one year and after more than one year; *interest paid on financial debts* corresponds to category "13.a."
[a] Austria, Belgium, Denmark, Finland, France, Germany, Italy, Japan, Netherlands, Portugal, Spain, Sweden.
[b] Belgium, Finland, France, Germany, Italy, Japan, Portugal, Spain.
[c] Belgium, Finland, France, Germany, Italy, Japan, Netherlands, Portugal, Spain.

thanks to its multisecular international vocation. Except for these cases, state institutions are still instrumental in shaping banking structures.

Impact of banking concentration on small business

Small business depends on banks for its financing. Smaller firms rely less on equity for financing than do larger firms. A nine-country average shows an 11 percentage-point difference in the own-funds ratio between small and large firms (table 7.5). Instead, smaller firms rely on bank debt twice as much as larger firms, and spend a larger proportion of their income paying interest on the debt. The recent emergence of new stock markets specializing in the financing of SMEs (Neuer Markt in Frankfurt, OTC List in Stockholm, Nouveau Marché in Paris, and AIM in London) should provide easier access to markets, though only for a small number of highly innovative SMEs with strong growth potential.

The switch from price fixing during the postwar period to market clearing in recent decades is likely to have negative distributional consequences for small firms. Under price fixing, the group that was likely to suffer the most from tight monetary policy was still small business; large business could look to the money market as an alternative. This was truer in Anglo-Saxon than in continental countries, especially after, rather than prior to, 1960. But because credit policy was run by the government and political parties were eager to indemnify small business for bearing the brunt of disinflation, notably through the subsidization of specialized state credit banks, the distributional impact of tight monetary policy was somewhat balanced. It was balanced in the sense that small business could appeal to political parties to have their market power raised on a par with their electoral power. The removal of the partisan option, which accompanied the switch from price fixing to market clearing, ruptured that balance. The strengthening of the money market favored large business more than small business, at the same time that the compression of the state credit sector directly cut into small business' access to credit.

Once the framework that made possible the selective allocation of credit at subsidized rates was removed, small borrowers were left to turn to regular banks. Banks initially were happy to oblige. Throughout the 1980s, the largest ones in Britain, Germany, France, Italy, Scandinavia, and Japan expanded their retail banking operations with an eye, on the assets side, to scoop up the loan-to-small-business market.[34] Following deregulation and enhanced price competition in the Nordic countries, the banks threw caution to the winds and chose, instead, to build up their portfolios, with devastating consequences for the overall liquidity of the banking system as a whole.[35]

Ten years and one banking crisis later, those banks have reconsidered what turned out to be a losing strategy. Deutsche Bank, the universal bank par excellence, spent the last five years of the century searching for a way out of retail banking, unsuccessfully so. Large banks enjoy no comparative advantage in lending to small business in countries with strong local banking networks. Moreover, small firm owners dislike the fact that their branch manager – who they feel best understands their problems – has to refer to a higher authority in granting loans. The Crédit Agricole may be one of the largest banks in the world, but its mutual status ensures that lending decisions are made at the branch level. Accountable to a board of stockholders, commercial banks cannot afford comparable decentralization.

As banks grow larger, they abandon lending to small business. The distance between the banker and each individual borrower widens,

[34] On Japan, see Fries 1993, p. 9 and Pempel 1998, p. 23. On Germany, see Sabel et al. 1993, p. 23. On France, see Ganne 1995. On Italy, see Cesarini 1994, 45. On Scandinavia, see Drees and Pazarbasioglu 1995, p. 18.

[35] Drees and Pazarbasioglu argue that deregulation in Norway and Sweden triggered a move from "relationship banking" to "transaction-based banking that weakened banks' ability to assess credit risks and monitor borrowers" (1995, p. 18).

increasing the need for arms' length, standardized information. Standardization impoverishes the quality of the information, quality on which lending to small business relies. These hypotheses were directly tested in a study of US banking. Analyzing a sample of over 1.6 million individual loans to domestic businesses by US banks, Berger et al. (1995) found that large banks tend to lend to medium and large business borrowers, while small banks tend to specialize in lending to small business. They also found evidence that banking consolidation in the first half of the 1990s in the United States led to a contraction in lending to small borrowers.

A bank may abandon small lending without necessarily harming small business. Revisiting the same issue in a subsequent paper (Berger et al., 1998b), the authors found that the negative effects of consolidation on small business lending were generally offset by the reactions of other local banks. The authors found sufficient ground to conclude that bank consolidation has no negative net effect on lending to small business.[36] These findings illustrate two points. First, bank consolidation hurts small borrowers. Second, this problem is mitigated in the presence of a broad local banking sector. Absent such a sector, as is more likely to be the case in centralized countries, small borrowers find it more difficult to obtain bank credit.

A second recourse open to small business to make up for the vanishing state credit sector is to lobby for new state subsidies. However, the return to balanced budgets implies that any new subsidy must be paid by tax returns, a stiff condition making subsidies in general more difficult to legislate.

Budget constraints forced central governments to compress the sums traditionally devoted to regional development policies, with local and regional communities left to bear the burden of change. Local communities are pressed to make themselves attractive to savers and firms, both local and external. Regions are increasingly locked into a race of which the winners may well be those that, in addition to their natural resources, have the most policy instruments at their disposal.[37] Two of the most centralized governments (Britain and France) have embarked on the road of institutional decentralization. The French state devolved to local governments the power to guarantee loans to local business.[38] The British and French devolution programs, however, are quite modest in comparison to what is being done in federal countries. In Germany, beginning in the 1970s, the

---

[36] Note that this conclusion is somewhat weakened by the failure to control for the price of credit. Given that price is a negative function of the length of a bank–firm relation, a fact empirically demonstrated using the same data by Berger and Udell (1995), switching banks in the wake of a bank merger is bound to raise the price of credit for the affected firm in the short run.

[37] See Keating 1997 and Deeg 1997.   [38] See Ganne 1995.

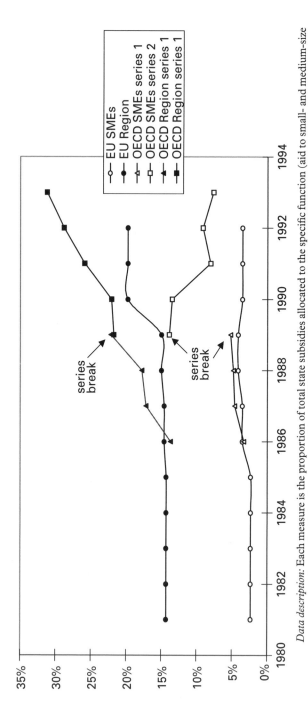

Data description: Each measure is the proportion of total state subsidies allocated to the specific function (aid to small- and medium-size enterprises, aid to regional development) within the EU and the OECD respectively. The EU dataset includes ten countries for the period 1981–85, twelve for the period 1986–92. The OECD first series (1986–89) includes twenty-two countries, the second series (1989–93), twenty-four countries.

Sources: OECD (1992, 1996); European Commission (1989, 1990, 1992, 1995).

Figure 7.5. Shares of regional aid and aid to SMEs in EU and OECD countries, 1981–93

Länder adopted subsidies to help the *Mittelstand* with consulting, technology, and exports. Some of them also created their own banks, the *Landesbanken*, to provide small firms with loans for startups, modernization, and innovation.[39]

The subnational government is an increasingly attractive level of organization and lobbying for small business. The same firms that, until recently, identified themselves as small business, and organized small business federations to lobby the central government, are now more concerned about lobbying their respective local governments – the small has become the local. This redefinition has actually affected the way governments target subsidies to business, away from aid to small and medium-sized business, toward aid to regional growth. This trend is visible in figure 7.5, which provides the relative proportion represented by these two types of aid among EU countries and among OECD countries. Notwithstanding the change in methodology in OECD series, both datasets exhibit a rise in the share of aid allocated to regional development, and a decline in the share allocated to small business. The recipients are the same; they are the small and the local. Only the channels have changed; they have been decentralized. The local governments are becoming the main suppliers of relief to small business.

Conclusion

The supply shocks of the 1970s led to the deregulation of money and credit. Thirty years of regulatory frost were succeeded by thirty years of deregulatory deluge, at the end of which financial institutions could sell just about anything, to anyone, anywhere. We are back to the pre-Depression days, when central governments did not directly intervene in financial markets. Yet, deregulation does not mean market competition. The shakeup of the newest regulatory sediments has not opened the way to a flood of market entrants but, in many cases, has merely revealed a bed of hardened, older restraints, which are difficult to eradicate, for they are rooted in state institutions. Consequently, for-profit banks must still make do with a substantial amount of sectoral segmentation, being excluded from local markets in which they can neither open a branch nor buy the local monopolist. This situation prevails in decentralized countries, where central governments lack the institutional wherewithal to impose their will on local governments. Rather than yielding convergence, deregulation is revealing differences of a structural nature.

[39] See Deeg 1997.

8   The globalization of banking

Banking became international for the first time in the nineteenth century when the international money market grew large enough to enable banks to refinance themselves on that market. Until World War I, the international money market rested on bankers' international acceptances – trade bills endorsed by reputable London merchant banks. The banking crisis of the 1930s put an end to that era. In the immediate postwar years, cross-border flows took the form of direct investment (FDI) by multinational firms; this was an instrument of marginal financial importance, for it was neither mediated by banks nor traded on markets. International banking took off again with the emergence of the Euromarkets, initially a London-based offshore interbank market in short-term dollar-denominated deposits. The Euromarkets made possible a rapid expansion of international banking. Banks lent or borrowed liquidity on the Euromarkets at rates that were more advantageous than those obtained on regulated domestic markets.

Banking internationalization was at first hindered by the Keynesian–Phillips synthesis that dominated macroeconomic policy. It was generally believed that wages were sticky and full employment unreachable without government managing consumers' demand for goods. Governments, seeking the right mix of price stability and employment, viewed cross-border flows as an irritant. Inflation led most OECD countries to restore capital controls in the 1960s and 1970s. Euromarkets developed on an offshore basis, in breach of acceptable economic practice. It is only in the 1980s that internationalization became a deliberate policy, which governments pursued to improve the efficiency of their financial system.

Internationalization had redistributional effects. It made banks dependent on world markets for both funding and investment, forcing them to improve asset quality. It placed firms that did not enjoy direct access to money markets at a relative disadvantage. This redistributional effect is important in understanding the cross-national variation in internationalization. I show that the degree of banking internationalization

156

is, today, as in the past, a function of the degree of centralization of the state.

The present argument concedes little to US hegemony in promoting internationalization.[1] With its decentralized institutions, the United States has a relatively protectionist banking community, undermining US leadership. The present argument does not contradict the current emphasis on competitive deregulation, but merely points to the greater immunity of unconcentrated banking systems to such pressure.[2]

I first retrace the origins and development of the international money market, and then consider its consequences for financial politics.

Macromanagement and offshore banking

Keynesian-style management works best in a closed economy. Openness enlists monetary policy for the exclusive defense of the currency, depriving governments of one of their most efficient policy tools. The demise of Keynesian macromanagement corresponded with the gradual opening of product and capital markets. The paradigmatic change occurred in the 1980s, under the initiative of two conservative governments – Thatcher's in Britain and Reagan's in the United States. Both allowed unemployment to shoot upward to squash the dramatic wage inflation of the 1970s – they endorsed monetarism and rational expectations, a theoretic mix that rejected the Phillips tradeoff between price stability and employment. The French and Spanish Left's embrace of monetarism in 1983 sanctioned the advent of post-Keynesian politics. Rather than reflating a weak economy, they opted for price stability at the cost of unemployment, to avoid the greater evil of financial closure.

Certainly, in small economies, trade openness long predated, out of necessity, such a paradigmatic shift. This is why their governments established comprehensive welfare systems to insure workers employed in import-sensitive industries against the hazards of foreign competition.[3] The exemplar was the Swedish Rehn–Meidner plan, according to which wages were negotiated nationwide irrespective of the industry of employment, thereby forcing non-competitive import-sensitive sectors out of business, while the state took on the cost of retraining and finding new jobs for laid-off workers. Social corporatism eventually floundered upon the need to decentralize wage negotiations and abandon capital controls.

---

[1] This argument is endorsed by Strange 1986, Goodman and Pauly 1993, Gill and Law 1993, Helleiner 1994, p. 201, and Sobel 1994.

[2] This argument appears in various guises in Helleiner 1994, p. 196, Strange 1986, p. 26, Plender 1987, 41, Andrews 1994, Bryant 1987, and O'Brien 1992.

[3] On this, see Katzenstein 1985.

This did not happen until the mid-1980s, explaining why Sweden was the last OECD country to authorize its banks to open branches abroad and permit entry by foreign banks.

The incompatibility between macroeconomic management and internationalization explains the offshore origins of the international money market. Throughout the 1950s, international banking was what it had always been before – onshore. New York banks were lending to the Mexican government, British banks were financing trade from Scandinavia and India, and so forth. Foreign branching was limited, except for American banks, which were following their multinational clients abroad. Irrespective of nationality, banks were subject to host-country regulations. It is only with the return of obstacles to cross-border capital flows in Britain and the United States at the turn of the 1960s that the largest banks began to think of foreign banking as a way to bypass restrictive domestic regulations. The offshore Euromarket was the paradoxical offspring of the focus of Keynesian-style macroeconomic management on internal aggregates, to the neglect of external constraints.

In the 1950s and 1960s respectively, the British and US governments refused to curb capital flight by conventional means – by raising interest rates – but groped, instead, for a stopgap in the form of capital controls. They feared deflation might throw them off target with respect to unemployment. The reluctance to divert monetary policy to the defense of the currency away from the fine-tuning of the inflation/unemployment tradeoff led to the reintroduction of capital controls. Yet, because each government was also afraid of losing support from bankers, they allowed for enough loopholes to permit bankers to move international lending to a de jure offshore platform – the Eurodollar market in London.

Indeed, after the British government in 1957 had prohibited banks from lending pounds to finance non-British trade, the banks began financing the same trade by attracting dollar deposits and lending dollars instead of pounds. Because stringent regulations prevented the non-sterling transactions from affecting domestic-asset markets, the British government was willing to take a laissez-faire attitude toward the banks' foreign-currency activities. Foreign-currency liabilities were free from reserve requirements, lending was free from exchange controls, and both borrowing and lending were free from interest-rate ceilings. London also had the peculiarity of being open to foreign banks. US bankers moved their international dollar business to London. Supportive of bankers, US regulatory agencies refrained from extending domestic regulations to offshore lending.[4]

---

[4] On the origins of Euromarkets, see Helleiner 1994. See also Kelly 1976.

The Eurodollar market thus developed free of bank reserve requirements and interest-rate regulation. With the progressive relaxation of exchange-rate controls throughout the 1960s, all large banks in the world began to patronize the Eurodollar market. Similar markets developed for all major currencies, with the significant exception of the Deutschmark – fearing imported inflation, the Bundesbank made the DM deposits held by the foreign branches of German banks subject to reserve requirements. Three centers developed besides London – Luxembourg, Paris, and Brussels. Euromarkets offered banks a means to evade the shortage of loanable resources – to which they were subject at home, by governments intent on keeping interest rates artificially low in order to promote home investment – while at the same time using bank reserve requirements to contain inflation. In countries with narrow short-term markets, the Euromarkets provided banks with a supplementary channel for securing funds and expanding volume and profits. The market moved from being an exclusively interbank market, in which banks distributing consumer credit borrowed from the giro institutions of the savings and cooperative banks, to one open to all large players.[5]

From a tolerated method of rule evasion in the 1960s, the international money market came to play a central role in assisting the rise of international banking in the 1970s. The move from fixed to flexible exchange rates reduced official reserve transactions. Bankers stepped into the breach, assuming the task of financial intermediation on a worldwide scale. The oil crisis further added to the developing countries' need for foreign credit, increasing bank involvement in the recycling process of short-term funds from capital-rich, oil-exporting countries to capital-scarce, oil-importing countries. The rise of budget deficits in the 1970s and 1980s also led governments in OECD and developing countries to borrow on the international credit market with a view to limiting the crowding out of private investors from domestic credit markets. The rise in demand for traditional foreign banking happened at the same time as floating exchange rates, inflation, and interest volatility considerably increased risk in international banking. Banks responded to this challenge by relying more and more on the Euromarkets to hedge against currency and interest risks by means of swaps and futures contracts.

Banks' reliance on the global interbank market was increased by the debt crisis, which converted large volumes of loans into frozen assets. Not

---

[5] The Eurosecurities markets also benefited from distinctive advantages over onshore international banking: bonds were in bearer form and paid interest gross rather than net of tax. Securities also paid dividends gross. Finally, none of these transactions was subject to sales tax.

only were banks forced to make provisions against actual and anticipated losses, but tougher standards adopted by bank regulators across the OECD also forced them to increase capital. Increasing capital, however, proved to be tricky. Banks could not issue equity, because markets had priced down their shares. They could not borrow long term, because rating agencies had cut their credit ratings. They could not retain earnings, for there were none. Instead, the banks resorted en masse to the Euromarkets, through bonds and floating-rate notes. They also lost corporate clients, who, enjoying higher credit ratings than their bankers, found it more advantageous to sell commercial paper directly on the Euromarkets. The upshot was a surge in the issuance of international paper, fueled by banks and ex-clients.

Last, international branching received a boost from regulators. Worried that deregulation would trigger concentration, they welcomed foreign entry as a way of exposing domestic banks to the competition of foreign banks. This was a new development, for, until the 1980s, foreign banks seeking to branch out abroad faced restraints in almost all OECD countries. From the perspective of a central bank trying to reach a monetary target, foreign banks were too independent because they could rely on international sources of funds. In countries like Japan or France, where the government used monetary policy to finance the debt or allocate credit, foreign banks were seen as less pliable to the will of the government. In only a handful of countries could foreign banks set up a branch or take majority control without restriction – Britain, Switzerland, and the United States. Following the deregulation of domestic banking and financial markets in the 1980s, most government regulators began to see benefits in allowing an onshore foreign presence. In the case of small countries, foreign competition was seen as a healthy check against concentration. For instance, the Canadian Bank Act of 1980 indicated that authorization be granted to foreign operators provided they contributed to competitive banking in Canada.[6] In Australia in 1984, the federal government invited applications from foreign banks for banking licenses, granting fifteen of forty.[7]

Governments of large countries wooed foreign banks, not so much to increase competition at home as to enhance the international role of the home market. Inviting in the Citibanks of the world was a quick way of bringing a backward money market up to an international grade. Practiced all along by the United States, Britain, the Netherlands, and Luxembourg, this attitude became dominant in France, Belgium, and within the scope of the European single market. However, governments

---

[6] See Pecchioli 1983, p. 187.   [7] See Ackland and Harper 1992, p. 50.

were not always able to convince domestic banks of the fairness of such a course. Nationals understandably asked for reciprocity – the practice of restricting a foreigner to conducting only those activities the government of the other nation allows foreigners to conduct on its own territory. Switzerland, despite a significant presence of foreign banks, and the European Common Market with respect to non-member states made foreign access contingent on reciprocity.[8] Canada, Japan, and Spain (until 1994) not only requested reciprocity, but their legislation still discriminated against foreign entrants.

Few governments would have succeeded in attracting foreign banks without the international money market. Foreign banks rarely open a foreign branch to tap deposits and make loans, at least not at first, because of the monopolization of the retail banking market by domestic institutions. Their competitive advantage, if any, lies in the wholesale business, which they owe to their superior capacity to tap the Euromarkets.

A new approach to the management of assets and liabilities

The turn of the twentieth century exhibited a strong association between internationalization and the standardization of financial instruments (chapter 4). A similar correlation is visible at present. The international money market has transformed the way banks do business; modern banks rely on shorter borrowing than their predecessors; they match assets with liabilities; they standardize assets; and they develop market-related services.

A first trend is the shortening of bank liabilities. Banks finance less of their investments through individual deposits. The proportion of deposits collected from households and non-financial firms has dropped. Calculated on a sample of nine European countries, the share of deposits in all liabilities dropped from an average of 64 percent in 1981 to 49 percent in 1997 (table 8.1). The drop was especially marked in Spain and Portugal. Offsetting the drop in individual deposits is a greater reliance on the global interbank market through certificates of deposit, bonds, and notes. Interbank deposits are shorter than individual deposits. Being issued for three or six months, they have to be repaid at maturity; there are no core deposits staying indefinitely, as is the case with demand deposits. Bonds are longer – they are designed to meet capital adequacy guidelines. Still, even then, banks have preferred to issue floating-rate notes – long-term notes with a variable, and thus de facto short-term, interest rate. All

[8] See Pecchioli 1983, p. 78.

Table 8.1. *Non-bank deposits as a proportion of total bank liabilities (1981, 1997)*

	1981	1997
France (large commercial banks)	0.42	0.30
Switzerland (large commercial banks)	0.49	0.41
Sweden (commercial banks)	0.55	0.43
Germany (large commercial banks)	0.57	0.48
Finland (commercial banks)	0.64	0.55
Norway (commercial banks)	0.71	0.51
Spain (commercial banks)	0.72	0.44
Portugal (commercial banks)	0.80	0.46
Greece (commercial banks)	0.82	0.79
Average (unweighted)	0.64	0.49

Source: Bank Profitability, various years.

these alternative liabilities are priced by efficient markets, offering banks little possibilities of rents.

A second trend in banking is a greater awareness of the need of matching assets with liabilities. Until the 1960s, banks were not in the business of matching assets and liabilities in the short term. On the liabilities side, most items were individual deposits that paid regulated interest rates, providing banks with a comfortable margin between interest charged and interest paid. On the assets side, banks were usually able to pass any cost on to the borrowers. As a result, banks refrained from individually pricing all services they provided, preferring, instead, bundling and cross-subsidization.

Things changed in the 1980s. Deregulation increased competition for borrowers among banks on the one hand, and, as far as very large firms are concerned, between banks and markets on the other. Large depositors, at first, then all depositors a decade later, began to expect market rates on deposits. Forced to pay higher rates on deposits, banks became less able to pass on expensive liabilities to borrowers. The point was demonstrated in the wake of the debt crisis, which left many a large bank with a downgraded credit rating. Forced to pay higher borrowing rates on the Eurocurrency markets, the banks were progressively priced out of the market for corporate external capital. The corporate clients of the banks found it less costly either to self-finance their investments or to resort to the bond market.

The thinning of interest margins forced banks to refine their cost–profit analysis. The currency volatility of the 1970s led banks to hedge short-term currency mismatches by matching currency on both sides of the balance sheet, mostly by issuing or buying dollar-denominated liabilities.[9] The interest volatility of the 1970s also led them to match assets and liabilities in terms of interest-rate structure. Banks passed the interest risk on to the borrowers by shortening all loans and rolling them over, or, simply, by adopting variable-rate lending. The banks were helped in the task of asset–liability matching by the development of derivatives markets in foreign exchange and interest rates. By means of futures and swaps, banks could hedge just about any currency or interest-rate risk.[10]

Banks have also paid greater attention to maturity matching. The marketization of liabilities, already noted, has led to a shortening of assets. Banks have to worry about their credit rating, which determines the price they pay. Banks have a growing preference for assets that are easily disposable, not only to be able to unload them in case of interest hikes, but also because disposable assets have a market value that is directly – and more favorably – assessable by Moody's and Standard & Poor's.

Most banks have settled for the strategy of asset standardization. Asset standardization makes bank assets less risky and more valuable, because they are more easily disposable. This explains the recent success of "asset-backed securities," by which banks securitize some of their loans. Banks typically collect a large portfolio of bank loans that are then used as collateral for new bonds. It works because markets can price certain bank loans better – and thus higher – than single banks, provided first, that these loans occur in large pools for which past experience can be used to predict default rates and, second, that claims over collateral are easily transferable. Only a few categories of bank assets so far meet these requirements: credit card receivables, corporate receivables, automobile loans, mortgages, leases, and home equity loans.[11]

The rise of securitization, along with the declining retention of loans on the balance sheet, has led banks to increase their so-called off-balance-sheet items – market-oriented financial services (such as standby credit, backup facilities for the placement of paper, or any kind of commitment contingent on a future event) that generate fees as opposed to interest. Off-balance-sheet business was particularly sought by banks that had their credit ratings downgraded in the wake of the debt crisis. Securitization allowed these banks, Harrington (1987, p. 141) wrote, "to lend in excess of what capital resources would permit, in the knowledge that some of the lending can be sold to third parties." A computation of off-balance-sheet items held by the largest banks in the OECD (with total assets above or equal to US$ 1 billion) during the 1990s points to a significant increase;

---

[9] Harrington 1987, p. 46.

[10] Swaps are traded on the interbank market. Futures, in contrast, are traded on specialized exchanges.

[11] On the securitization of bank loans, see Thompson 1995.

in relation to total assets, these items leapt from 20 percent in 1991 to 34 percent in 1998.[12]

Financial disintermediation does not imply that money markets are replacing banks, but that banks are redefining their role away from intermediation toward market facilitation. Their role is to facilitate the placement of short-term paper by providing backup facilities and keeping the market liquid. They also use these markets to hold more negotiable assets and to fund themselves through marketable issues. Among the banks' best clients for off-balance-sheet services, indeed, are banks themselves; the need for banks to dress their balance sheets and win a good rating increases their dependence on negotiable assets.[13]

Winners and losers from internationalization

A foreign bank that wishes to enter the wholesale market, a market that entails relatively low fixed costs, will open a branch in the financial center. A foreign bank that targets the retail market, in contrast, will prefer to merge with or take over an existing branch network. This is because retail banking requires an investment in a costly branch network that will not generate profits immediately.

Holding everything else constant, all banks, whether private or public, center or local, stood to lose from opening up the home market to foreign competition. However, some categories of banks were easier to convince than others, provided they were offered the right quid pro quo. Generally, the largest center banks were willing to accept foreign competition in exchange for reciprocal treatment abroad. Large commercial banks in Europe and Australasia were also willing to withstand foreign competition in exchange for being freed from shouldering the burden of financing the public debt. The typical quid pro quo was between the banks and the treasury. As long as the treasury used the banks as a cheap way of financing the public debt, they would not face foreign competition. With the deregulation of government bond market and, concomitantly, the liberalization of branching and securities trading, it became difficult for banks to oppose foreign competition. In Australia, Canada, Sweden, Norway, Spain, Greece, and Portugal, foreign competition was imposed as a quid pro quo for deregulation.[14]

---

[12] The figures were calculated on the 1,316 large banks featured in the Bankscope database; see Fitch-IBCA 2001.

[13] Harrington 1987, p. 131.

[14] For evidence of this in Canada and Australia, see Pauly 1988. On Spain, Greece, and Portugal, see contributions to Gibson and Tsakalotos 1992. The opening of branches by foreign banks was not allowed in Sweden and Norway until the mid-1980s, when interest rates were freed and ceilings on advances abandoned.

Remnants of the center banks' opposition to foreign competition were still visible in the privatization of nationalized banks. In France, Italy, Spain, Greece, and Portugal, the transfer of ownership of the largest center banks from the state to private shareholders was hedged with precautions to avoid banks falling under foreign control. Many European governments, France in particular, adopted the practice of so-called *noyaux durs* (stable shareholders) and strategic alliances in the form of bank–customers cross-ownership.[15] The Amato Law went further than the French practice, placing the shares of three of the top ten Italian banks in bank foundations whose members are appointed by their respective local governments.[16] In two other cases, Rome included in the bylaws a cap on the voting shares that any shareholder can hold.[17] In still other cases, privatization was nominal: 30 percent of Istituto Mobiliare Italiano (IMI) shares were placed with three public sector banks.

In contrast to large center banks, local banks never had a reason to support internationalization. This was most evident in countries combining local banking with a large international presence – the United States and Switzerland. Lobbying by US regional banks in California and New York, two states in which foreign bank branches were active, was critical to the passage of the 1978 International Banking Act – a protectionist piece of legislation curtailing foreign banks from engaging in interstate banking.[18] In Switzerland, where local banks are heavily vested in mortgage lending, competition from foreign banks is hampered by explicit restrictions on foreign ownership of domestic real estate.

Local non-profit banks in Germany, Austria, Italy, Spain, and Scandinavia were also opposed to foreign entry. The threat of foreign entry, however, was subsumed under the question of privatization, already covered in the previous chapter. The only way for an outsider to penetrate a local market is by taking over a local bank. If the target is a non-profit bank, such a move is, depending on the country, either illegal or impossible to achieve without the consent of the target. Hence, as long as non-profit banks manage to maintain their non-profit status, they are immune to foreign takeover bids.

Mutuality is so efficient at preventing unwanted takeover bids that France used it to shelter its largest previously state-owned bank against a potential foreign takeover. When the French government privatized the

---

[15] The European Commission decided to refer Portugal to the European Court because of the restrictions imposed on foreign investors in its privatization program.

[16] The three banks are the Istituto Bancario San Paolo di Torino, Banca Nazionale del Lavoro, and Banca Monte dei Paschi di Siena.

[17] This was the strategy pursued in the privatization of two large Italian commercial banks in 1994, Credito Italiano and Banca Commerciale.

[18] On this case, see Pauly's clear presentation (1988, p. 51).

Crédit Agricole, the second largest bank in the world in 1986, it turned it into a mutual bank. Mutuality – the fact of being owned by one's local member banks – enabled the Crédit Agricole to buy private banks (Indosuez, Banque Française pour le Commerce Extérieur), and purchase strategic positions in others, while preventing private banks from buying it.[19] The Crédit Foncier – the first state credit bank – was also mutualized, being taken over by Caisses d'Epargne, in turn mutualized in 1999.

Local governments may or may not lose from cross-border financial flows. It depends on what direction these funds tend to flow. Local governments welcome capital mobility when it brings a multinational company to open a plant in their districts.[20] However, they tend to lose from the internationalization of banking, for, in most cases, it implies shedding resources to financial centers. Free entry for foreign banks reinforces competition and thus concentration among banks, accelerating the disappearance of country banks. The internationalization of money markets not only absorbs large quantities of national, and thus local, savings, but it also emancipates local banks from the collection of local savings, somewhat diluting their dependence on (and loyalty to) local economies. Last, the growth of large international money markets fuels the growth of securities markets around the world, accentuating their centralization in each country and specialization across countries (this point is developed in the next chapter).

In two special cases, local governments welcomed foreign banks. Australia and Canada are two countries in which the regulation of nonbanks (finance companies) is decentralized among provincial governments; the regulation of banks, in contrast, is entrusted to the federal government. In both cases, provinces were keen to attract foreign banks to expand the pool of local business at the expense of the financial center.[21]

The effects of internationalization on borrowers are more difficult to identify. Financial internationalization is not an issue on which firms are asked to take a position by governments. Moreover, the effects of internationalization of firms are so much entwined with the effects of bank concentration (addressed in the previous chapter) and disintermediation (addressed in the next chapter) that few firms are likely to entertain a position on the issue of internationalization per se. On experience of past trends, it is possible to offer a few speculations. The internationalization of the money market has made banks more sensitive to their credit

---

[19] *The Banker* January 1995, 22.
[20] Provided, of course, that they manage to attract FDI, an outcome that is sometimes quite elusive; on this, see Thomas 1997.
[21] See Pauly 1988.

rating. Managing the rating has forced banks to restructure their investments away from long- and medium-term loans. Banks cannot afford to
keep renewing advances to long-term clients as much as previously. Nor
can they afford anymore to take equity positions in non-traded companies
with the hope of reselling them at a profit three years later after a rejuvena-
tion of management. They must abandon this task to venture capitalists
and investment companies. The latter, however, are unlikely to pay much
attention to sectors or companies with little or no market appeal. This
means that companies operating in sectors other than high-tech and the
internet will be left aside – a point that is further developed in the next
chapter. Outside these high-growth sectors, only firms with the critical
size to access the new markets for commercial paper on their own will
be able to benefit from the reinvigorated money markets. Today's banks
are as likely to compete for good paper drawn on good borrowers as their
nineteenth-century ancestors did. And they do it for the same reason, to
burnish their image as a reliable borrower. Therefore, firms that depend
on renewed bank loans to finance their working capital are likely to be
relatively worse off.

This survey of the respective winners and losers of internationalization across government levels and among banks reinforces the tentative
conclusions that we reached after analyzing the consequences of domestic financial deregulation (see previous chapter). Internationalization has
detrimental consequences for local banks, if not yet on their borrowers.
In a general equilibrium, we should expect these banking sectors (and
perhaps their clienteles as well) to appeal to their political representatives
to resist the harmful trends. Their capacity to do so should depend in
turn on these groups' capacity to coordinate and mobilize the support of
enough legislators to veto internationalization. These conditions are met,
I argued in the previous chapter, in decentralized polities. In sum, there
are good reasons to expect that the past correlation between centralization, a large center bank sector, and internationalization should still be
observable today. The last section probes the existing evidence.

Evidence

There are two independent variables – market segmentation and state
centralization – which are presumed to show a relation with financial
internationalization. I use three different measures of internationalization. The first variable is *foreign bank penetration*; it measures for each
country the proportion of bank assets belonging to foreign banks. The
second is *foreign assets and liabilities held by banks*; for each country, it measures the amount of external bank assets and liabilities (added together

and weighted by GDP). Given that most of these items are generated by interbank transactions, it gives a sense of the size of cross-border money markets among EU countries. The third is *international bonds* – the volume of international issues weighted by the equivalent volume of domestic issues. All variables are calculated circa 1990.

The first and third measures exist only for a small number of countries – between ten and twelve; the second measure is available for twenty-one countries. Still, they are preferable to other measures which may have a wider geographic coverage, but do not reflect the argument of this chapter. FDI, for instance, has a wide coverage, but it does not reflect foreign bank competition and reliance on Euromarkets as much as multinational corporations' strategies in a low-tariff world.[22] Alternatively, capital control – a measure of regulatory openness calculated by Quinn and Inclán (1997) – fails to capture informal means of protection of the type discussed in this work – market saturation and local monopolies. I correct for the small number of observations by bootstrapping standard errors and confidence intervals.

In all regressions, I control for economic development (measured as GDP per capita), since wealth favors internationalization. I use country size (proxied by population) in the regression having international bonds as the dependent variable to control for inherent scale economies; small countries (with the exception of Switzerland) are more likely to issue bonds in the currency of a large country (US dollars, Deutschmarks, British pounds, French francs) than the opposite.

I first consider the relation between market segmentation and internationalization. The hypothesis that internationalization is associated with the existence of a banking system dominated by center banks is confirmed by the data (table 8.2). Foreign bank penetration in regression 1 is both strongly and significantly affected by the market share of domestic center banks – a one-(unbootstrapped)standard-deviation difference in center market share corresponds to an equivalent difference in foreign market share (regression 1). This result confirms the intuitive idea that a large local non-profit sector blocks foreign entry.

Center banking is marginally associated with bank holdings of foreign assets and liabilities (regression 2). The impact is of the order of 50 percent – a one-standard-deviation difference in center banking corresponds with half-a-standard-deviation difference in foreign holdings. The volume of international bond issues shows no association with the

---

[22] And yet, despite this imprecision, FDI does correlate with center banking and state centralization; see Verdier 1999.

Table 8.2. *Internationalization and market segmentation, circa 1990*

	Dependent variable			
Independent and control variables	*Foreign bank penetration, 1987*	*Foreign assets and liabilities, 1990*	*International bonds, 1990*	
	1	2	3	4
Center banking sector, 1990	1.12	2.07	28.60	61.52
	(0.25)***	(1.01)*	(32.68)	(5.44)***
	[0.37]**	[1.32]*	[44.35]	[8.51]***
GDP per capita, 1990	5×10^{-5}	0.0001	0.0006	0.004
	(1×10^{-5})**	(5×10^{-5})**	(0.02)	(0.0003)***
	$[2 \times 10^{-5}]$**	$[6 \times 10^{-5}]$*	[0.03]	[0.0006]***
Population, 1990			−0.39	−0.72
			(0.34)	(0.06)***
			[0.42]	[0.08]***
Intercept	−1.20	−2.10	3.14	−63.48
	(0.31)***	(1.10)*	(36.89)	(6.88)***
Num. obs.	10^a	21^b	12^c	11^d

Methodology: Ordinary least squares with standard errors and bias-corrected confidence intervals calculated on 1000 bootstraps. Each cell reports values of observed coefficients and corresponding regular and bootstrapped standard errors in parentheses and brackets respectively. Confidence intervals using bootstrapped standard errors are bias-corrected; *, **, *** indicate coefficients situated in the 90%, 95%, and 99% confidence intervals respectively.

Data description and sources: Foreign bank penetration is the ratio of foreign bank assets over all bank assets. It was calculated for 1987 by Steinherr and Gilibert (1989, table 6). *Foreign assets and liabilities* refers to the external balance sheet items held by banks in each country weighted by GDP in 1990; the source is IMF 1995. *International bonds* is the stock of international bonds outstanding as a percentage of domestic bonds in 1990; it was calculated by Danthine et al. (1999, p. 38). For *center banking sector*, see appendix 2. For *GDP per capita* (in US$) and *population* (in millions), see *National Accounts*.

[a] Belgium, Denmark, France, Germany, Ireland, Italy, Netherlands, Portugal, Spain, UK.
[b] Australia, Austria, Belgium, Canada, Denmark, Finland, France, Germany, Greece, Ireland, Italy, Japan, Netherlands, New Zealand, Norway, Portugal, Spain, Sweden, Switzerland, UK, USA.
[c] Austria, Belgium, Finland, France, Germany, Ireland, Italy, Netherlands, Portugal, Spain, Switzerland, UK.
[d] Same as previous note minus Switzerland.

independent variables in regression 3. A look at the outliers points to Switzerland as a strong outlier. For reasons that I ignore, Switzerland scored the lowest value on the international bond variable. A rerun of the regression without the Swiss observation yields statistics in line with the results (regression 4). Though significant, the impact of center banking on international bond issuance is moderate; the largest effects are registered by the two control variables, wealth and country size. Note that, in all regressions so far, the wealth variable (GDP per capita) is also positively associated with internationalization. Overall, there is little doubt that banking systems featuring a large center banking sector are more internationalized than those with a large local and non-profit banking sector.

Evidence for the second hypothesis, that internationalization reflects state centralization, is not as clear cut. I use the same variables as before, only substituting state centralization for center banking. The OLS procedure picks up a weak relation between state centralization and foreign bank penetration – the coefficient for that variable is different from zero at the 90 percent (bias-corrected) confidence level (regression 1, table 8.3). A look at the partial regression plot for the state centralization variable reveals a case of heteroscedasticity (see figure 8.1). Centralization is a necessary but not sufficient condition for foreign penetration. Decentralization is associated with limited foreign presence, but so is centralization, notably in the Dutch and Italian cases. Although it is true that the measure I use for centralization (the distribution of revenue between central and local governments) overestimates the degree of Italian centralization, this is not the case for the Netherlands. The explanation for the low Dutch value is to be found in the strength of Dutch banks, dominated by three all-purpose groups – ING, ABN Amro, and Rabobank. Dutch banking is as much internationalized as Belgian banking. The fact is that Dutch banks themselves, ING and ABN Amro at least, though coded as domestic, are the vehicle of internationalization. This point is easily confirmed by the other regressions in table 8.3, where the Netherlands no longer figures as an exception but falls in line with our expectations.[23]

State centralization is significantly and firmly associated with foreign holdings only after the exclusion of the Swiss case (regressions 2–3, table 8.3). The Swiss observation is an outlier, here, for the usual reason – the centralization and extroversion of its financial system are out of line with its federal institutions. Considering regression 3, a one-standard-deviation change in state centralization is associated with a change equivalent to 70 percent of a standard deviation in external holdings. Economic

---

[23] The reason why the Dutch case did not appear as an outlier when market segmentation was regressed against foreign bank penetration (in table 8.2, regression 1) is that Rabobank, one of the top three banks, is a mutual association of local banks (and is thus coded as a local bank).

Table 8.3. *Internationalization and state centralization, circa 1990*

Independent and control variables	Foreign bank penetration, 1987 1	Foreign assets and liabilities, 1990		International bonds, 1990 4
		2	3	
State centralization, 1990	0.91	0.71	3.39	86.89
	(0.56)	(1.65)	(1.08)***	(28.03)**
	[2.82]*	[2.50]	[1.36]**	[40.07]**
GDP per capita, 1990	3×10^{-5}	0.0001	0.0001	0.003
	(2.3×10^{-5})	(8×10^{-5})	(5×10^{-5})**	(0.002)*
	$[6.5 \times 10^{-5}]$	$[8 \times 10^{-5}]$	$[5 \times 10^{-5}]$**	[0.003]
Population, 1990				−0.67
				(0.23)**
				[0.28]***
Intercept	−1.06	−1.22	−3.77	−86.59
	(0.70)	(2.28)	(1.42)**	(40.48)*
Num. obs.	10^a	20^b	19^c	12^d

Methodology: Ordinary least squares with standard errors and bias-corrected confidence intervals calculated on 1000 bootstraps. Each cell reports values of observed coefficients and corresponding regular and bootstrapped standard errors in parentheses and brackets respectively. Confidence intervals using bootstrapped standard errors are bias-corrected; *, **, *** indicate coefficients situated in the 90%, 95%, and 99% confidence intervals respectively.

Data description and sources: State centralization is defined in appendix 3. All the other variables are defined in table 8.2.

^{a} Belgium, Denmark, France, Germany, Ireland, Italy, Netherlands, Portugal, Spain, UK.

^{b} Australia, Austria, Belgium, Canada, Denmark, Finland, France, Germany, Greece, Ireland, Italy, Japan, Netherlands, Norway, Portugal, Spain, Sweden, Switzerland, UK, USA.

^{c} Same as previous note excluding Switzerland.

^{d} Austria, Belgium, Finland, France, Germany, Ireland, Italy, Netherlands, Portugal, Spain, Switzerland, UK.

development (GDP per capita) moderately contributes to the outcome (to the tune of 53 percent in terms of parallel changes in standard deviations). State centralization is also associated with international bonds issuance. Both control variables – GDP per capita and population – have a leverage at least twice that of state centralization.[24] In sum, the

[24] Note that the Swiss observation, which was an outlier in regression 4, table 8.2, is no longer one in regression 4, table 8.3, because of the already-noted discrepancy between the state centralization and market segmentation variables, a discrepancy that is unique to the Swiss case.

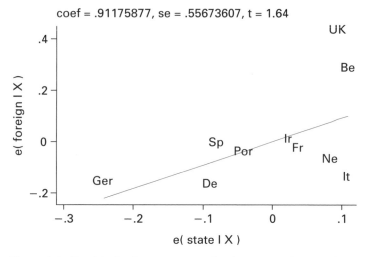

Figure 8.1. Partial plot for state centralization, regression 1, table 8.3

nineteenth-century relation between state centralization and financial internationalization is present, though probably not as clearly as it was then.

Conclusion

The internationalization of the money market did not force deregulation on OECD countries. The Euromarkets were offshore anomalies that were tolerated by governments as long as they did not threaten monetary policy. The currency speculation that attended the collapse of the Bretton Woods system led to a restoration of capital controls to protect the policy tradeoff between inflation and unemployment. The ensuing stagflation made capital controls redundant and inefficient. They were dropped, along with kindred prohibitions on foreign bank entry, in order to restore bank competition and price stability. The social-democratic attempt to prevent stagflation through corporatist bargaining between encompassing producer associations merely postponed the reckoning by a handful of years.

The rise of the internationalization of finance, along with its deregulation, has revolutionized banking. Having to borrow most of their resources on the international money market, banks closely manage the risks they take in order to maintain a good credit rating. Their willingness to immobilize resources in relatively unknown firms is consequently lower. Firms that are dependent on these loans have to find an alternative. This alternative is more readily available in countries with large non-profit banking sectors, which, benefiting from a state guarantee, need not worry about their credit rating. Non-profit sectors are still strong at the local level in decentralized countries. This is why internationalization of banking is correlated with state centralization.

9   The growth of securities markets

> [H]olding large corporate loans on a bank's book is a very effective way
> of destroying shareholder value.
>
> Raphael Soifer, *The Banker* October 2000, 118.

Securities markets are growing again. From 1980 to 1996, listed stock
capitalization doubled in the United States, quadrupled in France,
Germany, and the UK, and increased by a multiple of twenty-six in
Portugal, though, in this case, the initial value was very low. Although
most of this increase was spent recovering from two poor decades – US
market capitalization, for instance, did not regain its 1961 GDP-weighted
value until 1993 – the surge is sufficiently pronounced and ubiquitous
enough to be considered a qualitative change.

Market growth implies a relative decline in the role of banks, with predictable redistributional effects. Disintermediation reduces the twofold
capacity that the financial system has to overcome information asymmetry and insure firms against cyclical financial vicissitudes. Although
there is no evidence of a "Macmillan gap" yet, the trend toward securitization has the potential to hurt firms that are small or engaged in
traditional sectors. We should not be surprised, therefore, to observe that
disintermediation and securitization are not pursued to the same length
in all countries, but, instead, that the largest stock markets, today as
prior to the Great Depression, are found in financial systems that exhibit a low degree of segmentation and in countries with centralized state
structures.

Still, we should not expect the 1913 patterns to reemerge intact. Half
a century of state intervention in industry does not get easily shaken out.
Despite current privatization programs, state control over industry still
lingers in many countries, impeding stock market growth, for governments, unlike private investors, do not consider shareholder value to be
their primary goal. As Levy (1999) argues in his study of France, the
success of dirigism in the postwar decades preempted the development
of banks and markets, making it impossible for the state to fully disengage

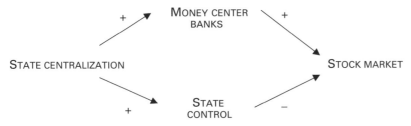

Figure 9.1. Impact of state centralization on stock market

itself from industry in the 1980s. The states that were the most susceptible to dirigism after World War I were among the most centralized ones.

Thus state centralization today has an ambiguous effect on market growth, which it did not have a century ago. On the one hand, state centralization is associated with dominant center banks, which fuel the development of integrated financial markets. On the other hand, state centralization is correlated with state control, which hinders the growth of stock markets. The net effect is null (see figure 9.1).

After describing the changes of the last twenty years, I provide systematic evidence of this dual effect on a cross-sectional population of twenty OECD countries. The results also show the indirect effect of the origins of the legal system.

Origins and magnitude

The development of corporate stock markets paralleled the growth of money markets. Central banks in the 1970s and 1980s retooled their monetary kit, discarding price-fixing instruments in favor of market-clearing ones (chapter 7). In so doing, they encouraged the development of a domestic money market, on which treasury bonds were usually the main instruments to be transacted. Tax reductions and budget deficits, first in the United States, then Britain, and later continental Europe, forced state treasuries to finance their growing debt on the bond market. Treasuries sought to ease the refinancing of the debt by pursuing deflationary policies, thereby reviving the moribund bond market for corporate borrowers at the expense of bank lending. The privatization of state-owned companies in European countries also led governments to promote stock markets, passing legislation making the purchase of securities more attractive to individual savers.

The deregulation of capital markets was met by a rising demand for securities. Households are more willing today than in the past to hold a larger share of their financial wealth in the form of stock exchange

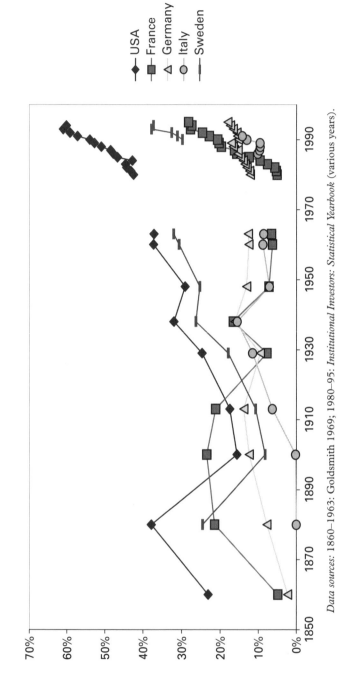

Data sources: 1860–1963: Goldsmith 1969; 1980–95: *Institutional Investors: Statistical Yearbook* (various years).

Figure 9.2. Market share of institutional investors (in % of financial assets)

securities, as both investment and insurance for their retirement. The growing privatization of pension plans in some countries, associated with a deep-seated aging of populations, is responsible for the growing assets of insurance companies and pension funds. The latter, along with investment companies, have stepped into the market to intermediate this new demand for securities, becoming the dominant holders of financial assets and increasingly important participants in capital markets.

Institutional investors are not new. They emerged in the nineteenth century in response to the public's demand for risk insurance, but were temporarily displaced by the creation of social insurance programs run by states on a pay-as-you-go basis. Since the 1980s, however, the weight of institutional investors in the financial system has sharply increased. This upturn can be glimpsed in figure 9.2, in which I plotted the market share of institutional investors in five countries – France, Germany, Italy, Sweden, and the United States.

The most spectacular increase was recorded by corporate securities markets. To get a sense of the magnitude of the increase, consider figure 9.3, reporting annual data on stock market capitalization over the 1980–97 period. The data are an unweighted average calculated over a pool of seventeen OECD countries for which time series are available. Market capitalization relative to GDP quadrupled in seventeen years (from 19 percent in 1980 to 90 percent in 1997). Another indicator of this rise is the growth in traded value relative to GDP – it rose from 4 to 60 percent over the period. To make sure that the rise in traded value was not a mere reflection of the increase in value of the stocks thus traded, but reflected a genuine surge in activity as well, I divided value traded by capitalization. The resulting series also shows an upward increase, from roughly 13 percent to 70 percent, confirming the idea that volume, not just value, has also increased (it has quintupled).

"Big Bangs" and muffled ones

Regulators allowed deposit banks to engage in investment banking, that is, the underwriting of equity, private placements, and the provision of advisory functions in mergers and acquisitions. Some large commercial banks have recently acquired well-known investment banks.[1]

---

[1] To name only the most visible deals of the last decade, Bankers Trust acquired Alex. Brown & Co., Deutsche Bank acquired Bankers Trust and Morgan Grenfell, ING acquired Barings, Dresdner acquired Kleinwort-Benson and Wesserstein Perella, Commerz acquired Hambro, SBC acquired Warburg, Crédit Suisse acquired First Boston and Donaldson, Lufkin & Jenrette, and the Crédit Agricole acquired Indosuez, while Citicorp merged with Traveller and its investment and brokerage arm, Salomon Smith Barney.

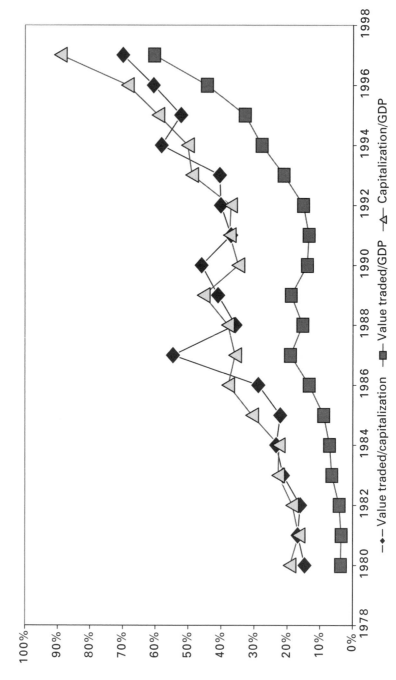

Figure 9.3. Development of capital markets, 1980–97 (unweighted average values for seventeen countries)

Banks also successfully lobbied governments for the deregulation of stock brokerage. Securities brokers lost their traditional monopoly over brokerage. Fixed brokerage commissions were abandoned, new securities commissions were created, new securities laws were enacted, floor trading gave way to automated trading, and markets in futures and options were established.

In some countries, exchanges were consolidated and supervision centralized. In Australia, the six state stock exchanges were integrated into a single stock exchange in 1987. In France, the Ministry of Finance centralized trading from the six regional exchanges to Paris. In Switzerland, four local exchanges were closed down in 1990–91, leaving behind only the exchanges of Zürich, Geneva, and Basle. The cantons were the main regulators of stock exchanges until 1995, when they transferred this function to the federal government. Portugal still has two stock exchanges, one in Lisbon and the other in Oporto. In 1994, they agreed to specialize, transferring the cash spot market to Lisbon and making Oporto the site of a futures market. In Canada, the provinces of Vancouver and Alberta merged their exchanges. Montreal agreed to specialize in derivative products and small share stocks, conceding the market for blue-chips to rival Toronto.

In most deregulatory battles, the rift ran between brokers, who defended their secular monopoly, and other financial sectors, who contested the monopoly. This was especially the case in Britain and France – two centralized countries. In Britain, the deregulation of stock brokerage was promoted by the Bank of England and pitted the corporation of stockbrokers against commercial bankers, insurers, and trust and pension fund managers – all dwellers in the City.[2] In France, the measure was imposed by the state, at times without consultation with banks.[3] In both countries, the political debate was restricted to center-based actors and institutions.

In some decentralized countries, however, the debate between brokers and non-brokers blended with another, pitting a center championing deregulation against a periphery backing the status quo. This was most visible in Germany. The "Frankfurt Coalition," including no less than Federal Finance Minister Waigel along with the four largest banks and Hessen (Frankfurt's *Land*), pushed to have stock markets play a larger part in corporate financing. They were opposed by the seven smaller exchanges and their supervisors – the respective *Land* governments.[4] The local coalition opposed computerized trading, the opening of a futures market, and the creation of a central supervisory agency. They feared the

---

[2] See Moran 1991 and Sobel 1994.
[3] According to Cerny 1989, 183. William Coleman (1993) offers a concurring opinion in his survey of French banking reforms.
[4] See Lütz 1998 and Story 1997.

centralizing impact of these measures and the eventual impoverishment of their local economies. The local coalition, however, was divided. The largest local banks, such as NordLB in lower Saxony, had already set up an office for securities trading in Frankfurt. The prospect of opening, alongside the main market in Frankfurt, a parallel market for smaller firms wanting to go public was more likely to fulfill their needs for investment banking than the beefing up of existing regional stock exchanges. Eventually, in 1992, the Frankfurt Coalition overcame the status quo, but at the price of a compromise that recognized some of the claims of the peripheral coalition. Part of the deal was the creation of the Neuer Markt, a parallel, less strictly regulated market for smaller stock issues – the large cooperative and public-sector savings banks' turf.[5]

A similar, though much less known, conflict between local and central authorities occurred in Italy – another de facto decentralized country. The large commercial banks and the Stock Exchange Council favored the creation of a national over-the-counter market. They were opposed by the Chambers of Commerce and a number of regional trade associations, which preferred the promotion of local securities markets. Law 1/1991, on the financing of medium-sized firms, took a compromise position, providing both for the creation of local securities markets and the creation of a national over-the-counter market.[6]

Canada is another country in which securities regulatory power is lodged with each provincial government. The Canadian debate proceeded along the center–periphery cleavage, pitting against each other the provincial governments of Ontario and Québec. The lineup, however, was paradoxical, reflecting the near-balance between the two rival financial centers. Toronto – the political center – was opposed to deregulation, whereas Montreal – the political periphery – championed it. The large banks of both provinces rooted for the Québec government against the Ontario government. They won eventually – the Ontario securities firms were bought out by the banks.[7]

Unlike in Germany and Canada, securities in the United States are regulated at both the state and the federal level, with federal regulation taking the lead. Hence, the main point of contention between the states and Washington was not the opening up of securities brokerage, as it was in the other decentralized countries. At issue, instead, was the repeal of the Glass–Steagall Act, legislation prohibiting deposit banks from underwriting securities. The debate pitted banks against the securities

---

[5] The fear that the Neuer Markt would be run from London caused opposition by the cooperative banks to the proposed merger between the London and Frankfurt stock exchanges; see *International Herald Tribune* May 20–21, 2000.

[6] See Mondello 1994, 198.   [7] See Harris 1996.

industry (brokers and underwriters). While banks wanted a piece of the growing securities business, brokers wanted to be sure that they would be granted full rights to buy into the commercial banking industry, just as banks were being promised unrestricted access to Wall Street.[8] Although large banks were willing to accede to that request, small banks were opposed to it. They feared an increase in banking concentration, for brokerage firms, unlike banks, could maintain nationwide branch systems.[9] Moreover, being too small to provide investment banking services, community banks did not want their larger rivals to provide them either, as this would place the former at a competitive disadvantage. They finally feared that the dismantling of the barrier between deposits and securities would bring down the barrier between banking and insurance in its wake.

From the 1980s on, the three financial regulators (the Federal Reserve Board, the Comptroller of the Currency, and the Federal Deposit Insurance Corporation) consistently supported the New York and California banks' demand for repeal, against the opposition of the smaller rural banks and their representatives.[10] Although the latter successfully blocked all legislative initiatives in Congress, where they had the power to do so, they were unable to prevent the erosion of the Glass–Steagall prohibition through the regulators and the courts. The Federal Reserve Board interpreted Glass–Steagall as permitting banks to underwrite corporate securities on a limited basis through affiliates. The legalization of interstate banking in 1994 also removed an important reason for local banks to resist the repeal of the Glass–Steagall Act. The act was eventually repealed in November 1999, along with key portions of banking law that had prevented banks from underwriting insurance. Interestingly, the repeal legislation was held up for more than a year by the "community compromise," which was forced upon the legislators by the Community Reinvestment Act, obligating banks in poor neighborhoods to redline a certain amount of deposits for loans to local borrowers.[11]

In sum, the so-called Big Bangs, which blasted open the gates of the securities markets to all financial institutions, had implications beyond the financial center. In countries where the center–periphery cleavage intersected with the banker–broker cleavage, the "Bangs" were muffled. To reach working compromises with their local rivals, the stock exchanges of Frankfurt and Milan had to accept limitations that hindered them in their competition with international rivals. It took US money center banks about thirty more years than French, Belgian, and English banks

---

[8] *American Banker* March 3, 1995, 3.   [9] See *American Banker* February 15, 1995, 7.
[10] See Reinicke 1995, pp. 57–123.   [11] See *Time* November 8, 1999.

to be allowed to underwrite securities, because community banks feared the resulting concentration. There is no doubt that the local resistance reflected the existence of vested institutional interests – the local regulators' fear of losing authority, the local stock exchanges' fear of losing business to the center, the local banks' fear of being displaced by the competition of center bank branches. It also reflected the fact that securitization has negative implications for small business. I develop this point in the next section.

The redistributional implications of disintermediation

Securitization and its corollary, disintermediation, have negative implications for market efficiency. Disintermediation eliminates two comparative advantages that banks have over markets. First, banks can overcome information asymmetry better than markets by maintaining long-term relationships with firms. As banks become more dependent on markets, both to secure resources and to dispose of assets, they have an incentive to neglect loans that are firm-specific and illiquid, and that would invariably drag their credit ratings down. Indeed, relational information (the private information that a bank is able to gather on a firm through a long-term relationship with that firm) does not readily transfer to other creditors, thereby making these loans' market value – the only value that Standard & Poor's fully recognizes when rating a bank – systematically inferior to their real value.

The banks' lesser capacity to reduce information asymmetry is not compensated by a greater aptitude of markets to do so. Improvements in information technology may facilitate the dissemination of public information; more information may be available on borrowers for whom there is information to begin with. But new technology does little for the gathering of relational information. There is no one else, besides bankers, to monitor firms. Institutional investors typically hold highly diversified portfolios with small stakes in hundreds of companies for short periods; they are unlikely to assume the role of monitor.[12] Credit-rating institutions such as Moody's and Standard & Poor's are not designed to gather relational information.

The second comparative advantage enjoyed by banks, but threatened by securitization, is the capacity to insure a firm against cyclical financial vicissitudes. As Rajan and Zingales (1999, p. 9) put it, long-term bank–firm relationships are "a form of insurance; a firm in trouble gets credit at

---

[12] Porter 1992, 69. There are exceptions, involving US public-employee funds; see Philip Davis 1995, p. 192.

a below-competitive rate in return for which it pays the premium by giv-
ing more of its business to the relationship bank in good times." Markets,
in contrast, not only put strains on the social relationships that form the
primary source of insurance, but markets' exclusive reliance on complete
forms of contracting – of little use in a situation of uncertainty characterized by few precedents and little prior knowledge from which to estimate
risk – disqualifies them from providing new forms of insurance. "In good
times," Rajan and Zingales continue, "the greater allocative efficiency of
the market papers over the lack of insurance ... But in major downturns,
the political pressure from the large masses of losers becomes hard to
resist" (p. 10). The rise in market competition between banks means that
banks have an interest in eliminating past cross-subsidization between
large and small loans, leaving firms with no hope of finding a functional
substitute in financial markets. In fact, it has been argued that competition
from the money market is leading banks to practice cross-subsidization
in reverse, lending to large clients at the interbank rate while lending to
smaller clients at a much higher rate.[13]

Disintermediation and securitization affect large and small firms differently. Large firms benefit from greater access to capital markets. Being
listed on a stock exchange inflates a company's assets; making the grade
to being a component of a stock index inflates them even more. Irrespective of whether stock prices convey perfect or semi-perfect information
about the real value of a firm, the sentiment that other investors may buy
its stock increases the attraction of that stock in the eyes of an investor.
Like the players of a coordination game, who look for the focal point,
investors plump for the most traded stocks.

Small firms, especially those involved at the present time in sectors
other than communication and information technologies, do not benefit
from expanding capital markets. They are too small to enable market investors to evaluate their earning potential with a modicum of confidence,
but must instead rely on bank loans. Mistrust on the part of the investor
is usually reinforced by the unwillingness on the part of the owner, often
the founder or the founder's heirs, to yield control over the company
or comply with the transparency and disclosure rules following exchange
listing.[14] As a result, small firms are generally less capitalized and more indebted than large firms.[15] Moreover, small and medium-sized companies

[13] Danthine et al. (1999, p. 71) present evidence to that effect in the case of Italy.
[14] This is the "number one" problem identified in a European Commission communication
1997a.
[15] Evidence for the United States, Japan, and eleven European countries can be found
in European Commission (1997b, pp. 26 and 29). Two notable exceptions over the
1986–95 period were Spain and the UK.

have to rely much more heavily on short-term external financing by banks or other sources than larger companies.[16]

Many countries have opened parallel markets in which small and medium-sized domestic companies are listed. The largest parallel markets in absolute terms are found in Germany, France, and Sweden. With the exception of the relatively inconsequential London AIM, such markets are not found in Anglo-Saxon countries. The second board for local stocks not listed nationally in Sydney was established in 1985 but closed in 1992. Parallel markets exhibit a low turnover. Their size remains modest, with a capitalization of the order of 1 to 20 in comparison with main markets.[17] They provide easier access to markets for only a small number of innovative firms, with strong growth potential.[18]

The move toward a single currency on the European continent is expected to tilt the scales in favor of large firms for several years. European institutional investors have traditionally faced restrictions that force them to invest primarily in their domestic market. The Third EU Directive on Life Insurances, for instance, stipulated that insurance companies are required to hold 80 percent of their assets in the currency of denomination of their liabilities, typically the home currency. Pension funds in Denmark, Finland, and Germany also have an 80 percent currency-matching rule. Estimates in 1997–98 for pension-fund money held in foreign equities varied: for Germany, between 2 and 6 percent, for France, between 3 and 4 percent, and for Spain between 1 and 3 percent.[19] Italian data are either not available or believed to be precisely zero. The advent of the single currency will remove the currency restrictions and encourage broad diversification across European stock markets.

The rebalancing of domestic portfolios is likely to occur to the benefit of the larger companies and at the expense of the smaller ones. The big French funds will unload French smaller stocks to buy into large German companies, such as DaimlerChrysler or Siemens. German funds will go into Fiat or Telecom Italia, and so forth. Large companies benefit from their greater visibility and stability. The creation of pan-European stock indices is likely to drive up their prices. In contrast, the demand for smaller company stocks may be undermined. The benchmark for what constitutes a large company might also be revised upward. As an

---

[16] European Commission 1997c, 27.

[17] For statistics on parallel markets, see FIBV *Annual Report*.

[18] For a more positive assessment of the role of parallel markets, especially since the creation of national Nasdaq markets in the last years of the twentieth century, see Posner 2001.

[19] The higher estimates are reported in Danthine et al. 1999, p. 66; the smaller estimates are from Lynn 1999.

investment banker cited by Lynn (1999) declared about the creation of a single European equity market:

It may . . . end up redefining what are large- and small-cap stocks: a blue-chip in the Dutch market may become a midcap in a euro-zone market.[20]

The 2000 proposal to merge the London Stock Exchange and the Deutsche Börse to create "iX" would have further widened the gap between the very large companies and the rest. The merger proposal, which eventually failed to be approved by the members of both exchanges, would have consolidated the market for blue chips in London and that for growth stocks in Frankfurt. The project drew the support of the world-class investment banks because of the trading volumes and increased liquidity that a single market would yield, and the top 300 or so European companies that would make the main market in a reconfigured London. The project drew the expected opposition of smaller players – the Alternative Investment Market's (AIM) proponents in London and the savings and cooperative banks in Germany.[21] The main point of the consolidation was to increase the liquidity pool for blue chips in London and for high-growth tech stocks in Frankfurt. But for the companies which would not have been listed on either market – the overwhelming majority – "the result," in the words of the London-based Centre for the Study of Financial Innovation, "could be a fragmentation of liquidity – and exclusion from increasingly crucial indices."[22]

It is difficult to provide evidence that smaller firms are suffering from securitization. Complicating the picture is the fact that the predicted equilibrium may not have been reached yet. Another equilibrium, equally plausible in the short run, is that large commercial banks may try to make up for the flight of their largest clients to market instruments not by beefing up their investment banking facilities, an option available only to a handful, but by lending more to small and medium-sized enterprises, often against real estate collateral. Although such a strategy eventually leads to illiquidity and downgrading by rating agencies and is thus unsustainable in the long run, it was actively pursued by many banks in Japan, Germany, Scandinavia, France, and Italy with the expected negative consequences.[23]

---

[20] The author goes on to speculate that the winners will be, first, the countries that seem to be good at producing huge companies – France, Germany, and the Netherlands – at the expense of Portugal, Ireland, or Finland, and, second, big companies in general at the expense of smaller stocks.

[21] *International Herald Tribune* May 20–21, 2000.

[22] *The Banker* September 2000, 10.   [23] See chapter 7.

In sum, there are grounds to believe that disintermediation and the securitization of both short- and long-term debt have negative consequences for small and medium-sized firms. The available evidence is not decisive, but the presumption of mischief is strong enough for governments that owe their political survival to the support of local firms and community banks to buck the trend. Therefore, securitization is unlikely to revolutionize extant banking structures. Although securities are assuming a greater importance in relation to bank loans in all countries, this trend is probably unfolding at a lower speed in decentralized countries. Centralized countries are likely to move there faster, on account, first, of the relatively small size of the local banking sectors and, second, of the relatively weak power of local regulators. Today, as in 1913, stock market size should reflect state centralization.

This simple thesis is likely to suffer one exception, however. Since the 1930s, state centralization also enables governments to intervene in the economy, a policy that hurts stock markets.

State control of industry

Stock exchanges need stocks to trade. The wider the range of stocks they can offer, the more possibilities for diversification they make available to potential investors. Moreover, each stock must occur in a sufficiently large quantity, guaranteeing a constant trading volume. Last, in order to insure liquidity, the stock must be visible, able to focus investors' action. Indeed, market liquidity is comparable to a coordination game, in which a player trades a stock only if she thinks that others will trade that same stock.[24] The existence of a focal point helps solve coordination problems to every participant's benefit. Famous stocks, such as Microsoft, Dell Computer, Cisco, and GE Financial have the wherewithal to attract transactions. Their price includes a liquidity premium. They are the workhorses of the exchange in which they are listed, providing brokers with their daily bread. Five percent of the stocks listed on the NYSE represented 51 percent of trading value in 1998, 60 percent in London, and 86 percent in Frankfurt.[25] Stocks that are unknown and with little prospect of becoming known are unlikely to be listed. The companies that tend to get listed are either very large, present in growth sectors, or both.

In many European countries many of the companies that would fit that profile are owned by the state. Until twenty years ago, nine of ten

---

[24] The problem is aptly defined by Rajan and Zingales as "a chicken and egg problem ... people will not trade in a particular market unless they think the market is liquid, but the market will not be liquid unless they trade" (1999, p. 17).

[25] FIBV *Annual Report* 1998, 88.

of the largest companies in European countries were in that situation. Sectors such as railways, telecommunications, postal service, coal, gas, petroleum, electricity, air transport, shipbuilding, and banking were in many cases part of the public sector.[26] State ownership denied stock markets an adequate capital base.

There was no hard and crisp logic behind the creation of public sectors. Most nationalizations in most countries were unplanned, but occurred because the government sought to salvage an unprofitable private firm from bankruptcy. The firm may have been involved in a sector deemed strategic for security reasons, or it may have been a large firm, employing a numerous and politically sensitive workforce – or both, as with railways.[27] Once public, many of these firms stayed public, not out of post facto rationalization, but because the state could not dispose of their assets – capital markets were too narrow.

The incorporation of a public company is a necessary but not suffi-cient condition for stock market growth. The state also has to abandon control, both direct in the form of majoritarian – and sometimes even minoritarian – participation, and indirect, through the appointment of a core-controlling group (the French *noyau dur*) of companies linked toge-ther through mutual cross-shareholdings. Although cross-shareholdings artificially boost the capitalization of the stock market – the same shares are counted twice – they also curb trading by the core shareholders, who cannot sell for a determinate period. Investors are also unlikely to find the stock attractive, as the management team of the company is shielded from external takeover bids. Unlikely to fail, a state-controlled firm is equally unlikely to maximize shareholder value. In the end, state control is a cause for thin trading.

A cause of state control is centralization. Centralization provides the central government with the capacity to increase its power over the econ-omy. Since a major industrial rescue threatens local governments with a roundabout way of tilting the constitutional balance between the federal state and its constituent parts, state control is an unlikely occurrence in decentralized countries, where local governments possess extensive pow-ers of veto.[28] Therefore, today's capacity for exchanges to list attractive

---

[26] The steel sector in Austria, Belgium, Britain, France, and Italy was state-owned. In the automobile industry, Renault, VW, SEAT, Alfa Romeo, Jaguar, British Leyland, Rover, and Rolls-Royce ended up being state-owned at one point.

[27] IRI, the Italian state holding company, was initially created in the 1930s to take over the industrial holdings of the three virtually bankrupted main Italian banks; see Posner and Woolf 1967. IRI ended up producing, among various things, Christmas *panettone* and 25 percent of Italian *gelato*.

[28] Note that a similar logic has been used to account for the dearth of privatization programs in decentralized countries; see Heald 1989, p. 46. The claim is that, in decentralized

stocks is a negative function of state control, in turn a positive function of state centralization.

To recapitulate the last two sections, state centralization has a mixed, and thus indeterminate, effect on stock market growth. On the one hand, state centralization positively affects stock markets, for it denies local governments the capacity to stem the flight of financial capital to the center. On the other hand, state centralization negatively affects stock markets, for it enables politicians to maintain some form of state control over large industrial concerns.

Evidence from twenty OECD countries

I now try to assess the validity of the argument. I embed it in a broader system, including alternative hypotheses and plausible control variables. Consider the flow chart drawn in figure 9.4. At the core is the diamond-shape argument of figure 9.1 – a system of variables with effects working in opposite directions suppressing each other.[29] A correlate of the model is the absence of any direct relationship between state centralization and stock market (represented by a 0 coefficient).

To this, I added the common law argument.[30] Financial markets, according to this argument, need a legal system that is flexible enough to adapt property rights to financial innovation. Yet flexibility opens the gate to political discretion. Common law solves the dilemma by interposing the judge between the state and the market, reassuring private actors that the rules of the game are modified according to a logic that escapes politics and clientelism. In contrast, the civil law system relegates the judge to a subaltern position, leaving property rights to hinge a lot more on who governs. In the worst case, the system is corrupt. In the best of cases, formal rights are rigid and a poor match for market reality. Two versions of the common law argument exist, differing with respect to the causal path: (1) Rajan and Zingales' argument that common law *indirectly* bolsters stock markets through the mediation of state control (two negative arrows, the first running from common law to state control, the second, from state control to stock market); (2) La Porta et al.'s argument that

---

countries, privatization threatens to rob local governments of an important power base, if not a source of revenues. Although this argument does suggest that decentralized countries are less likely to evince large privatization programs, which is true, it fails to take into account the fact that decentralized countries do not have large public sectors to begin with.

[29] This type of system is usually referred to as a "suppressor" or "inconsistent" system; see James Davis 1985, p. 57.

[30] See La Porta et al. 1997a and 1998, and Rajan and Zingales 1999.

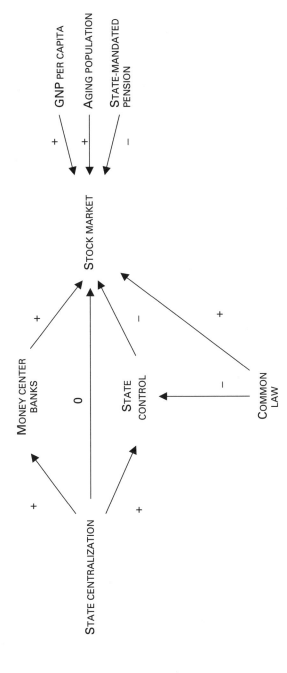

Figure 9.4. Complete model

common law *directly* strengthens stock market (a positive arrow directly connecting common law and stock market).[31]

Given the supply-side bias of all these variables, I included three variables to control for the demand side: greater wealth (GNP per capita) and a larger old-age population dependent on pension investment funds should raise the demand for stocks. In contrast, the presence of a well-developed, pay-as-you-go, state-mandated pension system should reduce the demand for pension funds.

I now describe the variables. The dependent variable is the market value (i.e., capitalization) of the exchanges weighted by GDP. Calculated by the International Federation of Stock Exchanges, the measure offers the advantage of aggregating various national stock exchanges, to include only shares of domestic companies, and to exclude investment funds and companies whose only business goal is to hold shares of other listed companies. The measure has the drawback of double-counting cross-shareholdings, which are known to be higher in Japan, Germany, and France than in Britain or the United States. Note, however, that cross-shareholdings have an offsetting dampening impact on market activity, thereby making the net impact on capitalization indeterminate.[32]

State centralization is measured by the proportion of government revenues drained by the central government. The degree of concentration of the banking system is measured by the proportion of assets controlled by money center banks. Legal origins is a dummy variable coded "1" for common law countries and "0" for others.

State control is a difficult variable to measure. I used an indicator constructed by Nicoletti et al. (1999, p. 74) and described as capturing "public ownership" (in turn taking into account the "size" and "scope" of the public sector, "control of public enterprises by legislative bodies," and "special voting rights") and "(state) involvement in business operation" (in turn including "price controls" and "use of command and control regulations"). The indicator ranges from 0.55 for the United Kingdom to 3.92 for Italy.

---

[31] In my review of the literature (Verdier 2002), I identified two other arguments: (1) Levy's argument that state control (*dirigisme*) harms stock market, and (2) Weingast's and Root's argument that centralization *indirectly* harms market growth. These two arguments are encompassed by the diamond-shaped model: Levy's can be represented by the negative arrow running from state control to stock market, while Weingast's and Root's can be represented by the positive arrow running from state centralization to state control (absolutism) and the negative one running from state control to stock market.

[32] An alternative measure of stock market size would be to use turnover. This measure raises problems of comparability, as stock exchanges treat offmarket transactions differently to compile turnover statistics. Turnover statistics are also subject to demand shocks – some related to the business cycle, others to changes in the fiscal treatment of capital gains – difficult to root out without multiyear averages.

I include three control variables – GNP per capita to control for cross-sectional variations in demand for stocks related to wealth; the relative size of the population sixty-five years of age and above to control for the demand for pension funds; the relative importance of state-mandated pension plans to control for the same fact. All the data are supplied in appendix 5.

I run several OLS regressions, each reflecting a causal articulation of the argument as sketched in figure 9.4. The use of ordinary (as opposed to two-stage) least squares is justified by the absence of any pairwise correlation among regression residuals.[33] The population is a cross-national panel of twenty OECD countries for the year 1991, the largest number and latest year for which I have the required data. The number of observations is still too small to satisfy the limit theorem condition. It also makes the results vulnerable to outlying observations. I compensate for these weaknesses by resorting to the graphic representation of bivariate relations as much as possible, and to that of partial relations to spot outliers.

Regression results are listed in table 9.1. The first regression shows the close association between centralized state institutions and a large money center banking sector. The bivariate relationship (shown in figure 9.5) points to Switzerland as potential outlier. Switzerland is a country where the large amount of international business handled by the center banks artificially boosts the relative importance of that sector. Note the size of the coefficient (0.58), which suggests that a one-standard-deviation change in state centralization (about 17 percentage points) raises center banking by 10 percentage points (about 56 percent of a standard deviation). The coefficient reaches 0.80 in the absence of the Swiss observation (results unreported).

The second regression registers the positive impact of state centralization on state control, while controlling for legal origins. The bivariate relation between state centralization and state control helps visualize the regression (figure 9.6). The relationship is both positive and heteroscedastic: centralization is a necessary but insufficient condition for state control – also required is a legal system other than common law. Indeed, all the common law countries – and only they – line up along the x-axis, suggesting that common law has a strong negative impact on state control. The coefficients of the state centralization and common law variables in regression 2 point to a normalized impact of 42 percent and negative 65 percent respectively.

---

[33] Also, Breusch–Pagan tests of independence on all specifications show a chi^2 close to zero, with a probability close to 1.

Table 9.1. *Cross-sectional OLS estimates of the model, 1991*

	Money center banks	State control	Stock market capitalization		
	1	2	3	4	5
Independent variables:					
State centralization	0.58	2.22	0.33	0.21	0.25
	(0.20)***	(0.78)**	(0.31)	(0.36)	(0.36)
Common law		−1.34	−0.05	−0.01	−0.002
		(0.31)***	(0.12)	(0.13)	(0.04)
Intervening variables:					
Money center banks			0.61	0.69	0.63
			(0.23)**	(0.26)**	(0.29)**
State control			−0.24	−0.23	−0.22
			(0.06)***	(0.06)***	(0.07)***
Control variables:					
GNP per capita			22×10^{-6}	20×10^{-6}	20×10^{-6}
			(8×10^{-6})**	(8×10^{-6})**	(8×10^{-6})**
Aging population				2.08	2.26
				(2.83)	(2.94)
State-mandated pension					−0.01
					(0.03)
Intercept	0.26	0.87	−0.17	−0.41	−0.38
	(0.15)	(0.61)	(0.36)	(0.49)	(0.51)
Adj. R squared	0.28	0.59	0.70	0.69	0.68
Correlation between regression residuals		2/1: 0.023	3/1: 0.00 3/2: 0.00	4/1: 0.00 4/2: 0.00	5/1: 0.00 5/2: 0.00

Notes: $N = 20$. Values of standard errors are given in parentheses; *, **, *** indicate coefficients situated in the 90%, 95%, and 99% confidence intervals respectively. Data are for 1991; they are described in appendix 5.

The last three regressions bring together the two opposite effects of state centralization – the positive effect of banking centralization and the negative effect of state control – while varying controls. Regression 3 controls for GNP per capita alone, regression 4 for GNP per capita and the size of the senior population, and regression 5 for all the above plus the relative size of the state-mandated pension system. The coefficients for the three control variables have the expected signs, but only that of

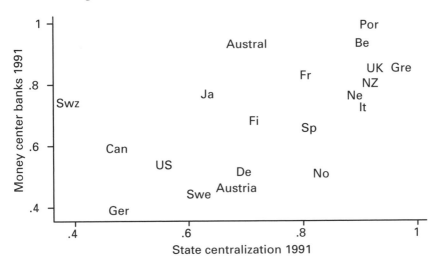

Figure 9.5. Center banks and state centralization: bivariate 1991

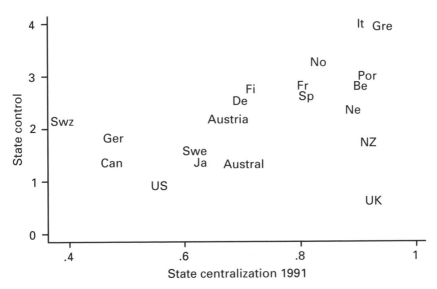

Figure 9.6. State control and state centralization: bivariate 1991

wealth can be said to be significantly different from zero with 95 percent confidence.

The coefficients for the intervening variables (money center banks and state control), positive and negative respectively, are significant at the 95 percent confidence level across specifications. The presence of both the independent and intervening variables in regressions 3 to 5 allows us to assess the relative importance of the direct and indirect effects of the independent variables. First, consider state centralization. Significantly different from zero in regressions 1 and 2, it is not any more in regressions 3 to 5. Such results confirm our belief that state centralization operated indirectly and inconsistently through more than one path; they provide an indirect confirmation of the diamond-shaped, suppressor system.

Then, consider the common law dummy. Its coefficient is negative in regression 2 but not significantly different from zero in regressions 3 to 5. This result tends to support the idea that common law operates on stock markets through the mediation of state control (Rajan and Zingales' hypothesis) rather than directly (La Porta et al.'s hypothesis).

I try to detect outliers by plotting the partial relations. I use a cleaned-up version of regression 3 (rid of the two statistically insignificant independent variables). The three plots of figure 9.7 show no major outliers, only five countries for which the model is still insufficiently specified (Japan, the UK, and Greece, whose stock values are consistently located above the three regression lines, and Finland and Australia, consistently below). The business cycle may have been responsible for the overvaluation of the Japanese stock market in 1991 and its undervaluation in Australia.

A visual analysis of the plots suggests a few revealing two-by-two comparisons. Consider the United States and the UK. The United States – the largest absolute stock capitalization in the world – owes its large market, holding banking centralization and wealth constant, to its low level of state control (top right-hand graph of figure 9.7), in turn a reflection of both its decentralized polity and its common law tradition (it is overdetermined, as suggested in figure 9.6). But the rather decentralized structure of US banking, which reflects federalism (figure 9.5), holding state control and wealth constant, has a negative impact on the stock market (United States y-axis value in top left-hand graph of figure 9.7 is below the mean). Like the United States, the UK has common law and a low level of state control (figure 9.6), but, unlike the United States, it has a centralized banking system, which it owes to its centralized polity (figure 9.5). Holding wealth constant, bank centralization in Britain is sufficient to hoist British market capitalization more than two standard deviations above the mean (top left-hand graph in figure 9.7).

Consider now Germany and the United States. The two countries share a decentralized polity, causing the banking system to be decentralized (figure 9.5) and keeping state control to a minimum (though slightly higher in Germany than in the United States in light of the different legal tradition [figure 9.6]). Holding wealth and state control constant, both

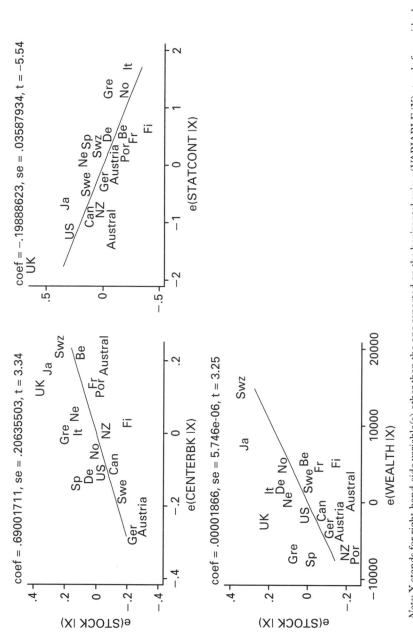

Note: X stands for right-hand-side variable(s) other than the one reported on the horizontal axis; e(VARIABLE |X) stands for residuals of VARIABLE regressed against X. It is a property of partial regression plots that the coefficients, standard errors, and *t* statistics for each plotted independent variable should be the same as in the corresponding regression.

Figure 9.7. State control, banks, and law: partials

countries score below average stock market values on account of bank decentralization (top left-hand graph in figure 9.7). Last let us contrast Belgium and the UK. The two countries have a centralized banking system, but differ on state control (high in Belgium because of both state centralization and civil law). Although Belgium's stock score is almost as high as the UK's on account of its banking system (top left-hand graph in figure 9.7), the Belgian stock score on account of state control is quite low, holding wealth constant (top right-hand graph in figure 9.7).

Conclusion

This chapter examined the current relation between state and financial markets. It argued that state centralization has two inconsistent effects on stock market size. On the one hand, state centralization facilitates the emergence of dominant money center banks, fueling the development of the capital market, whereas state decentralization allows blocking coalitions of small banks, small firms, and local governments, with an interest in keeping finance local, to maintain the existing privileges of local banks and to restrain the geographic centralization of finance. On the other hand, state centralization enables the government to extend its control over large firms, tolerate a lower return on capital, and make the shares of these firms unattractive to investors. The government of a decentralized state, in contrast, is unlikely to extend control over large firms in the first place.

The analysis also shows that state control of markets is lessened in the presence of common law. It is impossible, however, to say whether the legal origin variable is the cause of market development or merely a symptom of a broader syndrome with deep roots in culture, history, and geography.

10   Choosing the right product mix

> In investment banking, you either mount an offensive to take over the world or you cash in your chips and stick to commercial banking.
>
> Jules Stewart, *The Banker* April 2001, 104.

Banks are in the course of redefining their product mix. Concentration allows banks to serve bigger accounts; internationalization opens up possibilities in currency trading and export finance; securitization calls for underwriting, brokerage, and the provision of mutual funds (asset management); and the removal of barriers between bank and insurance invites the development of bancassurance or Allfinanz. The availability of new options does not imply that all banks will pursue them all; it is not clear whether the trend is toward a broader or narrower product mix. Nor is it clear yet what universalism and specialization refer to in today's banking practice.

I survey the initial rush to diversify that greeted deregulation and then the more recent, gradual, and uneven movement toward a new form of specialization. I point to the logic that, I believe, is causing this realignment. I identify an emerging dichotomy between the two historical prototypes – Britain and Germany. I also examine two developments – bancassurance and banking via the internet – and their potential impact on the product mix. I argue that universal banking is destined neither to prevail over nor to lose to specialized banking, but that the two models, instead, are likely to be distributed across countries according to a rule that should be now familiar to the reader: centralization favors specialization, decentralization favors universal banking.

In the absence of historical distance, any argument about the present, let alone the future, is bound to be tentative. It took fifty years, from 1850 until 1900, for prewar observers to discern an equilibrium different from the English model.[1] Still, we are not left to engage in mere mental

---

[1] The first academic defense of universal banking as a plausible alternative to English-like specialization dates back to Riesser (1977, p. 547) in response to the critics of German banking, notably to Adolph Wagner, who argued in favor of the English system.

speculation. Drawing from our knowledge of the prewar financial system, which, very much like the present one, was subject to concentration, internationalization, and securitization (though not bancassurance), it is possible to steer one's way through the maze of ambiguous information that characterizes today's financial writings.

The initial trend toward diversification

The initial effect of deregulation was to release a repressed desire for diversification. For thirty years, banks were forced to respect a form of specialization inherited from the 1930s consensus that mixing long- and short-term banking activities had caused or worsened the banking crisis. Specialization became a sort of dogma, embraced by all national regulators, though with due allowances made for historical differences. The main activity of the commercial banks was, along with other giro systems, to insure payments, open deposit and checking accounts for individuals, lend short to corporate business, and handle international banking. State credit banks were set up to lend long to commerce and industry. Underwriting, in the few countries where it persisted, was the realm of investment banks or, in the case of Germanic countries, the largest commercial banks. The savings banks were given pride of place in domestic personal and consumer banking, including savings and housing loans – with the exception of Anglo-Saxon countries, where mortgages were sold by separate institutions known as building societies. In countries with large savings bank sectors, such as Germany, Austria, and the Scandinavian countries, saving banks were local specialists, communicating with each other through the mediation of regional banks, and with the rest of the financial system through a central giro bank. Cooperatives, wherever they existed, and locally chartered banks in the United States concentrated on the lower rungs of corporate lending. The wealthiest individuals banked with private bankers. Insurance and brokerage were activities considered separate from banking. New forms of lending, such as leasing and factoring, were not developed by banks but by separate financial companies.

Based on what was considered appropriate in the 1930s, the decreed specialization soon became artificial. Commercial banks lost part of their corporate clientele to financial companies and international issuers because of restrictions on lending imposed by central banks. Commercial banks also lost part of their individual deposit base to savings banks or financial companies because they were not allowed to open new branches. Conversely, investment banks, savings banks, and financial companies were targeting new clienteles with their products. The deregulation of finance, which began as a trickle in the 1960s and turned into a deluge in the 1980s, opened a period of all-out competition between financial institutions. Commercial banks tried to recover lost ground, while their competitors sought to consolidate their new acquisitions. Everyone also sought to develop the new market-oriented instruments.

In a first relaxation of the rule, commercial banks moved into investment banking in non-Germanic countries. Starting in the 1960s in Belgium and France, and followed in Britain in the 1970s, banks began to offer medium-term loans to companies. In France, Paribas and Suez, the two largest investment banks, responded by buying up non-nationalized and regional deposit banks.[2] The nationalized banks developed their own investment arm and eventually overtook the investment banks; the Crédit Agricole acquired Suez while Paribas went to BNP. In Britain, the clearing banks either acquired existing merchant banks or developed their own investment banking division. In the area of corporate lending, many a large commercial bank, such as the clearing banks in Britain, the nationalized banks in France, Deutsche Bank in Germany, and the city banks in Japan, launched special lending programs designed to attract small business financing, in competition with local and specialized state credit banks.

Simultaneously, commercial banks moved into personal and consumer banking. They extended their branch networks outside financial centers and competed with savings and specialized banks for deposits and housing loans, notably in Belgium, Australia, and the Nordic countries. In the wake of the Big Bangs, commercial banks reinforced their personal banking divisions by offering depositors securities brokerage facilities and mutual funds. In Canada, for instance, the banks absorbed all the mutual funds. With the breakdown of walls between banking and insurance in Europe, banks such as Barclays, Deutsche Bank, the Dutch ABN Amro, the Swedish SEB, and the Swiss UBS and Crédit Suisse started offering their own insurance policies to their clientele, while other banks allied with insurers whose products they distributed.

In most countries, savings banks (and building societies in most Anglo-Saxon countries) responded to the prospect of deregulation, along with the competition from commercial banks, by moving into corporate business, including not just lending, but also underwriting, leasing, factoring, and so forth. The largest savings banks, their girozentrale especially, became regular players in wholesale markets. During the debt crisis, top ratings allowed these banks to be money-market intermediaries. More importantly, traditional discipline broke down within savings

---

[2] Suez took over Crédit Industriel et Commercial and Indochine, whereas Paribas bought Banque de l'Union Parisienne and Crédit du Nord.

sectors. In Austria, Norway, Denmark, the Netherlands, Italy, and Spain, savings banks began to transgress territorial boundaries, invading each other's physical area by opening branches or through outright mergers. The vertical division of tasks that existed in Germany, Austria, and the Scandinavian countries, according to which the savings banks' girozentrale handled the investment and international business of the savings banks, splintered under the pressure of the largest savings banks, eager to develop their own corporate business and to open branches in London, New York, and other financial centers. In Denmark, the savings bank girozentrale was sold by the savings banks in 1988, complete with branch network, to an insurance company. In Sweden and Norway, the savings girozentrale merged with a subset of savings banks, putting an end to its role as supplier of services to all savings banks. In all Nordic countries, the smaller savings banks lost their external agent and had to choose partners and channel business through larger savings banks. In Austria, the savings girozentrale simply became an investment bank.

Many large savings banks have become commercial banks. All the British savings banks merged to form the Trustee Savings Bank (TSB), later purchased by Lloyds. The largest building societies in Britain and Australia became commercial banks. Furthermore, many large savings banks merged with commercial banks. In Belgium, for instance, after a century and a half of separation, Generale Bank, the heir of the prewar Société Générale, was reunited with its past savings bank, the large, state-owned Belgian savings bank, ASLK–CGER, under the aegis of the Fortis Group. BACOB, a private savings bank, took over Paribas-Belgium, an investment bank (to form Artesia). In Austria, the largest savings bank, "Z," took over the two largest commercial banks in the country, including the once-famous Creditanstalt. In Italy, the Cassa di Risparmio di Roma took over Banco di Roma (to form Banca di Roma). Cariplo, the largest savings bank in the country, formed Banca Intesa, a group including a commercial bank (Banca Commerciale).

Although cooperative banks have not participated in the movement toward diversification as actively as savings banks have, there is one fore-runner in Rabobank, the merger of all cooperative banks in Belgium. Rabobank merged with Robeco, a fund manager, and Interpolis, an insurer, to create a broad personal banking group. Across the French border, the Crédit Agricole, which the state turned into a cooperative in 1988, took over an investment bank – Indosuez.

The diversification that accompanied deregulation opened the prospect of cross-national convergence on the universal banking model. As commercial, investment, savings, and mutual banks and brokerage and insurance companies were to become similar within each financial system, many an observer predicted that financial systems would become similar across countries. The universal banking model was championed by the adversaries of the Glass–Steagall Act in the United States.[3] The Second Banking Directive of 1988, enacted at the beginning of 1993, allowed all European Community credit institutions the right to supply deposit taking, wholesale and retail lending, leasing, stock and bond dealing, fee-based advisory services, portfolio management, custody, and payments. It was perceived by most as a clear victory for the universal banking principle.[4]

Yet, the wide-ranging diversification that attended deregulation is not necessarily tantamount to universal banking. The functional specialization imposed in the 1930s no longer matched the postwar market reality. Deregulation made possible, after forty years of regulatory freeze, a re-assignment of tasks on the basis of market competition. Whether market competition will lead firms to narrow their product range or, instead, widen it to the point of becoming financial "supermarkets" is not something that can easily be predicted at this point. Only through a sustained process of experimentation, interaction, and trial and error will banks identify where their respective comparative advantages lie. Though it is too early to discern the final equilibrium of present market competition, several tendencies are nonetheless visible. They are the subject of the following section.

A new specialization: retail versus investment

All-out diversification is not a sustainable equilibrium in the long run. There are no sufficiently compelling economies of scope to justify that banks supply all products to all customers. Eventually, banks have to specialize, either along functional lines, as in so-called specialized banking systems, or along customer or geographical lines, as in universal banking systems. In this section, I point to an emerging functional specialization, keeping the issue of geographic specialization for the next section.

Poor performance is leading banks to consolidate their product mix – to develop their "core competence" in current corporate parlance. The immediate consequence of diversification was asset growth. Banks increased the size of their balance sheets. This emphasis on growth led banks to increase their debt and the corresponding fraction of capital mandated by the Basle Accord. The higher cost of that debt, allied with shrinking profit margins in lending and the securitization of the most

---

[3] See, among others, Calomiris 1995, Saunders and Walter 1994, Kroszner and Rajan 1994, and Benston 1990.
[4] See, for instance, Underhill 1997a, p. 110.

liquid, low-risk instruments, enticed banks to find high-yielding, high-risk assets to offset the rise in funding costs. The surge in risky assets caused some of the problems banks faced in the late 1980s and early 1990s. Commercial banks and savings and loans in the United States and banks in Japan and Scandinavia found themselves overextended in a sinking real estate market.[5] The Crédit Lyonnais was another victim of careless expansion abroad and purposeless acquisition of blocks of shares in non-financial companies.[6] Crises taught commercial banks to limit the extent of their commitment to real estate and pare down their holdings of shares in industry.

A second valley of sorrows was lending to small business. Large commercial banks tried to make up for the flight of their largest clients to market instruments by lending more to small and medium-sized enterprises (often against real estate collateral). This strategy was actively pursued by many banks in Japan, Germany, France, and Italy with the expected negative consequences.[7] Center banks learnt at their own expense the risks of lending to small and medium-sized companies without access to local intelligence and prolonged monitoring.

If losses are an obvious reason for afflicted banks to rid their balance sheets of losing assets and adopt a more circumspect attitude toward any further expansion, losses remain exceptional. They either affect too few banks to induce methodical learning among all banks or are too concentrated in time to prevent regulators from interfering with market competition. A less conspicuous, yet more pervasive, source of market adaptation – Adam Smith's "invisible hand" – is profitability. Always important, profitability is decisive when banks rely heavily on efficient money markets to fund their investments, for profitability determines the price banks pay for funding. Profitability, indeed, determines the speed at which a bank can increase its capital over time, first, to meet the Basle capital adequacy ratios and, second, to improve its credit rating. The credit rating determines how much and at what cost a bank can borrow. To the extent that a continuous stream of dividends also helps sustain the value of bank shares, profitability further contributes to capital growth, and thus lending capacity.

Banks' twofold dependence on money markets and credit ratings today plays a role similar to the nineteenth-century fear of a depositors' run on the bank, which forced banks to stay liquid. In those days, the liquidity guarantor, in countries where there was any, was pledged to maintain

---

[5] On US banks, see Boyd and Gertler 1993. On Scandinavian banks, see Drees and Pazarbasioglu 1995, p. 18. On Japanese banks, see Fries 1993, p. 9.

[6] On the Crédit Lyonnais, see Story and Walter 1997, pp. 198–210.

[7] See chapter 7.

the stability of the financial system as a whole, but not of any individual bank or firm. The fear to be the first one to go instilled a sense of discipline among bankers. The threat of a depositors' run on individual banks vanished with the introduction in the 1930s of depositor insurance in the United States and an implicit state guarantee of individual deposits in all other countries. It survives in a minor form in the realm of wholesale deposits, which do not benefit from any state guarantee.[8] Bank runs, however, are blind, cyclical, and unlikely to produce an effect except over several decades and numerous bank failures. In contrast, by deciding where a bank's competitive advantage lies, credit ratings offer a stronger incentive for banks to manage assets and liabilities so as to maximize profitability.

Credit ratings have two effects on a bank's business. First, a rating determines at what cost the bank can refinance itself on the money market. A top-rated bank can borrow on the Euromarket at base rate and then re-lend the proceeds to subrated borrowers at a premium. At a time when individual savings are lured away by the mutual fund industry, banks that do not have access to the capital markets are condemned to stagnate. Second, ratings have an effect on off-balance sheet activities. Off-balance sheet activities do not involve the purchase or sale of an asset or liability (at least not immediately), but are services that a bank performs for a fee or commission. They include all advisory services and, most importantly, the extension of letters of credit or any form of guarantee to customers. Through a letter of credit a bank pledges to substitute itself for the debtor in case of default on the latter's part, thereby enhancing the credit of the debtor and the marketability of the debt itself. Letters of credit are notably used to transform loans and mortgages into securities (securitization), an activity of growing importance in times of disintermediation. They also provide the backbone of foreign trade finance.[9] A bank's letter of credit, however, is only as good as its credit rating. Banks with only "fair" or "poor" ratings are excluded from this lucrative market. Today, as in the past, the best paper – the least risky and most sought after by institutional investors – goes to the most creditable banks, leaving the less desirable material to banks with poor ratings.

Certainly, there are expedients to which banks can resort to dress up their balance sheet and improve their credit ratings. For instance, given

---

[8] A textbook case is the run on Continental Illinois in May 1984, the biggest bank failure in the United States, halted by a $14 billion rescue package.

[9] The letter of credit by which a banker turns a low-grade, unmarketable debt into a high-grade, easily marketable bond is similar to the old acceptance business, by which a banker of world repute would put his signature on a bill, thereby making the bill tradable in the London bill market and eligible for rediscounting with the Bank of England.

that credit agencies weigh each single bank asset by risk, they can reweigh risk through the use of costly derivatives. Banks can also dispose of risky assets and write off the loss. Regardless, the only sure way of raising a bank's rating over the long run is by generating profits, and thus refocusing a bank's activity on what it does best.

Profit-maximizing strategies typically fall into two categories: mass production, emphasizing low unit cost, and product differentiation, which is more quality-oriented. Nineteenth-century commercial banking was an illustration of product standardization; investment banking, in contrast, is a specimen of product differentiation. Commercial banking involved the sale of short and low-risk loans – a relatively standard product, addressed to a wide market, open to competition, and generating thin profit margins. Only center banks with countrywide branch networks managed to survive in such a competitive environment, for they alone could handle large volumes, using surplus deposits in one town to discount paper in another, and pooling individual deposits into large sums to be lent on call to brokers or other banks. Investment banking, in contrast, presented characteristics opposite of mass production. Pricing a bond issue – the main activity of investment banking back then – so that the entire issue was subscribed, the borrower's repaying capacity was left undamaged, and the underwriter's travail was more than adequately rewarded was a qualitative, unsystematic business, replete with asymmetrical information and political maneuvering. A good investment banker was a man with many friends in high places and access to privy information, and who relished the trust of a select clientele. In the cases where underwriting failed, the banker absorbed the unsold shares and directly managed the company. Investment bankers were also involved in the supply of countless services, including the management of large estates, membership in shareholder boards, subsidiary help with diplomacy, and, in the case of J. P. Morgan in the United States, central banking responsibilities in times of credit crunch. They had to know everyone who could help them and their clients. They were the concierges of grand capital.[10]

The development of financial markets in our times is pointing to a similar divide among banks between investment and retail banking. Investment banking, today, is characterized by product innovation – swaps, complex derivatives, asset-backed securities, any synthesis thereof, and countless lesser-known financial instruments all come out of the capital

---

[10] Bagehot (1991, p. 131) wrote of London private bankers: "There has probably very rarely ever been so happy a position as that of a London private banker; and never perhaps a happier."

market divisions of a handful of New York investment banks. Once created and tested, these products become adopted by other banks and sometimes standardized, forcing their creators to innovate anew. The freeing of international trade and investment has turned mergers and acquisitions into today's most lucrative activity – an information-sensitive, reputation-based line of business, largely dominated by the so-called bulge bracket: Morgan Stanley Dean Witter, Merrill Lynch, Goldman Sachs, Salomon Smith Barney, and Crédit Suisse First Boston.[11] In such a qualitative, reputation-based, and R&D-intensive line of business, profit is not made on volume, as in commercial banking, but reflects monopolistic pricing – the capacity to extract a rent that accrues to the firm with a headstart in the development of a product popular with customers. Moreover, as in the past, famous investment houses are privileged underwriters for $100-million-and-over international bond issues, highly profitable deals reflecting the scale economies (and logarithmic risk) inherent to issuing.[12] The entrepreneurial nature of investment banking, indeed, its social and political embeddedness, makes it a very different animal from retail banking.

In contrast to investment banking, retail banking is based on the marketing of standard products to millions of individuals and thousands of firms. In addition to checking and savings accounts, today's banks are expected to supply individuals with credit and debit cards, brokerage, mutual funds, insurance policies, housing mortgages, and car loans. To corporate business, they offer payment services, loans, and, on a fee basis, cash management and letters of credit, and perhaps the underwriting of rated commercial paper for their best clients. Retail banking also includes leasing and factoring, by which a firm sells at a discount (or for a fee) its account receivables to a bank.[13]

[11] Competition to be considered as part of the bracket is tough, accounting for the takeovers in 2000 of two boutique investment firms, Wasserstein Perella and Donaldson by Dresdner and Lufkin & Jenrette by Crédit Suisse, and the acquisition of J. P. Morgan by Chase Manhattan.

[12] The main issuers in 1999 were CS First Boston, Deutsche Bank, J. P. Morgan Securities, Morgan Stanley Dean Witter, Goldman Sachs International, BNP Paribas, Lehman Brothers, UBS Warburg, Schroder Salomon Smith Barney, Merrill Lynch International, Chase HSBC Markets, Nomura Securities, and Chase Manhattan International.

[13] The divide between investment and retail banking is not clear cut. Commercial and investment banking have several products in common. Commercial banks, for example, offer foreign exchange services to firms to finance trade, while investment banks provide foreign exchange for investment. Swaps are another example, with commercial banks offering swaps to their customers to hedge interest or currency risk, and investment bankers issuing new assets with swapped interest or currency. For more on this, see *The Banker* January 1987, 26. Another area in common is capital management and private banking, upscale personal banking services that also provide investment banks with the ability to place offerings of shares and bonds.

Though a specialization, retail banking is also subject to further separation. How and why reflects a variety of factors, escaping simple
systematization. No more than it was possible to predict why bill brokers
kept separate from clearing banks in nineteenth-century Britain, whereas
in Paris the two roles were undifferentiated, it is not possible today to
predict the degree of specialization within the retail banking profession.
Specialization among retailers will reflect, besides the size of the market
and the intensity of competition, regulation and technology (how much
of currently unprofitable activities, such as lifeline banking, banks can
outsource). What is certain is that, unless regulators decide otherwise,
the distinction between the for-profit and non-profit sectors is bound to
disappear. Savings banks, cooperative banks, and commercial banks all
do retail banking.

Evidence of a respecialization of banking activities along the invest-
ment-retail banking divide is fragmentary. A first piece of evidence is
the crowding of commercial banks out of the international investment
market. In 1997, two London clearing banks decided to sell the investment banking facilities which, like every other large bank, they had en-
thusiastically promoted in the wake of deregulation. Barclays dismantled
and sold BZW, thereby exiting the equity capital market and mergers-
and-acquisitions advisory businesses. The same year, NatWest followed
with its investment unit, NatWest Markets.[14] The two banks regrouped
their activities around, in the words of NatWest's chief executive, their
"core banking business," that is, retail, corporate, mutual funds, and, for
Barclays, international bond issues through a slimmed-down Barclays
Capital group. Of course, two exits do not make a trend, especially when
so many other banks are entering investment banking. Still, as *The Banker*
judiciously remarked, "the UK capital market is the largest where universal and specialist banks meet in direct competition" – and the most
likely, therefore, to point the way of the future.[15] HSBC is the only universal bank present in the UK retail market through Midland Bank, the
third clearing bank. Lloyds TSB (the merger of the insurer with the old
trustee savings banks) is an essentially UK-focused retail financial group,
that gave up its long-standing and profitable international banking and
corporate banking activities to concentrate on retail banking in the UK;
that is also true of the rest of British banking.[16]

Dutch banks seem to be following the British trajectory. In 2000, ING
Group sold most of its investment banking in the United States to its

---

[14] See *The Banker* April 1998, 22.   [15] *The Banker* January 1987, 23.
[16] The French market, in contrast, is still going through the deregulatory phase, with four
universal groups – BNP Paribas, Crédit Agricole Indosuez, Société Générale, and CDC –
fighting it out.

rival ABN Amro and cut back deeply in Asia and Europe. Six months later, ABN Amro said it wanted to allocate less capital to investment banking and invest more in retail banking.[17] Dutch banks are moving out of investment banking.

The second fragment of evidence that I have to offer to substantiate the claim of a reemergence of a specialization along the investment–retail divide is the crowding of commercial banks out of retail banking in Germany, Austria, Italy, and Spain. Savings and mutual banks, along with postal savings, wherever they are strong players, make it hard for money center banks to maintain a profitable presence in retail banking. This phenomenon is especially advanced in Germany, where two out the three remaining *Großbanken* – Deutsche Bank and Dresdner Bank – made it clear, in March 2000, during negotiations of a merger that eventually failed to materialize, that they sought a way out of retail banking.[18] Hemmed in by an overgrown local non-profit sector and an overbranched banking sector, these two banks have, of late, been unable to make a profit from their retail business. Part of the deal, had it been approved by shareholders, involved selling the two banks' retail networks to Allianz, an insurance company. The two merged banks, in contrast, would have become a specialist bank, with a global investment focus.[19]

Crowding out also occurs when a savings bank takes over a commercial bank. In Austria, the largest savings bank ("Z") successively took over two commercial banks – Landerbank and Creditanstalt – to form Bank Austria. Moves in that direction are surfacing on the Italian scene as well, though much more tentatively. The Rome savings bank took over Banco di Roma, while Cariplo (the large Lombardy-based savings bank) took over Banca Ambrosiano Veneto and Banca Commerciale. In Spain, the commercial banks have been losing market share to the savings banks for the past twenty years. The largest Spanish savings bank is located in Barcelona. There are no large commercial banks in Catalonia. With domestic expansion thus constrained, the Spanish commercial banks have turned their sights toward Latin America.[20] ING, a retail bank made up of an insurance company and a savings bank in the Netherlands, is pushing the sole commercial bank left, ABN Amro, out of the domestic private savings sector.[21]

---

[17] *Wall Street Journal Europe* August 27, 2001.
[18] See *The Banker* April 2000, 28 and May 2000, 14.
[19] Roy Smith and Ingo Walter welcomed the initial announcement of the offer with an op-ed in the *Financial Times* entitled "The Death of Universal Banks" (March 14, 2000). See also *The Economist* December 19, 1998, 130.
[20] See *The Banker* December 1997, 27.   [21] Berendsen 1999, p. 473.

Why bridging investment and retail banking is a bad idea

If a new specialization is separating investment from retail banking, why are banks trying to combine the promotion of shares – a core investment banking activity – with the placement of shares among investors – a retail banking activity that is alternatively subsumed under brokerage, asset management, or private banking?[22] Irrespective of what is being done at present, I argue in this section that the promotion of shares is incompatible with the management of investors' assets.

Many banks are justifying acquiring both an investment capacity and a brokerage (or asset management) capacity by pointing to scope economies. On the one hand, investment banking provides raw material for the creation of mutual funds and their retailing to investors; on the other hand, the asset management division provides the investment banking division with the investors they need for the issues they promote. The justification is spurious. The union of investment with asset management presents a classic conflict of interest, as an investment banker is expected to work for the borrower and a broker for investors. Since investment banking makes more money than brokerage, the bringing of the two roles together under integrated management is bound to make investors suspect that their broker is, in Wall Street parlance, a "sell-side broker." Investors are likely to suspect that banks will use their brokerage and asset management unit to place their worst merchandise – the shares that elicit little demand on the market, but for which the bank must find takers to satisfy its corporate clientele. The conflict is further compounded if the bank has extended loans of dubious quality to the firm in which they are offering shares, since the bank could have the firm reimburse the loans by issuing shares and adding them to the mutual fund offerings. With or without this complication, in equilibrium the investor will not buy in the mutual fund offered by the bank unless the banker can allay the investor's suspicion. How can she do that?

In order to defuse that fear, the bank can pursue one of three strategies. First, the bank could try to establish a reputation for promoting only good companies. This is what J. P. Morgan did a century ago, at a time when corporate securities were still perceived as risky investments and difficult to place outside personal networks of wealthy investors.[23] Whenever Morgan made a mistake, he would take over the management

---

[22] Brokerage is the brokering of securities, asset management is the sale of mutual funds, and private banking is the same as the other two for the wealthy.

[23] On J. P. Morgan, see de Long's (1991) favorable evaluation and Sabel's more sober assessment (following de Long's contribution).

of the failing company and try to steer it out of trouble. Although Morgan was able to live up to his reputation, the basis of his success perhaps was unique. Morgan issued securities in sectors that were highly concentrated and where prices could be fixed, such as railroads, and, when this could not be achieved, he would seek an entente between competitors (steel, electrical engineering, shipping).

A second strategy is to insure investors against a drop in the value of their portfolio; the bank may offer to buy it back at a predetermined price. After doing just that during the "bubble economy" period of 1985–90, Japanese banks ended up disbursing large sums of money afterward. Although no bank failed and the taxpayers footed the bill, the government decried the practice and passed rules to insure against a reoccurrence. No government, not even the Japanese, wants to or can extend a guarantee of that sort to banks. Unlike its ancestor, this new form of universal banking is unlikely to be stabilized by the creation of a lender (in this case buyer) of last resort.

A third strategy is to keep the investment and brokerage units separate. The bank builds "firewalls" between the two and is universal only in name. Crédit Suisse took a step in that direction by allowing its asset management unit (CS Asset Management) to build up its in-house research capability; it hired a large complement of industry analysts who duplicate the work of industry analysis in its investment unit (CS First Boston), but are answerable only to the portfolio managers.[24] Although a bank may succeed in convincing investors in such a way, the firewall strategy is strictly dominated by the specialization strategy.

So why are commercial banks so tenaciously combining corporate lending with investment banking and asset management? Certainly not to free up scope economies between the retail and investment banking sides. An alternative answer is that banks have no intention of keeping them all in the long run. Banks are merely trying to increase profitability by adding money-making activities to their existing profitless ones – first and foremost, investment banking and, secondarily, asset management. This interpretation is upheld by the one-way direction in which diversification has proceeded so far: commercial banks have sought to acquire investment banks and brokerage firms; some brokerage firms have tried to acquire investment banks only; investment banks have not tried to acquire anyone.[25] Where they will go next is, of course, unpredictable,

---

[24] *International Herald Tribune* August 30–September 1, 2000, 18. CS's direct competitor, UBS, seems to be pursuing the very opposite strategy of integration, justifying its acquisition of PaineWebber in 2000 by the opportunity to sell the stocks it creates.

[25] The only reason for a brokerage firm to bid for a commercial bank would be to acquire the trust department. For instance, Charles Schwab acquired US Trust.

but it should not be ruled out that, once the process of diversification is sufficiently advanced, the banks will divest from unprofitable activities and focus on what they do best.

A role for state structures?

State structures affect the way center banks choose their product mix. In countries where sheltered banks dominate, i.e., in decentralized countries, the center banks are forced out of the retail market. In countries where exposed banks are dominant, in centralized countries, these banks are still strong in retail banking.

Consider the German prototype again. Students of federalism have been quick to point to the strengthening of state regulation, especially in light of the creation of a supervisory agency for securities trading under the jurisdiction of the Federal Ministry of Finance.[26] Local governments conceded this fight, but they have resisted on others. A bone of contention at the present moment is the status of the *Landesbanken* – regional banks owned in part by local savings banks and each local state. Should they be treated like any other bank, i.e., allowed to branch out outside their state of origin and denied the benefit of local government guarantees, or should their special relationships with local governments be recognized? The question no longer is contained to German governmental circles, but has spilled out to Brussels, where the European Commission has ruled that the capital contribution which WestLB received from the state of North Rhine Westphalia was illegal and had to be repaid.[27]

The German *Landesbanken* enjoy an unlimited guarantee that has in the past enabled Standard & Poor's and other rating agencies to base the ratings of *Landesbanken* exclusively on the credit strength of their public sector owners, that is, top. At a time when commercial banks throughout the world, including Citigroup and Deutsche Bank, cannot maintain a triple-A rating, the *Landesbanken* enjoy an unfair advantage over private banks, allowing them, among other things, to corner the wholesale business, on which intermediation rests now that mutual funds are siphoning individual savings. Under threat to take the issue to the European Court of Justice, the Commission convinced the German government to remove state guarantees for its public banks starting in July 2005. It is generally

[26] In a survey of recent developments in the German and US financial federal systems, Deeg and Lütz (2000) concluded that there was a strengthening of central state regulation in these two countries.

[27] In March 2000, Lütz (2000, p. 17) reports, the conflict about subsidies escalated when representatives from several German states threatened to block the EU's enlargement process in the Bundesrat if Brussels did not leave the *Landesbanken* alone.

believed, however, that the *Landesbanken* will be more affected by the removal of the state guarantees than the savings banks, which are still mainly financed through client deposits.[28]

Landesbanken and savings banks enjoy greater market advantages in Germany than in Britain. This is the explanation for the above-mentioned reverse specialization movement observed in these two countries. In Britain, the country with the most developed capital market and the smallest local banking sector, the commercial banks are abandoning investment banking to concentrate on retail banking. Conversely, in Germany, the country with the least developed capital market, ceteris paribus (see chapter 9), and the largest local banking sector, the commercial banks are seeking refuge in investment banking outside retail banking.

The fact that Britain has a centralized state and Germany a federal constitution is no coincidence. Being at either end of the state centralization continuum, the two financial systems were the first to give in to the pressure of competition; they merely show others the way of the future. As competition among banks intensifies, specialization will move from the outliers on the state centralization continuum toward the mean. Stepping in German footsteps among decentralized countries are Spain and Italy. In both countries, savings banks have managed, so far, to circumvent the spirit of European directives. In the case of Italy, the sole legislative attempt at applying the European Commission's directives has changed little. Even though the Amato Law turned all savings banks into joint-stock companies, savings bank stocks failed to change hands. Following the British model among centralized countries are the Netherlands and Belgium. Dutch and Belgian savings banks, like their British equivalents, were stripped of all remaining privileges. Consequently, they abandoned the non-profit format to become commercial banks and merge with existing commercial banks.

If decentralization helps us understand why savings banks are more successful than commercial banks in retail banking activities, it does not quite allow us to predict that universal banking will predominate in decentralized countries. The strategy of the three German commercial banks in the past ten years has been to break away from the universal banking model to become global investment banks. This international strategy is reminiscent of the original raison d'être of Deutsche, founded in 1870 to finance overseas trade and foreign investment in competition with London banks.[29] Internationalization is a strategy of specialization, and

---

[28] It is likely that the savings banks will substitute an insurance fund for guarantees. See *The Banker* September 2001, 111.

[29] On the beginnings of Deutsche Bank, see Gall 1995.

could hardly be otherwise in light of the magnitude of the market. Were the present strategy to succeed, it would free the space for *Landesbanken* and large savings banks to monopolize personal banking and most of corporate lending. But were Deutsche, Dresdner, and Commerz to fail to find admittance in the "bulge bracket," or were a prolonged business downturn to flatten that bracket, Deutsche might fall back on its time-tested universal banking strategy – to be the one-stop financial provider to large companies in Germany. This is what happened in 1890, after Deutsche failed to challenge the London banks' international dominance; Deutsche expanded from financing overseas trade and investment to financing domestic industrial investment and underwriting corporate stocks and bonds.[30]

The large banks' move out of retail banking is less advanced in the United States than in Germany, having been hindered until recently by 1930s restrictions. Still, there is no doubt that, for the large banks, investment banking is more profitable than retail banking. As a result, banks have a common goal, but opposite strategies. The investment banks (Goldman Sachs, Morgan Stanley Dean Witter, and Merrill Lynch) want to stay away from corporate lending and stick, instead, to Wall Street's most profitable business lines – underwriting stocks, advising on mergers, and investing capital for themselves and their clients.[31] In contrast, the deposit banks want to diversify into investment banking. Under the prohibition of the Glass–Steagall Act in the 1980s, two deposit banks, Bankers Trust and J. P. Morgan, exited retail banking to transform themselves into full-fledged investment banks. During the 1990s, at a time when the repeal of the prohibition was foreseeable, Citibank merged with Traveller to form the first universal banking group in the United States. The actual repeal in 1999 made it possible for large deposit banks to take over smaller investment banks; Chase took over J. P. Morgan. It is conceivable that other deposit banks such as Bank of America, Bank One, and First Union, as well as large foreign banks seeking a presence in Wall Street, will seek to increase their profitability by making similar bids for the few remaining independent investment banks and that investment banking

---

[30] The large Swiss banks have managed to remain global banks over the long run. The international strategy worked thanks in part to the risk of war, which made Switzerland a natural haven for capital in neighboring countries. However, the end of the Cold War and the pressure exercised by the EU countries for Switzerland to conform with general standards of disclosure are cutting into this comparative advantage and have forced the banks to reinvent themselves as multinational investment banks.

[31] The following anecdote is revealing of the limited appeal of retail banking in the United States: "Recently ... Ford Motor pressed Goldman Sachs to provide not just advice or a quick underwriting but part of a credit line. Goldman Sachs politely declined" (*Wall Street Journal Europe* September 14, 2000).

will soon become a subsidiary activity of commercial banking. It is unlikely, however, that the profit motive in a competitive and large financial market will justify integrating the retail and investment activities, lest the former degrades the profitability of the latter.

So strong is the state embrace of the financial system in France that the banking system is not evolving in any discernible direction. The state is still active in proffering help and advice to large banks and protecting them from being targets for takeover by foreign rivals. The Crédit Lyonnais is still in 2001 in the hands of a hard core of shareholders and the Crédit Agricole, though private, is an unlisted, impregnable *mutuelle*; Caisses d'Epargne was privatized (mutualized) in 2000 only to be merged a year later with a rehabilitated Caisse des Dépôts et Consignations (CDC Finance), with the French Treasury owning 50.1 percent of the conglomerate.[32] Overall, four out of the six largest banks in France are state-engineered universal banks.

Bancassurance

A new area of competition between private and non-profit banks is the provision of insurance products to savers. Bancassurance – the distribution of insurance products by banks – is a fast-growing segment of both the banking and insurance markets. Although some banks initially created their own insurance products, bancassurance is not so much an arena of competition between bankers and insurance brokers as a matter for a reciprocal partnership to help bankers and brokers compete within their respective category. Bankers and brokers teamed together, the former to carry new products popular with their clienteles, the latter to increase the size of their distribution networks. The partnership has evolved through three characteristic phases. In a first phase, banks and brokers signed non-exclusive commercial agreements. In a second phase, the agreements became exclusive, backed up by reciprocal participation or joint ventures. In a third phase, which has been reached only in the Benelux and Nordic countries, the tie-up matured into full-fledged merger.

Bancassurance may give a competitive edge to the for-profit banking sector over the non-profit sector. Concentration is generally greater in insurance than in banking. Since insurers look for size when considering a tie-up, they are more likely to seek one large center bank than a multiplicity of local non-profit banks. Moreover, in countries where banking concentration is moderate, bancassurance is still undeveloped. According

---

[32] *International Herald Tribune* June 26, 2001.

to analysts at Salomon Smith Barney, the countries in which the concentration movement in banking is "incomplete" – Germany, Italy, France – are also those countries in which few or no bancassurance mergers have taken place yet. AXA, Allianz, and Generali – the largest insurers in Europe – have been more interested in using banks, preferably more than one in each country and in more than one country, to sell policies on commission. In contrast, in the Benelux and Nordic countries, where hardly any room seems to be left for further banking concentration, mergers between banks and brokers are common.[33] Nationale Nederlanden insurance company took over NMB Postbank to form ING; Amev insurance company took over VSB savings bank (to form Fortis bank) and the Belgian ASLK-CGER savings bank and Generale Bank to become the dominant banking group in Belgium. Smaller insurance companies in Scandinavia formed joint ventures with, or were acquired by, banks.[34] Last, to the extent that low banking concentration reflects state decentralization, holding everything else constant, one would expect bancassurance in the future to be more prevalent in centralized than in decentralized countries.

Internet banking

PC-online banking is a further step in the decentralization of retail banking, coming on top of branching, automatic tellers, and telephone banking. Each innovation has had the effect of making previous ones obsolete, forcing the pace of amortization of previous investments in infrastructure.[35] Each step offered pioneers, often even startups, the possibility of breaking through a line of business otherwise protected by steep entry barriers, until established banks eventually adopted the innovation – often by purchasing the startup – and closed the market to further entry. The boom in information technology, however, has not led retail bankers to deviate from their long-standing profit-maximizing strategy. If anything, each new technology has intensified competition in the retail business, confirming the dominant strategy of mass production. The internet is likely to allow banks to skirt the branch office for a larger number of stereotyped products in the lower end of the market, allowing banks to

---

[33] *Life Insurance International*, Lafferty Publications, October 1999, p. 2; made available by Reuters *Business Briefing*.

[34] Britain stands halfway between the two groups: Lloyds acquired the Trustee Savings Bank, but NatWest's offer to take over insurer Legal & General failed.

[35] Telemarketing has high startup costs, requiring investment in technology for the call center, in people and training, and in advertising.

close bank offices.[36] Furthermore, with standardization comes special-ization. The internet helps clients shop around, undermining the banks' case for cross-selling products.

However, for more complex financial products, in which personal con-tact will continue to play a major role, banks will still need to keep their branch offices open. The internet may allow new competitors to enter consumer banking by offering low-priced, no-frills products. In the medium run, however, the maturing of their clientele will force these newcomers to move to the higher end of the market and open branches. Internet banking may not open a new area of specialization over the long term.

Conclusion

Deregulation opened a period of diversification, during which many banks sought to try their hand at new products. This initial period was followed by a period of consolidation, in which banks sought to improve profitability by focusing on what they do best. A new specialization be-tween investment banking and an expanded version of retail banking (including the collection of deposits, lending, and the provision of insur-ance, brokerage, and mutual funds) is emerging. Investment banking is falling into the hands of international banks while retail banking is be-coming the province of domestic (or "multidomestic") banks. The trend is visible in Britain, where commercial banks, enjoying plenty of elbow room in the domestic retail market, have withdrawn from investment banking, and in Germany, where the commercial banks are embracing investment banking as an alternative to a crowded domestic retail market.

---

[36] The cost-cutting trend is increasingly clear in the Nordic countries, the leaders in Europe in terms of internet and mobile-phone penetration; see *Distribution Management Briefing*, Lafferty Publications, May 2000, p. 16; made available by Reuters *Business Briefing*.

Conclusion

For the past century and a half, the rules governing the banking and financial professions have been shaped by the rivalry between two types of banks – banks that are relatively more exposed to market competition and banks that are somewhat sheltered from it. Exposed banks cannot afford to own risky or non-marketable assets, lest their financial costs rise, their profitability drops, and their share value suffers. Sheltered banks, in contrast, can afford to hold riskier or less marketable assets either because they benefit from a government guarantee or because they need not worry about maximizing profitability. What has varied over time is the membership of each group. Before World War I, the exposed group was made up of center banks, the sheltered group of local banks and postal savings. During the contraction of the middle century, state intervention added to the sheltered group a new category of bank – the special (state-run) credit bank. Today, the deregulation of finance has reduced the sheltered group to local banks again.

During the period under consideration in this study, the relative size of the exposed and sheltered sectors was a reflection of the relative power of their respective clients – large and high-growth firms on the exposed side; agrarians, small firms, and traditional industries on the sheltered side. The anti-competitive coalition was comparatively stronger in decentralized states, where they could rely on local governments to monopolize access to investment information and extract protection for local banks. The existence of a large sheltered sector allowed local governments to keep their local banks and defeat geographic concentration. Moreover, the existence of a large exposed sector opened a broader segment of domestic finance to a foreign presence. More foreign banks, with an interest in high-volume money markets, were attracted to the financial center. More capital was made available for foreign ventures. A larger sheltered sector, in contrast, kept a greater proportion of domestic savings invested in local ventures. A dispersed and shallow money market was unattractive to foreign bankers and investors.

A large exposed sector also meant a more disintermediated financial system, in which a relatively greater proportion of savings flowed through the markets than through the banks. Intermediation was higher in countries with large local banking sectors. A large exposed sector finally gave to the competition greater latitude in determining product mixes. Holding constant the existence of a liquidity guarantor, the broader the market was, the more specialized financial intermediaries were. In contrast, the presence of a large sheltered sector segmented the clientele along geographic lines, limiting the potential benefits of specialization within each segment.

Branching and concentration increased in the nineteenth century, were frozen by regulation in the 1930s, and increased again after 1960. Internationalization was suspended by World War I, came to a stop in the 1930s, and was resumed in the 1960s. Securitization followed the same trajectory, and therefrom arose capital mobility. Specialization was up in centralized countries at the end of the nineteenth century, declining in the 1920s; it was raised again by law in many countries in the 1930s, dropping suddenly in the wake of the deregulation in the 1970s and 1980s, and perhaps rising again in the past five years following a reorientation by individual banks of their product strategies.

Capital mobility is the capacity for an investor to transform firms' liabilities into financial instruments of any maturity that can be continually traded in deep, broad, and impersonal markets. Capital mobility is identical with securitization, and associated with spatial concentration and internationalization. Capital mobility is a direct function of the relative size of the exposed banking sector, and thus of state centralization. Capital mobility rose in the nineteenth century, declined between the wars, and rose again in the last decades of the twentieth century.

Paradigmatic shifts

The theory identified paradigmatic cases. The market-based versus bank-based dichotomy was the defining typology of the nineteenth century. Financial systems lined up along a continuum bounded by England at one end and Germany at the other. Center banks were dominant and financial markets first developed in England. France was not sui generis, in these days, but analogous to England. There existed a Franco-English model, in which large banks tapped savings nationwide through their networks of branches, used most of it to extend short loans to commerce, and lent the residual to securities brokers and investment bankers, who used it to underwrite large issues of bonds and equity by well-established national and international borrowers.

The counterpoint to the classic Franco-English ideal of deposit banking was given by Germany, Austria, and also Italy. Hindered by local banks in their attempt to tap individual deposits, the *Großbanken* used the current accounts of their corporate clients to make renewable, de facto long-term loans to these same clients. They accumulated risk without ever being able to fully pass it on to individual investors. Issuing equity merely transformed long-term, often dubious, loans into securities that either had to be held by the bank, or placed among a circle of reliable clients, or artificially sustained through timely market intervention. Relatively safe under the liquidity cover of the central bank, the large commercial banks managed risk through a close monitoring of firms' investment.

The second period saw the emergence of a new paradigm – France's – characterized by a large state credit banking sector. Market contraction left the German paradigm unchanged – markets had never been important in decentralized countries anyway. Market contraction hit the center banks in centralized countries hard. This is when France and Britain began to diverge; in France, center banks were displaced by state banks, whereas in Britain, firms were mostly left on their own to finance long-term investment. The rationale for the divergence between the two cases, I have argued elsewhere, was the relative electoral leverage of small business, higher in France than in Britain.[1]

What are the paradigms today? The present period, not surprisingly, shows a mix of the two preceding periods. State banks are disappearing, reopening the old feud between center and local banks, wherever the latter are still a force to reckon with. The previous divergence between the Franco-English and the German models is clear with respect to bank concentration and internationalization. It is not clear any more with respect to securitization and specialization. The state-banking legacy in France is preventing Paris from duplicating London. The two benchmarks, therefore, are the British and German cases once again: British finance is high on all dimensions – concentration, internationalization, securitization, and specialization – whereas German finance is low on all four. The French system occupies a median position. Concentration, internationalization, and specialization are restricted by the continuing role of the state-controlled Crédit Agricole and the state-owned Crédit Lyonnais, while the French stock market is shackled by lingering state control over industry. The future will tell whether state control is transitional or whether it has become an enduring trait of French finance.

---

[1] Verdier 2000.

Where does the case of the United States fit in this trinity? The US financial system is commonly associated with the English model. Washington does not intervene in credit allocation and Wall Street is home to the largest stock market in the world. Against this view, however, I claim that US finance has traditionally been more German than English. Local banking in the United States was protected until a very recent date, while internationalization and stock market development reached levels that are modest in light of the country's overbearing wealth. Germany and the United States only differed with respect to universal banking, which did not develop in the United States until the establishment of the Fed in 1913.[2]

Capital mobility and territory

There has been much talk recently about the deterritorialization of money or, to put it more dramatically, the "end of geography." Richard O'Brien (1992) and Benjamin Cohen (1996), among others, have pointed to the weakening relevance of the state to the management of money and finance. The claim is that capital mobility has weakened the territorial organization of the world economy. The present study suggests a more nuanced interpretation.

On the one hand, bank resources – the liabilities side of the balance sheet – have lost their past territorial foundation. The physical association between savings and territory was a creation of the nineteenth century; it took the form of the deposit bank, an institution in which a bank financed investments with deposits. Deposit banking made it possible for local economies to have their own banks and use local deposits to finance investments in local endeavors, rather than witnessing center bank branches tapping the money and draining it to the financial center. The deposit bank made the cross-sectoral mobility of capital – the capacity for investors to move capital across sectors – more or less identical with the territorial mobility of capital – the capacity for investors to invest their savings in projects other than local ones.

The association between bank resources and territory no longer exists. Money-market accounts are replacing checking accounts, while mutual

---

[2] This result contrasts with a standard claim of the literature on various types of capitalism (Hall and Soskice 2001). From this perspective, Britain and the United States belong to the same liberal variant, in contraposition with Germany and Sweden, which belong to the social-market variant. Banks and firms are said to entertain an arm's-length relationship in the liberal variant, but a long-term relationship in the social variant. In contrast, I argue that in the Germany–United States contrast, this distinction is generally valid for large firms and firms in growth sectors, but not for small, local firms, which in both Germany and the United States enjoy a long-term relationship with their local banks.

funds are replacing savings accounts. All savings are centralized in the money and stock markets. All banks, whether center or local, or located in Boston or Barcelona, finance their investments by borrowing on the money market. Cross-sectoral mobility no longer is coterminous with territorial mobility.

On the other hand, bank assets – the assets side of the balance sheet – are still territorially bound, at least in countries with strong extant local banking communities. Center banks cannot enter local bank markets, while local firms, with a handful of exceptions, cannot tap the securities markets. Local governments in decentralized countries remain the privileged channels for the mobilization of anti-market coalitions.

What is true of local governments in decentralized countries is also true of national governments in the world economy. If the growth of financial markets does not make local governments irrelevant in decentralized countries, a fortiori it does not make national governments irrelevant in a world that is best characterized as anarchic. Quite the contrary, it provides them with the task of compensating losers and deflecting mounting opposition. The more capital flows across borders, the greater the need to regulate these flows to limit inequity and negative externalities. Decentralization in any form is simply not good for the development of deep and broad financial markets.[3]

Is the past the key to the future?

I have argued that present financial systems are comparable in their structures and dynamic to their nineteenth-century equivalents. The advent of bancassurance and internet banking offers no reason to modify this assessment. Still, however useful the past may be to our understanding of the present, it says little about the future. A big unknown in today's finance is how far disintermediation will proceed. Securitization has already revolutionized bank funding – which is no longer based on deposits, but relies on borrowing in the markets. The traditional definition of universal banking as the use of individual deposits to finance investment banking operations is obsolete.

Disintermediation modifies the terms of the competition for resources between banks, thereby limiting the relevance of the past to our understanding of the future. Local banks are not in competition with center banks for raising liabilities directly anymore, but only indirectly – the type of bank with the most clients is the one that is the most profitable,

---

[3] Whether the existence of a deep and broad financial market is a good thing is an entirely different matter, which this book does not address.

that has the best credit rating and the highest stock price. In a fully dis-intermediated and global money market, therefore, a profitable bank is never starved of resources; the cost of its liabilities is not constrained by supply considerations – money-market prices are set globally – but is fully determined by the profitability of its assets. The supply (liabilities)-side approach, which proved essential to understanding the nineteenth century, is ancillary to the demand (assets)-side approach in a disinter-mediated world. Local banks matter not because they may starve the financial center of liquidity, but because they attract a sufficiently large number of good borrowers to prevent center banks from making profits in the field of retail banking. The more advanced disintermediation gets, the less there is to learn from the study of the nineteenth century.

But how far is disintermediation likely to go? Current fascination with markets is untested. Historically, markets crashed regularly, resuming activity soon afterward. Before they were put out of their misery in the 1930s, stock markets dropped precipitously five or six times on average during the period lasting from 1850 until 1930. Meanwhile, individuals assumed market risk. It is unclear how much risk individuals are willing to bear today. Experts are in two minds about it, reflecting the basic in-vestor's tradeoff between risk and efficiency. On the one hand, individuals are more likely to accommodate market risk if that risk is limited. This implies moderating tax cuts and deflecting attacks on the welfare state, for such attacks can only have the effect of transferring too much risk to the poor, thereby undercutting mass support for markets. On the other hand, any form of insurance is a source of moral hazard, limiting the market capacity to sustain severe price shocks. A financial market cannot quickly recover from a crash if the other markets, on which economic recovery depends, are inflexible. The protracted crisis in which Japan has found itself since the end of the bubble economy in 1991 testifies to this point. Finding the right combination of welfare insurance and market flexibility is probably one of the greatest challenges of present times.

Appendix 1: A model of core–periphery relations in the financial sector

The model builds on the basic two-sector–two-region core–periphery model offered by Fujita, Krugman, and Venables (1999, ch. 5). This model is customized to reflect two peculiarities of the financial sector: the financial sector uses its own output in addition to capital as inputs; the manufacturing sector uses the output of the financial sector in addition to labor as inputs. Figure A1.1 maps physical flows in one region.

Consumption

The representative consumer in each region has Cobb–Douglas preferences over manufacture M and financial service F, with F a constant-elasticity-of-substitution (CES) aggregate of the differentiated financial varieties F_i

$$U = M^{1-\mu} F^{\mu}, \qquad 0 \leq \mu \leq 1, \qquad\qquad 1$$

with

$$F = \left(\sum_{i=1}^{n} F_i^{\xi} \right)^{\frac{1}{\xi}}, \qquad \xi = \left(1 - \frac{1}{\sigma} \right), \qquad \sigma > 1, \qquad\qquad 2$$

and σ is the elasticity of substitution between varieties (ξ is a convenient form of σ, which can also be interpreted as an index of homogeneity). A good is differentiated when there are many varieties of it on the market. Financial products are differentiated, as consumers take advantage of variety to diversify their portfolio. Modeling a good as a composite of varieties rather than treating each variety as a different good is justified by a discrepancy between what producers and consumers perceive to be a sector. From the producer's perspective, the products are two varieties of a good that require similar factor inputs and thus belong to the same sector. From the consumer's perspective, in contrast, the two varieties are like two different products in their own right, of which they are in equal need. Note that expression 1 reduces to a standard Cobb–Douglas

222

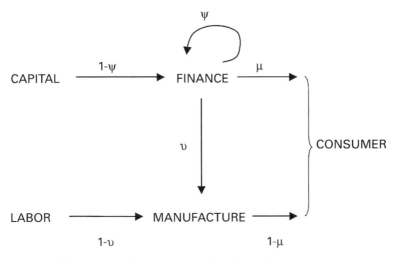

Figure A1.1. Factor and product flows in one region

function with homogeneous goods if the varieties for each good are in-finitely substitutable, that is, if $\sigma \to +\infty$ and $\Sigma_i^n F_i = F$. For any lower value of σ, the firm that produces this variety exercises some degree of market power.[1]

From 2, we derive F_{i11}, the demand that a firm producing variety F_i in region 1 faces in market 1,

$$F_{i11} = \frac{E_1^F}{G_1}\left(\frac{p_1^F}{G_1}\right)^{-\sigma} = E_1^F\left(p_1^F\right)^{-\sigma}(G_1)^{\sigma-1},$$

3

then F_{i12} the demand that it faces in market 2,

$$F_{i12} = E_2^F\left(p_1^F\right)^{-\sigma}(\tau)^{1-\sigma}(G_1)^{\sigma-1};$$

4

and thus in market 1 and 2 combined

$$F_{i1} = \sum_{s=1}^{2} E_s^F\left(p_1^F \tau_{1s}\right)^{-\sigma} \tau_{1s}(G_1)^{\sigma-1},$$

$$s = 1, 2, \quad \tau_{1s} = 1 \quad if \quad s = 1,$$

5

where E_s is the expenditure on the financial composite in market s, and p_1^F is the price of financial variety F_i in region 1. G_1 is the price index of the financial goods consumed in region 1. The price index is the price of

---

[1] For a demonstration that this market power determines the scale at which firms produce, see Helpman and Krugman 1985, p. 134. The ratio of average to marginal cost is not the result of some exogenous technology, but, along with the choice of that technology, is a function of the pattern of demand as defined by σ.

one unit of a composite good once the choice of each variety is optimal.[2] τ_{1s} is an information cost incurred by financial services in region 1 when delivered to a firm or consumer located in another region s. Formally, with $s = 1, 2$, we have $\tau_{12} = \tau_{21} = \tau > 1$ and $\tau_{11} = \tau_{22} = 1$. The idea is that information costs increase with distance. Note that distance is not essential to the definition of the problem, as regions could be easily redefined as information networks, with information circulating freely within each one, but at a cost between each other.[3] τ takes the so-called iceberg form: if a unit of the financial service is provided by a bank in region r to a consumer in s, only a fraction, $1/\tau$, of the original unit arrives.[4]

Aggregate demand for M in region 1 is

$$M_1 = \frac{(1 - \mu) Y_1}{p^M}$$

6

$$\text{with } p^M = 1,$$

and where Y_1 is the income of region 1. p^M is the price of manufacture, which is used as numeraire.

---

[2] The price index can be obtained by solving the problem of minimizing expenditure on the n varieties F_i under the constraint of buying one unit of the composite good F:

$$\min_{F_i} \sum_1^n F_i \, p_i \qquad s.t. \left[\sum_1^n F_i^{\frac{\sigma-1}{\sigma}} \right]^{\frac{\sigma}{\sigma-1}} = 1.$$

The result is

$$\sum_1^n F_i \, p_i = \left(\sum_1^n p_i^{1-\sigma} \right)^{\frac{1}{1-\sigma}} = G.$$

With two regions

$$G = \left[\sum_{r=1}^2 \left[\left(\sum_{i=1}^n p_{ri}^{1-\sigma} \right)^{\frac{1}{1-\sigma}} \right]^{1-\sigma} \right]^{\frac{1}{1-\sigma}}, \qquad i = 1, \ldots, n; \qquad r = 1, 2,$$

or

$$G_1 = \left[n_1 p_1^{1-\sigma} + n_2 (p_2 \tau)^{1-\sigma} \right]^{\frac{1}{1-\sigma}},$$

if we assume that all financial goods consumed in region 1 are priced p_1^F for those produced in region 1 and $p_2^F \tau$ for those produced in region 2. n_1 and n_2 are the number of financial varieties produced in region 1 and 2 respectively.

[3] For the sake of simplicity, I assume that information is perfect between investors and borrowers belonging to the same region, while imperfect between investors and borrowers belonging to different regions.

[4] A derivation of 5 can be found in Fujita et al. 1999, pp. 46–47.

Production

Manufacture is produced using a constant-returns technology. Production input is a Cobb–Douglas composite of *labor* and a CES aggregate of the differentiated financial varieties with total cost

$$C_1^M = w_1^{1-v} G_1^v q_1^M, \quad 0 \le v \le 1,$$ 7

where w_1 is the wage rate, and q_1^M the quantity of M produced, all in region 1. Assume that manufacture can be traded at no cost. In equilibrium, given that p^M is used as numeraire,

$$w_1^{1-v} G_1^v = p^M = 1.$$ 8

The *financial sector* has imperfectly competitive firms, producing differentiated products under increasing returns to scale. Technology is the same for all varieties in all locations, requiring the same fixed (α) and variable $(\beta q_{i,r})$ quantities of *capital* and a CES aggregate of the differentiated financial services with total cost

$$C_1^F = r^{1-\psi} G_1^\psi \left[\alpha + \beta q_1^F\right], \quad 0 \le \psi \le 1.$$ 9

The equilibrium is monopolistic competition; firms equate marginal return with marginal cost, free entry causes firms to be scaled so that they earn zero profits, and the elasticity of substitution σ is doubling in for the elasticity of demand.[5] Formally,

$$p_1^F \left(1 - \frac{1}{\sigma}\right) = r^{1-\psi} G_1^\psi \beta \Leftrightarrow p_1^F = \left(\frac{\sigma}{\sigma - 1}\right) r^{1-\psi} G_1^\psi \beta,$$ 10

where p_1^F here is the equilibrium price value of a particular financial variety. The expression $\sigma/(\sigma - 1)$ is the markup, that is, the price of a unit sold above the marginal cost; it tends to 1 as σ approaches infinity. We choose units so that the marginal input requirement β equals $(\sigma - 1)/\sigma$ and firms set price according to

$$p_1^F = r^{1-\psi} G_1^\psi.$$ 11

Forward linkage

Assume world supplies of $K = L = 1$. Define κ, region 1's share of world capital supply. The total value of financial production in region 1 is $n_1 p_1 q^F$, so the return on capital bill is a share $(1 - \psi)$ of this:

$$r_1 \kappa = (1 - \psi) n_1 p_1^F q^F, \quad 0 \le \kappa \le 1,$$ 12

---

[5] For an explanation of why the elasticity of demand is the same as the elasticity of substitution, see Helpman and Krugman 1985, p. 119.

with q^F the quantity produced by each financial firm within the national economy.[6] We choose units such that $q^F = 1/(1 - \psi)$, so that

$$n_1 = \frac{r_1}{p_1^F} \kappa. \tag{13}$$

Using 11 and 13, we can write the price indices for each country (n. 2), as

$$G_1^{1-\sigma} = \kappa r_1^{1-\sigma(1-\psi)} G_1^{-\psi\sigma} + (1 - \kappa) r_2^{1-\sigma(1-\psi)} G_2^{-\psi\sigma} \tau^{1-\sigma},$$

$$G_2^{1-\sigma} = (1 - \kappa) r_2^{1-\sigma(1-\psi)} G_2^{-\psi\sigma} + \kappa r_1^{1-\sigma(1-\psi)} G_1^{-\psi\sigma} \tau^{1-\sigma}. \tag{14}$$

Both expressions exhibit a forward linkage, $\partial G_j / \partial \kappa < 0$, $j = 1, 2$, magnified by input-output linkages, and according to which a concentration of capital in one region has the effect of lowering the price of financial goods in that region.

Backward linkage

Next, we build the "capital return equations" from the demand for a variety i. In equilibrium the quantity produced by a firm q^F is equal to the demand for the variety produced by that firm, F_{irs} (defined in 5). The inverse demand function for variety i produced in region 1 can thus be written

$$\left(p_1^F\right)^\sigma = \frac{1}{q^F} \sum_{s=1}^2 \frac{E_s(\tau_{1s})^{1-\sigma}}{G_s^{-(\sigma-1)}}, \qquad s = 1, 2, \ \tau_{1s} = 1 \quad if \quad s = 1. \tag{15}$$

Using the pricing rule from 10, we get the capital return equation

$$\left(r_1^{1-\psi} G_1^\psi\right)^\sigma = \frac{\sigma - 1}{\sigma \beta} \left[\frac{1}{q^F} \sum_{s=1}^2 \frac{E_s(\tau_{1s})^{1-\sigma}}{G_s^{-(\sigma-1)}} \right]. \tag{16}$$

Using the earlier choices of firm scale, $q^F = 1/(1 - \psi)$, and marginal input requirement, $\beta = (\sigma - 1)/\sigma$, expression 16 simplifies to

$$\frac{\left(r_1^{1-\psi} G_1^\psi\right)^\sigma}{1 - \psi} = \sum_{s=1}^2 \frac{E_s(\tau_{1s})^{1-\sigma}}{G_s^{-(\sigma-1)}}, \tag{17}$$

---

[6] It is an attribute of the model that the scale of each firm at equilibrium is a constant equal to $\alpha(\sigma-1)/\beta$. To find this result substitute the equilibrium value of p_1^F from 10 into the zero-profit condition

$$\pi_1^F = q_1^F p_1^F - r\left(\alpha + \beta q_1^F\right) = 0,$$

and solve for q_1^F.

or extensively and for each region

$$\frac{\left(r_1^{1-\psi} G_1^{\psi}\right)^{\sigma}}{1-\psi} = E_1 G_1^{\sigma-1} + E_2 G_2^{\sigma-1} \tau^{1-\sigma},$$

$$\frac{\left(r_2^{1-\psi} G_2^{\psi}\right)^{\sigma}}{1-\psi} = E_2 G_2^{\sigma-1} + E_1 G_1^{\sigma-1} \tau^{1-\sigma}. \qquad 18$$

Both expressions exhibit a backward linkage, $\partial r_j / \partial E_j > 0$, $j = 1, 2$, magnified by input-output linkages, and according to which a rise in demand leads to an increase in the nominal return on capital, thereby attracting more capital. Recall from above that, as more capital is attracted, prices for financial varieties drop (the forward linkage), thereby increasing both demand for and expenditure on financial products – the loop is closed.

The wage equations

From 8,

$$w_1 = \left(1/G_1^{\nu}\right)^{1/1-\nu},$$

$$w_2 = \left(1/G_2^{\nu}\right)^{1/1-\nu}. \qquad 19$$

The expenditures and income equations

Region 1's expenditures on financial services, E_1^F, equal

$$E_1^F = \mu Y_1 + \nu q_1^M w_1^{1-\nu} G_1^{\nu} + \psi n_1 p_1^F q^F. \qquad 20$$

The first term on the right-hand side is consumers' expenditure on financial services. The second is intermediate demand by the manufacturing sector, where we have used the fact that proportion ν of revenue (=costs) is spent on intermediates. The third is intermediate demand by the financial sector itself. After appropriate substitutions using 6 and 19,

$$E_1^F = \mu Y_1 + \nu(1-\mu)Y_1 + \frac{\psi r_1 \kappa}{1-\psi};$$

$$E_2^F = \mu Y_2 + \nu(1-\mu)Y_2 + \frac{\psi r_2(1-\kappa)}{1-\psi}. \qquad 21$$

The income of region 1 is

$$Y_1 = r_1 K_1 + w_1 L_1. \qquad 22$$

Given two earlier assumptions, $K_1 = \kappa K$ and $K = 1$, and making each region's share of world labor supply ($L = 1$) equal to $1/2$, regional incomes are

$$Y_1 = \kappa r_1 + \frac{1}{2}w_1,$$

$$Y_2 = (1 - \kappa)r_2 + \frac{1}{2}w_2. \qquad 23$$

Real returns

Capital moves to regions that offer a real return above average, while the fixed factor, labor, partly bases its policy position on its real return. Real return is equal to the nominal return divided by the cost-of-living index, $G^{\mu}(p^M)^{1-\mu}$, which, given that the price of manufacture is the numeraire, boils down to G^{μ}. Real return on capital is

$$\rho_1 = r_1 G_1^{-\mu},$$

$$\rho_2 = r_2 G_2^{-\mu}, \qquad 24$$

while real return on labor is, using 19,

$$\omega_1 = w_1 G_1^{-\mu} = G_1^{\frac{-[v+\mu(1-v)]}{1-v}},$$

$$\omega_2 = w_2 G_2^{-\mu} = G_2^{\frac{-[v+\mu(1-v)]}{1-v}}. \qquad 25$$

A fixed factor effect can be inferred from 25, where a drop in the price of financial services raises the real wage. Since the core–periphery pattern is characterized by a drop in the price of the financial good produced in the core (forward linkage), labor in the core is better off than labor in the periphery.

Numerical simulation

Equations 14, 18, 19, 21, 23, and 24 define the equilibrium. Numerical simulations show that, for high values of the cost of financial trade τ and assuming values of the other parameters to be later specified, the symmetric equilibrium obtains. As τ decreases, the symmetric equilibrium breaks down and a core–periphery pattern emerges, with one country absorbing the capital of the other as well as the entire financial sector. The three graphs in figure A1.2 plot the difference between the two countries' real factor rewards, $\rho_1 - \rho_2$ and $\omega_1 - \omega_2$, against κ, country 1's share of world capital supply. All three graphs are calculated for $\sigma = 5$, $\mu = 0.4$,

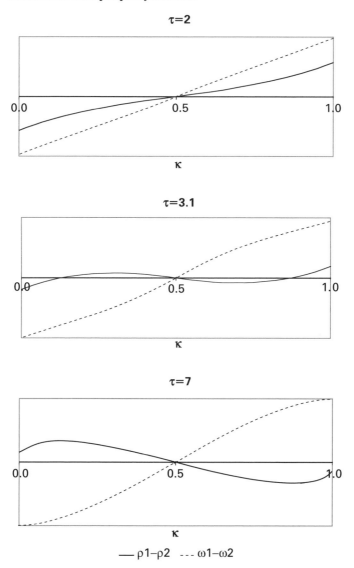

Figure A1.2. Regional differences in factor returns as a function of κ

$v = 0.3$, and $\psi = 0.2$.[7] Only the cost of doing business τ differs: the top graph shows a low cost case, $\tau = 2$, the middle graph an intermediate cost case, $\tau = 3.1$, and the graph at the bottom a high cost case, $\tau = 7$.

[7] $\sigma = 5$ is the value consistently used in Fujita et al. (1999, p. 75).

Consider first the mobile factor, capital. In the top graph, the capital return differential slopes upward in κ. This means that, if a country has more than half the capital stock, it is more attractive to capitalists than the other country, leading to a core–periphery pattern with all the financial sector concentrated in one country. In the graph at the bottom, by contrast, the rental differential is positive if κ is less than $1/2$, negative if greater than $1/2$. Having more capital makes a country less attractive to other capitalists. The countries converge to a symmetric equilibrium, in which finance is equally divided. Finally, the graph in the middle shows the intermediate case, with three locally stable equilibria, two core–periphery and one symmetric.

Now consider the fixed factor, labor. The three graphs show a wage differential with a strictly upward slope in κ: the larger the capital stock, the higher the wage of labor. There are two reasons for this correlation. First, the concentration of capital in a country makes finance less expensive to final consumers. Second, capital concentration makes finance less costly for firms in the manufacturing sector, thereby raising the productivity of labor. As a result, a prolonged deregulation of the financial sector, whether it causes or reflects a weakening of local banks, harms the fixed factor in the region that is drained from its endogenous capital.

The numerical example suggests that the maximum level of information asymmetry for which a core–periphery equilibrium is sustained is different from (higher than) the threshold below which a symmetric equilibrium breaks down. One must thus determine each point separately.

Determining the sustain point

When is a core–periphery pattern sustainable? Following the protocol laid out in Fujita et al. (1999), I posit a situation in which all finance is concentrated in region 1, $\kappa = 1$, and ask whether the real return to capital in region 1 is greater or less than in region 2. If $\rho_1 \geq \rho_2$ (or $\rho_2/\rho_1 \leq 1$) then the core–periphery pattern is sustainable, because capital will not move out of region 1. This condition can be rewritten

$$\frac{\rho_2}{\rho_1} = \frac{r_2 G_2^{-\mu}}{r_1 G_1^{-\mu}} = \frac{r_2}{r_1}\tau^{-\mu} \leq 1. \qquad\qquad 26$$

From 14 and 18 we can derive

$$G_2 = G_1\tau. \qquad\qquad 27$$

Using 26, 27, and 18, we have

$$
\left(\frac{\rho_2}{\rho_1}\right)^{\sigma(1-\psi)} = \left(\frac{E_1}{E_1+E_2}\tau^A + \frac{E_2}{E_1+E_2}\tau^{-A}\right)
$$

with

$$
A = 1 - \sigma(1-\psi)(1-\mu),
$$

$$
E_2 = \phi Y_2 = \frac{\phi}{2}w_2 = \frac{\phi}{2}(G_1\tau)^{\frac{-\nu}{1-\nu}},
$$

$$
E_1 = \theta G_1 + \frac{\phi}{2}G_1^{\frac{-\nu}{1-\nu}},
$$

$$
\phi = 1 - (1-\mu)(1-\nu),
$$

$$
\theta = 1 - (1-\mu)(1-\nu)(1-\psi). \tag{28}
$$

When $\tau = 1$ (no information costs), $\rho_2/\rho_1 = 1$; location is irrelevant. We consider a small information cost increase from that point by differentiating 28 and evaluating the derivative at $\tau = 1$, $\rho_2/\rho_1 = 1$. To that effect, we rewrite 28

$$
\left(\frac{\rho_2}{\rho_1}\right)^{\sigma(1-\psi)} = \frac{E_1\tau^A + \frac{\phi}{2}G_1^{\frac{-\nu}{1-\nu}}\tau^B}{E_1 + \frac{\phi}{2}(G_1\tau)^{\frac{-\nu}{1-\nu}}},
$$

with

$$
A = 1 - \sigma(1-\psi)(1-\mu) = \frac{1 - \sigma(1-\theta) - \nu}{1-\nu},
$$

$$
B = [\sigma(1-\psi)(1-\mu)(1-\nu) - 1]/(1-\nu) = \frac{\sigma(1-\theta) - 1}{1-\nu}. \tag{29}
$$

The derivative is

$$
\frac{d(\rho_2/\rho_1)}{d\tau} = \frac{A\left(E_1 - \frac{\phi}{2}G_1^{\frac{-\nu}{1-\nu}}\right)}{E_1 + \frac{\phi}{2}G_1^{\frac{-\nu}{1-\nu}}} = \frac{A\theta}{(1-\psi)\left(1 + G_1^{\frac{-1}{1-\nu}}\right)}. \tag{30}
$$

The denominator is positive, while the numerator is negative when $A < 0$ (i.e., $\sigma > 1/(1-\psi)(1-\nu)$). Assuming that this last condition is met, at small levels of information costs, agglomeration is therefore sustainable because $\rho_2/\rho_1 < 1$.

Suppose, on the other hand, that we consider a very large τ. The first term of the numerator in 29 (top) becomes arbitrarily small. There are two possibilities for the second term, B. Using L'Hôpital's rule, if $B < 0$ – or, more precisely, $1 - \sigma(1 - \theta) > 0$ – then this term also becomes arbitrarily small, so ρ_2/ρ_1, and thus ρ_2, tends to 0. A core–periphery pattern is always an equilibrium. If, instead, $1 - \sigma(1 - \theta) < 0$, then the second term becomes arbitrarily large and the core–periphery pattern is no longer sustainable. The condition for sustainability, which can be rewritten as $\xi > \theta$, is the equivalent in the present model of Fujita et al.'s "no-black-hole-condition" (1999, p. 58). In sum, at $\tau = 1$, $\rho_2/\rho_1 = 1$; then as τ increases slightly, ρ_1/ρ_2 drops downward, but then – provided that $-A > 0$ – turns upward. The point where it crosses 1 defines the sustain value of τ. Below this value the core–periphery pattern is an equilibrium and, above it, it is not.

Note that between the two conditions identified above, $A < 0$ and $B > 0$, the latter – the "no-black-hole condition" – is sufficient; if $B > 0$, then $A < 0$ always.

When is the symmetric equilibrium broken?

The break point occurs when the parameters are such that the $\rho_1 - \rho_2$ curve is horizontal at the symmetric equilibrium. We must evaluate $d("\rho_1 - \rho_2")/d\kappa$. Since we differentiate around the symmetric equilibrium, we know the values of the endogenous variables of the model

$$\kappa = 1/2,$$

$$G_1 = G_2 \equiv G, \quad E_1 = E_2 \equiv E, \quad r_1 = r_2 \equiv r, \quad w_1 = w_2 \equiv w,$$

$$Y_1 = Y_2 \equiv Y, \quad \rho_1 = \rho_2 \equiv \rho,$$

$$G_1^{1-\sigma(1-\psi)} = \frac{1}{2}(1 + \tau^{1-\sigma})r_1^{1-\sigma(1-\psi)},$$

$$G_1^{\sigma\psi} = \frac{(1-\psi)\left[E_1 G_1^{\sigma-1}(1 + \tau^{1-\sigma})\right]}{r_1^{\sigma(1-\psi)}}, \tag{31}$$

$$\Leftrightarrow 1 = \frac{r_1}{2(1-\psi)E_1} \Leftrightarrow E_1 = \frac{r_1}{2(1-\psi)} = \frac{r_1\kappa}{(1-\psi)}.$$

The last line of equivalencies was obtained by dividing the third by the fourth line. From the third line, we also have

$$\left(\frac{G_1}{r_1}\right)^{1-\sigma(1-\psi)} = \frac{1 + \tau^{1-\sigma}}{2}. \tag{32}$$

Define Z as an index of information costs, taking value 0 when there are no information costs ($\tau = 1$) and 1 when such costs are maximum ($\tau \to \infty$):

$$Z = \frac{1 - \tau^{1-\sigma}}{1 + \tau^{1-\sigma}} = \frac{1}{2} \left(\frac{G_1}{r_1} \right)^{\sigma - (1-\psi) - 1} (1 - \tau^{1-\sigma}). \qquad 33$$

Equating the expenditure equation with 31, one derives another useful set of expressions

$$r_1 = \frac{\phi}{1 - \phi} w_1 = \frac{\phi}{1 - \phi} G_1^{\frac{-\nu}{1-\nu}},$$

$$E_1 = \left(\frac{\phi}{2(1 - \phi)(1 - \psi)} G_1^{\frac{-\nu}{1-\nu}} \right). \qquad 34$$

We also take advantage of the fact that, for each endogenous variable,

$$dE_1 = -dE_2 \equiv dE$$
$$dG_1 = -dG_2 \equiv dG \qquad 35$$
$$etc.$$

The total derivative of the price indices (14) is

$$(1 - \sigma) \frac{dG}{G} = Z \left[\frac{d\kappa}{\kappa} + (1 - \sigma(1 - \psi)) \frac{dr}{r} - \sigma \psi \frac{dG}{G} \right]. \qquad 36$$

The total derivative of the capital return equations (18) is

$$\sigma (1 - \psi) \frac{dr}{r} + \sigma \psi \frac{dG}{G} = Z \left[\frac{dE}{E} + (\sigma - 1) \frac{dG}{G} \right]. \qquad 37$$

The total derivative of the expenditure equations (24) is

$$\frac{dE}{E} = \theta \left(\frac{d\kappa}{\kappa} + \frac{dr}{r} \right) + (1 - \theta) \frac{dw}{w}. \qquad 38$$

The total derivative of the wage equations (19) is

$$\frac{dw}{w} = \left(\frac{-\nu}{1 - \nu} \right) \frac{dG}{G}. \qquad 39$$

The total derivative of the real return on capital equations (22) is

$$\frac{d\rho}{\rho} = \frac{dr}{r} - \mu \frac{dG}{G}. \qquad 40$$

Using 39 to eliminate dw/w from 38

$$\frac{dE}{E} = \theta \left(\frac{d\kappa}{\kappa} + \frac{dr}{r} \right) + (1 - \theta) \left(\frac{-\nu}{1 - \nu} \right) \frac{dG}{G}, \qquad 41$$

and 41 to eliminate dE/E from 37

$$\sigma(1-\psi)\frac{dr}{r}+\sigma\psi\frac{dG}{G}$$
$$=Z\left[\left[\theta\left(\frac{d\kappa}{\kappa}+\frac{dr}{r}\right)+(1-\theta)\left(\frac{-\nu}{1-\nu}\right)\frac{dG}{G}\right]+(\sigma-1)\frac{dG}{G}\right],$$

42

we are left with a system of two equations, 36 and 42, in three unknowns. In matrix form we have

$$\begin{bmatrix} 1 & -Z\dfrac{1-\sigma(1-\psi)}{1-\sigma(1-\psi Z)} \\[4mm] Z\dfrac{1-\sigma\left(1-\frac{\psi}{Z}\right)+(1-\theta)\left(\dfrac{\nu}{1-\nu}\right)}{1-\sigma(1-\psi Z)} & \dfrac{\sigma(1-\psi)-\theta Z}{1-\sigma(1-\psi Z)} \end{bmatrix}$$

$$\times\begin{bmatrix} \dfrac{dG}{G} \\[3mm] \dfrac{dr}{r} \end{bmatrix}=\begin{bmatrix} \dfrac{Z}{1-\sigma(1-\psi Z)}\dfrac{d\kappa}{\kappa} \\[3mm] \dfrac{Z\theta}{1-\sigma(1-\psi Z)}\dfrac{d\kappa}{\kappa} \end{bmatrix}.$$

43

We use Cramer's rule to extract the values of dG/G and dr/r. Introducing these values into 40 yields

$$\frac{d\rho}{d\kappa}\frac{\kappa}{\rho}=Z\frac{\theta[1-\sigma(1-\psi Z)]-Z\left[1-\sigma(1-\psi/Z)+(1-\theta)\dfrac{\nu}{1-\nu}\right]-\mu\sigma(1-\psi)(1-Z\theta)}{\Delta}.$$

with $\Delta=[\sigma(1-\psi)-\theta Z][1-\sigma(1-\psi Z)]+Z^2[1-\sigma(1-\psi)]$

$$\times\left[1-\sigma(1-\psi/Z)+(1-\theta)\dfrac{\nu}{1-\nu}\right].$$

44

The symmetric equilibrium is stable if $(d\rho/d\kappa)(\kappa/\rho)$ is negative and unstable if positive. When Z gets very close to zero, both the numerator and the denominator are negative – the symmetric equilibrium is unstable. When Z approaches unity, however, the expression reduces to

$$\frac{\sigma(1-\mu)(1-\psi)(1-\nu)-1}{1-\sigma(1-\psi)},$$

45

of which the numerator is positive when the following condition is satisfied:

$$\sigma > \frac{1}{(1 - \mu)(1 - \psi)(1 - \nu)},$$

or

46

$$\xi > \theta,$$

negative otherwise. The denominator is negative when the following condition is satisfied:

$$\sigma > \frac{1}{1 - \psi}.$$

47

Condition 46 is sufficient, for it is stronger than condition 47. As already mentioned, 46 is the equivalent to Fujita et al.'s "no-black-hole condition." Hence, the denominator is negative whenever the numerator is positive. If 46 is not met, then the expression is positive for values of σ between 46 and 47. For values between 1 and 47, the expression is negative again (the numerator is negative and the denominator positive). Therefore, assuming 46 is satisfied, the symmetric equilibrium is stable at high values of τ.

Dependence of the sustain and break points on σ, μ, ν, and ψ

I use 44 to calculate the break point value of τ. Setting the numerator of the term in square brackets equal to 0, we have $d\rho/d\kappa = 0$ if

$$Z = \frac{\theta\left(1 + (1 - \nu)\dfrac{\sigma - 1}{\sigma}\right) - \nu}{\theta\left(\theta - \nu\dfrac{\sigma - 1}{\sigma}\right) + (1 - \nu)\dfrac{\sigma - 1}{\sigma} - \dfrac{\nu}{\sigma}},$$

50

and, given the definition of Z in 33, if

$$\tau = \left(\frac{1 - Z}{Z + 1}\right)^{\frac{1}{1 - \sigma}}.$$

51

The sustain point can be calculated as well by setting 29 equal to 1 and calculating the implicit value of τ.

A few numerical examples illustrate the dependence of the sustain point and break point on parameter values. The first line in table A1.1 provides baseline values of the two points for $\sigma = 5$, $\mu = 0.4$, $\nu = 0.3$, and $\psi = 0.2$. Then each new line increases the value of just one parameter each time. The endogenous values for the sustain point and the break point move in tandem. They drop with an increase in the elasticity of

Table A1.1. *Critical values of* τ

σ	μ	ν	ψ	Sustain point $\tau(S)$	Break point $\tau(B)$
5	0.4	0.3	0.2	4.21	2.40
6	0.4	0.3	0.2	2.73	1.94
5	0.5	0.3	0.2	13.50	2.94
5	0.4	0.4	0.2	7.02	2.69
5	0.4	0.3	0.3	8.95	2.77

substitution (σ), thus narrowing the range of information asymmetry for which a core–periphery pattern forms. This suggests that firms have a lesser incentive to agglomerate if they lose control over their markets, for they can no longer afford to sink fixed costs, forgoing the gains of scale economies. Conversely, the points move up with an increase in the share of financial goods in the consumer basket (μ), in the manufacturing sector's input (ν), and in the financial sector's input (ψ). An overall increase in the relative demand for financial goods facilitates agglomeration.

Theoretical limits of the model

Tractability imposes a constraint on what one can wish a model to accomplish. The present model does one thing very well: predicting the inverse relation between information asymmetry, understood as a product of physical, social, and political distance, and financial agglomeration. This feature directly speaks to two dependent variables in this study – the degree of agglomeration and the depth and breadth of financial markets.[8]

The other two dependent variables, the degree of internationalization and the degree of specialization, are not derivable from the model. Modeling internationalization as an endogenous variable would require a few amendments. One could build internationalization into the model by introducing a foreign country identical to the home country in all respects except for factor endowment – Home would be capital-abundant and Foreign labor-abundant. Capital would be country-bound, while the exchange of financial services between countries would take place between the two countries subject to information costs that would be lower between two cores than a core and a foreign periphery. Variation between

---

[8] Note that agglomeration – also referred to as geographic concentration – is different from sectoral concentration – the relative size of the two or five largest firms in the financial sector. The present model has nothing to say about sectoral concentration.

centralized and decentralized states would reflect different orderings in information asymmetry. For instance, assuming τ the information asymmetry between two regions of a country, τ_o the information asymmetry between two cores, and τ_o' the information asymmetry between a core and a foreign periphery, a decentralized country could be parametrized as a case in which $\tau_o' \geq \tau > \tau_o$ and a centralized as one in which $\tau_o' > \tau_o \geq \tau$. In both cases, $\tau_o' > \tau_o$, reflecting the fact that investments in the core are more transparent to foreign investors than investments in the periphery. The variation is with respect to τ, information asymmetry within a country, and whether it is superior (decentralized) or inferior (centralized) to any one of the other two.

It would be more difficult to make the degree of bank specialization endogenous. This limitation is due to a characteristic already mentioned in n. 6: the number of firms, n, and thus the range of product variety, is a function only of the preference and technology parameters (σ, α, β). It is not a function of agglomeration, κ, nor of the demand parameters (ψ, ν, μ), and thus not a function of the size of the market – one of Adam Smith's main findings as well as a stylized fact. Surely, it is very likely that an expansion in the size of the market would, in reality, correlate with an increase in the consumer's love for variety (lower σ) and the bank's fixed cost (higher α/β) – the last two being linked in equilibrium (see n. 1). However, the model does not support this feature, nor can it be modified to do so without upsetting its overall economy. The model is here to illustrate the most important aspects of the theoretical framework; it is no substitute for that framework.

Appendix 2: The four credit sectors

Definition

Financial regulation has evolved along two dimensions: center/periphery and for-profit/non-profit. Their intersection generates four banking sectors (see table 2.2, p.30).

The *center bank* category includes all commercial banks headquartered in the financial center(s), whether joint stock or partnership, whether nationalized by the central government or in private ownership. The central bank is not included. Joint-stock banks, with the central bank as primus inter pares, were created by private bankers, usually in the second half of the nineteenth century, with central government approval in the form of a charter. Many of these banks were nationalized after World War II and privatized in the last two decades of the twentieth century. Strictly speaking, it is incorrect to label these banks "for-profit" during the period when they were owned by the state, since they were not distributing dividends. But I kept this notation for convenience, because state ownership had little or no implication for the way the banks were run. Their directors enjoyed enough autonomy to pursue market-oriented strategies. Nationalization merely aimed at redistributing bank profits, not at reallocating bank credit. The private banks (a residual category, since most of them were incorporated as joint-stock banks in the nineteenth century) are also included in this category.

The *local non-profit bank* category includes savings banks, mortgage banks, credit cooperatives, and two categories of credit banks operated by local governments – the German *Landesbanken* and Swiss *Kantonal* banks. Local non-profit banks benefit from legal privileges, which allow them to compete with for-profit banks – they typically pay less or no taxes and enjoy a state or local government guarantee on their deposits. During the postwar era, they were spared from reserve requirements in all countries, except for Germany. Local non-profit banks differ from for-profit and state banks in terms of territorial scope – they are local institutions. City governments in the first half of the nineteenth century

238

initially chartered savings banks. They were (and quite often still are) local monopolies. Although the main investments of savings banks throughout the nineteenth century were mortgages, another category of non-profit bank specializing in mortgages also appeared in Anglo-Saxon countries (building societies in Britain, savings & loans in the United States). They were financed not by savings, like the savings banks, but by bonds. A third category of local, non-profit institutions comprises the credit cooperatives. They also appeared during the second half of the nineteenth century, extending to their members loans that they financed with membership fees. All the institutions included in the local non-profit category were grass-roots organizations. Although they grew over time into countrywide institutions, growth proceeded from the bottom up, through the creation of sector federations and clearing facilities. Savings banks and cooperatives that do not meet this definition are excluded from the local non-profit category. This is the case of the Belgian savings bank, which brought all savings banks under one government-controlled organization in the 1850s; they are included in the state sector until the 1993 privatization. The French Crédit Agricole is also included in the state banking category, until mutualization in 1988.

The *country bank* category in principle includes all the for-profit banks headquartered outside the financial center(s).

The *state banks* fall into two categories – savings and credit. State savings banks mainly include the postal savings, to which one must add the Canadian government savings banks and two national savings schemes (the British national savings accounts and the Belgian national savings system). State credit is the affair of separate credit banks. As already mentioned, state credit banks are not to be confused with the nationalized commercial banks, which are center banks. State credit banks enjoy state borrowing privileges, unlike nationalized banks, which must obtain their funds on the market like any other firm. State credit banks are usually specialized, lending to farmers (the French Crédit Agricole, etc.), to local governments (the Belgian Crédit Communal, etc.), to small firms (the French Crédit National, the Dutch Middenstandsbank, the Swedish AB Industrikredit, etc.), and heavy industry (Istituto Mobiliare Italiano, etc.).

The four sectors together cover the entire credit system, with the exception of the central bank and a residual category of specialized installment finance companies and specialized money market firms. Specialized stock brokerage firms and institutional investors are also excluded, brokerages on account of the insignificance of their aggregated assets, and institutional investors on account of their limited interest in financial regulation. Institutional investors include insurance companies, which were regulated as a category separate from financial institutions until very recently, and investment funds and pension funds, because of their complete lack of interest in financial politics until recently.[1]

Measurement

Although sectoral data are available, they present one difficulty. Separate data exist for state and local non-profit banks, but, for most countries, data for center and country banks are aggregated into what are generically called "commercial" banks – I prefer to call them for-profit.[2] Only in two cases – the United States and residually Australia – are country banks identified separately from center banks. Aggregating center and country banks into the for-profit category, except in the cases of the United States and Australia where they are distinct, I draw country-specific graphs representing the proportion of assets belonging to various sectors over the period 1910–95 for the years and countries for which data are available. Missing data points indicate that some or all of the relevant data are missing for that particular country-year. The graphs disaggregate the state banking sector into its savings and credit components.

The difficulty caused by the collapse of center and country banks in most countries is not insurmountable. Until the 1990s center banks everywhere except in the United States were allowed to open branches in the periphery and compete for deposits from country banks or merge with them. The trend was toward the amalgamation of country by center banks. The United States was unique in prohibiting interstate banking and, in many cases, branch banking within states as well. In light of this, I assume that for-profit banks, whether center or local, were center banks, except in the United States. This assumption does not always square with the qualitative historical record; it is quite problematic in the case of France prior to the Great Depression (see chapter 3).

The graphs illustrate the wide cross-sectional variety offered by OECD countries. For-profit (mostly center) banks are dominant in Britain, Canada, Australia, Ireland, Spain, and Portugal. Local non-profit banks are dominant in Germany, Austria, Denmark, and Sweden. State banks, though rarely dominant, were most developed in Belgium, France, the Netherlands, Greece, Norway, and New Zealand. US country banks held

---

[1] Even today in countries where they have reached gigantic proportions, investment and pension funds still are passive investors, with limited interest in corporate management and financial regulation.

[2] The phrase "commercial" has another meaning, that of a bank making loans, as distinct from "investment," which is used to qualify banks that mainly engage in underwriting securities.

a non-negligible share. Norway, Italy, and Japan show roughly equal proportions of center, state, and local non-profit banks.

Sources

GENERAL: Goldsmith (1969) provides comparative data for benchmark years 1880, 1900, 1913, 1929, c. 1938, 1948, 1960, and 1963; IMF 1962, League of Nations 1939a, b, Mitchell 1983, 1992, *Financial Statistics: Methodological Supplement* (various years), Société des nations 1931.

AUSTRALIA: 1913–70: Butlin et al. 1971, R. C. White 1973. 1976–81: *Official Year Book of Australia* (various years), *Australian Financial System* 1980. The 1982 breakdown of savings is from K. T. Davis 1985, p. 67.

AUSTRIA: 1960 and 1970: Diwok 1982, p. 26. 1977–91: Österreichische Nationalbank (various years). 1992–present: *Statistisches Handbuch für die Republik Österreich* (various years). *Bankiers* are included in *Aktien* since 1987.

BELGIUM: 1945–present: *Annuaire Statistique de la Belgique* (various years).

CANADA: 1869–1969: Neufeld 1972. 1970–present: *Canada Year Book* (various years), *Financial Institutions* (various years), and *Statistical Year-Book of Canada* (various years).

DENMARK: Johansen 1985, *Statistisk Årbog* (various years).

FINLAND: *Statistical Yearbook of Finland* (various years).

FRANCE: 1945–81: Conseil National du Crédit *Rapport Annuel* (various years). 1982–95: Banque de France a, b (various years), Bayliss and Butt Philip 1980.

GERMANY: 1876–1975: Deutsche Bundesbank 1976. 1976–present: *Statistisches Jahrbuch für die Bundesrepublik Deutschland* (various years).

GREECE: 1964–94: Petros Valamidas, Bank of Greece (personal communication), *Monthly Statistical Bulletin* (various months).

IRELAND: Central Bank of Ireland (various years), *Ireland Statistical Abstract* (various years).

ITALY: Banca d'Italia a, b (both various years), Garofalo and Colonna 1999.

JAPAN: Tamaki 1995, Bank of Japan (various months).

NETHERLANDS: Nederlandsche Bank n.v. 1987, Nederlandsche Bank n.v. *Annual Report* (various years), *Statistical Yearbook of the Netherlands* (various years).

NEW ZEALAND: 1885, 1910, 1940: Sheppard et al. 1990. 1957–84: G. T. Bloomfield 1984, *New Zealand Official Yearbook* (various years).

NORWAY: 1850–1908: Matre 1992. 1909–95: *Statistisk Årbok* (various years), *Bankstatistikk* (various years).

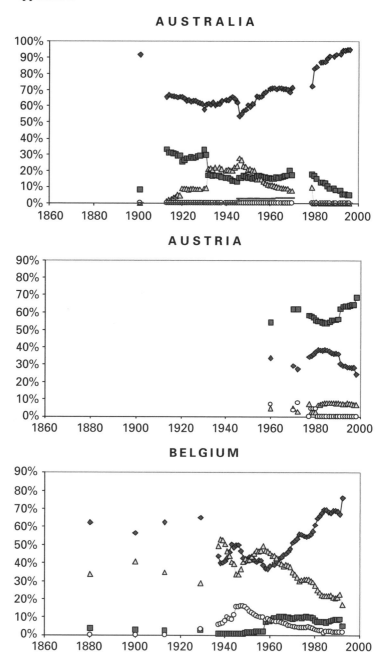

Figure A2.1. The four credit sectors in twenty-one countries
♦ all private banks (center and local), not including state-chartered
banks in the cases of Australia and the United States; ▪ local non-profit
banks; ○ postal savings and other state-run savings schemes; △ state
credit banks; – state-chartered banks in the cases of Australia and the
United States.

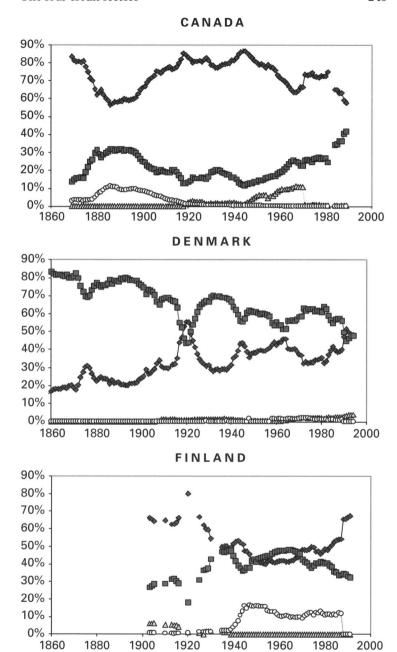

Figure A2.1. (cont.)

F R A N C E

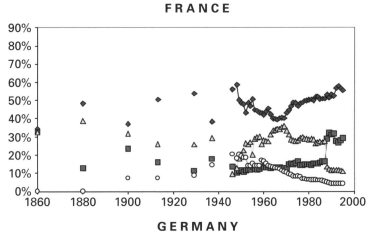

G E R M A N Y

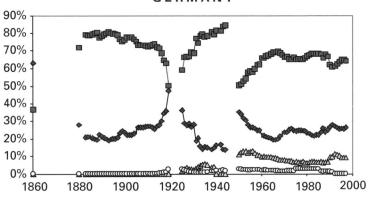

G R E E C E

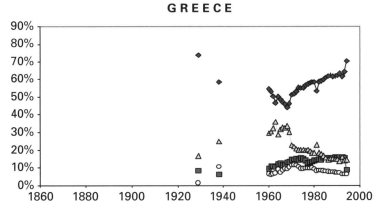

Figure A2.1. (*cont.*)

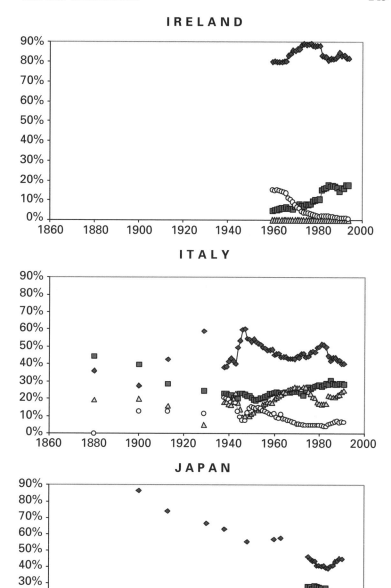

Figure A2.1. (*cont.*)

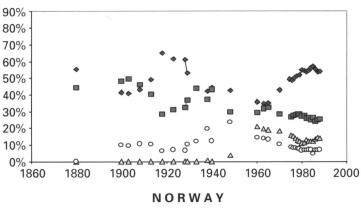

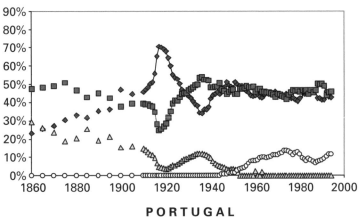

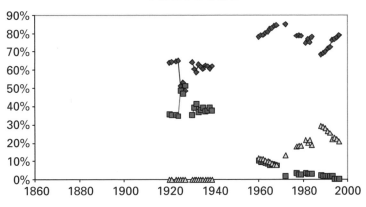

Figure A2.1. (*cont.*)

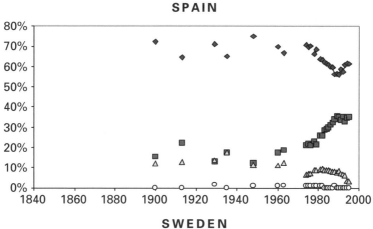

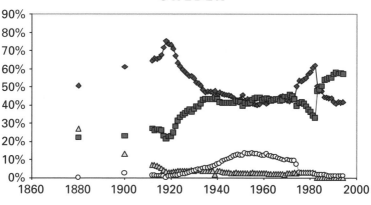

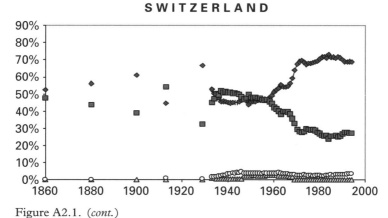

Figure A2.1. (*cont.*)

UNITED KINGDOM

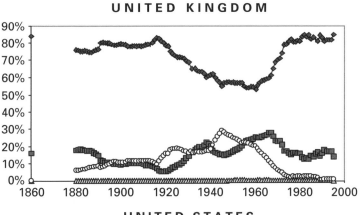

UNITED STATES

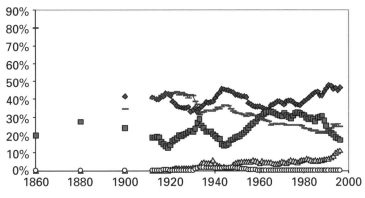

NEW ZEALAND

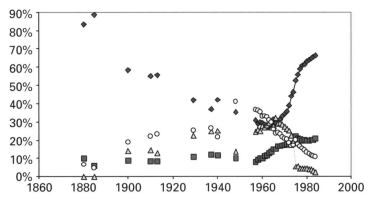

Figure A2.1. (*cont.*)

PORTUGAL: Nunes et al. 1994, *Estatística Financeiras* (various years).

SPAIN: Banco de España 1996, Martin-Aceña 1995.

SWEDEN: Sveriges Riksbank (various years), *Bankaktiebolagen* (various years), *Statistisk Arsbok för Sverige* (various years).

SWITZERLAND: Ritzmann 1973, Schweizerische Nationalbank (various years), *Statistisches Jahrbuch der Schweiz* (various years).

UK: Until 1959, commercial excludes colonial and foreign-owned banks with London offices. 1880–1966: Sheppard 1971. 1960–93: *Annual Abstract of Statistics* (various years), *Financial Statistics* (various years).

USA: 1896–1912: Board of Governors of the Federal Reserve System 1943, 1959. 1938–74: Board of Governors of the Federal Reserve System b (various years). 1955–87: Conference of State Bank Supervisors 1988. 1975–96: *Statistical Abstract of the United States*. 1986–96: data for commercial banks are estimated using the breakdown of principal assets in Board of Governors of the Federal Reserve System a (various years), with totals from FDIC 1991.

Appendix 3: A measure of state centralization

Definition

Levels of centralization were – and still are – not uniform across countries. Synthesizing different strands of macrohistory, Rokkan envisioned this map of Europe: at the center are the states located on the old trade-belt, stretching from Italy, crossing Switzerland, running along the Rhine toward the Low Countries, and then on to Scandinavia and the Hansean cities.[1] The high density of cities characteristic of this area made it impossible for centralized states to take root. Major state building, instead, took place on either side of the trade-belt – Sweden, Austria, Prussia, and Russia in the East; Britain and France in the West. Spain, a seaward state with a strong periphery, was an exception. Over time, state building proved stronger in the West, where the greater surge of commercial activity made it possible for state builders to extract resources easily convertible into currency, than in the East, where the only alternative partners for state builders were the owners of land, and the only resources that they could offer – food and manpower – were non-monetary.[2]

Meant for the eighteenth century, Rokkan's typology needs to be updated to the nineteenth. Political power remained decentralized in Switzerland and the United States. The French occupation of Spain and the Low Countries had a lasting centralizing effect, moving Belgium and the Netherlands into the same league as France and Britain. Its effect on Spain and Italy, however, was ambiguous. In both countries, centralization became associated with autocracy, and decentralization with republics and democracy. In both countries, fascism managed to impose a centralized rule, but its demise delegitimized centralization. The case of Germany is a bit more complex. The state that came out of unification – the empire – granted special privileges to the large states – Bavaria and

---

[1] Rokkan and Urwin 1983, p. 33.
[2] Rokkan's argument that trade kept trading states small and decentralized is echoed by Alesina and Spolaore 1997 who argue that increasing trade openness is associated with separatism, decentralization, or small size.

Württemberg. Although the debacle of World War I opened the way to a more centralized regime in the form of the Weimar Republic, centralization soon became associated with Nazi rule, and was then abandoned with the return of democracy in 1945.

The ex-English colonies developed in various directions according to no apparent logic. The United States rejected English centralizing autocracy, remaining a federal democracy. Loyal to the Crown, Canada, in contrast, was founded in 1850 as strong central state, a legacy of a colonial administration that was essentially a military apparatus. It is only over time that the confederal structure worked in the opposite direction to accommodate regional and linguistic diversity. A similar bifurcation occurred in Australasia, a set of seven dominions, which, by the turn of the century, rearranged themselves into two countries: New Zealand, which refused to join the Australian Commonwealth and thus became (or remained) a centralized state, and the six other states, which joined the Australian Commonwealth, a loose federation.

Limits: the weakness of a powerful variable

State institutions, like wealth, are a powerful constraint on the development of market institutions and regulatory policy, and state centralization is an aspect of state institutions. A powerful variable has advantages and drawbacks. Its main advantage is that it will correlate with many other variables. The drawback is that, by correlating *tout azimuth*, such a variable has multiple effects that are difficult to track, for they are indirect and sometimes cancel each other out. In the process of this study, I encountered two cases in which state centralization displayed inconsistent effects. First, on market segmentation in chapter 3: state centralization both reduced market segmentation by keeping local banks down and increased it by promoting state banks. Second, on stock market development in chapter 9: centralization favors capital mobility to the center, but hampers markets with state control over industry. Inconsistent effects of that sort reduce the policy relevance of the state centralization variable, but not its theoretical importance.

Measurement

State centralization is measured by the proportion of government revenues drained by the central government. I take out defense spending from central government expenditures since defense is essentially a central government item that varies in importance across countries according to circumstances extraneous to this study. I also take out social security transfers, which, irrespective of how they are distributed, leave government officials little room for maneuver.

Still, the fiscal decentralization variable presents the weakness of not weighing local expenditures according to the degree of discretion exercised by the local government; a substantial part of a local government's budget consists of transfers from the central government. To get a sense of how important this source of imprecision could be, I calculated two indices of fiscal decentralization: a *destination* index, which counts transfers as part of the destination government budget, and an *source* index, counting them as part of the originating government. The correlation between the two measures is high ($= 0.83$), justifying the use of one single index throughout this volume – the destination index. Note also that the OECD recently released systematic information on various degrees of local tax autonomy for nineteen countries, fourteen of which overlap with our dataset.[3] The correlation with the unadjusted revenue measure ($= - 0.77$) is good enough to justify using the more imprecise, yet more widely available, measure.

Subject to these caveats, it is possible to construct a measure of state centralization for a meaningful sample of countries for selected years during the past century. For each country, I divided the sum of central government receipts by the sum of all government receipts (social security payments excluded). I calculated this measure for years circa 1880, 1911, and 1930, and for the 1953–95 period. The exact formula for the latter period is of the form $(Central - Defense - Transfers_{C, P+L})/[(Central - Defense - Transfers_{C, P+L}) + (Provincial - Transfers_{P,C+L}) + (Local - Transfers_{L,C+P})]$, where *Central* stands for the central government, *Provincial* stands for any intermediate level of government between central and local, *Local* stands for local government, *Defense* stands for defense expenditures, $Transfers_{i,j}$ stands for transfers from level of government i to $j (i,j = C,P,L)$.

All available years are graphed in figure A3.1. Considering the oldest measure, circa 1880, the ordinal ranking matches Rokkan's qualitative assessment as amended above, with Belgium, France, and the Netherlands as most centralized, closely followed by Canada, Spain, and the United Kingdom. The Scandinavian countries and New Zealand are around the median. Italy and Germany belong to the decentralized category, along with Australia, Switzerland, and the United States, which show the lowest scores. After 1880, there was an almost imperceptible trend toward decentralization, except in Germany. World War I abruptly reversed this

---

[3] For each country, the OECD first provides "sub-central government taxes as % of total tax revenues" and then decomposes this figure into eight "types of tax autonomy." I used the decomposition to reweigh the first entry and create an adjusted figure of local tax autonomy. Note that the figures do not include governmental transfers; see OECD 1999, p. 26.

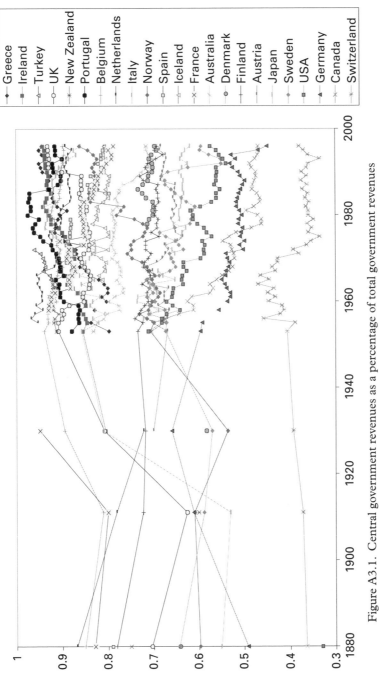

Figure A3.1. Central government revenues as a percentage of total government revenues

decentralizing trend for all the countries involved, Italy and the UK especially. World War II consolidated the centralizing trend, which peaked and then receded in the 1970s, earlier for decentralized countries, later for more centralized countries. Norway is the only country to show a steady centralizing trend, a clear artifact of the construction of the measure in light of the North Sea oil discoveries.

Data description and sources

For 1880, 1911, and 1930, I used central government revenues as percentage of general government revenues circa 1880, 1911, and 1930. Sources are: for Western Europe, excluding Spain, Flora 1983, p. 273. Data for Austria-Hungary could not be used, because of the exclusion of the non-Austrian part of the Empire. For 1913, for Spain, Bernis 1919, pp. 338, 347; for the United States, *Historical Statistics of the United States* 1975, p. 1119; for Canada, *Statistical Year-Book of Canada for 1889*, 1890, pp. 104, 117. Data for Australia are for 1907, Mitchell 1983, p. 802; *Official Year Book of the Commonwealth of Australia* 1908, p. 668. Data for New Zealand are for 1913, G. T. Bloomfield 1984, pp. 333, 352. For 1953 onward, the main source is *National Accounts* and the supplementary source, *Yearbook of National Accounts Statistics*.

Appendix 4: A measure of universal banking

Description and sources

Universal banking is measured by the ratio of own resources (capital, reserves) against individual deposits and savings. The numerator includes capital, reserves, and notes whenever appropriate. The denominator includes individual deposits and savings accounts. Unless otherwise noted, it excludes creditor current accounts, which exist for transaction purposes and are usually unremunerated. Interbank deposits (which usually constitute a relatively insignificant proportion of total liabilities) are excluded whenever possible. Data are for 1913 unless stated otherwise.

For the United Kingdom, 43 joint-stock banks of England and Wales, Sheppard 1971, p. 118. The numerator is "Paid-up capital and reserves." The denominator is "Deposits and other accounts"; it was not possible to separate current accounts from deposits. As a result, the ratio overstates the liquidity of UK banks.

For the United States, 7467 national banks, *Historical Statistics of the United States* 1975, Series X 634–55, p. 1025. The numerator is "Capital accounts"; the denominator is "Deposits" excluding "US government." It was not possible to separate current accounts from deposits. Consequently, the ratio overstates the liquidity of US banks, a bias that is further reinforced by the large number of banks included in the sample.

For Canada, all chartered banks, Urquhart and Buckley 1965, Series H 226-245, pp. 240–42. The numerator is "Capital and rest fund." The denominator includes "Notes in circulation," "Personal savings deposits," "Public notice deposits," and "Public demand deposits."

For Australia, 21 Australian trading banks, Butlin et al. 1971, pp. 114, 120, and 131. The numerator is "Shareholders' equity." The denominator includes "Bills in circulation" and "Deposits bearing interests."

For France, 4 *banques de dépôts* (Crédit Lyonnais, Société Générale, Comptoir d'escompte, Crédit industriel et commercial), archival document communicated to me in 1995 by Mr. Nougaret, Directeur des Archives Historiques du Crédit Lyonnais, Paris. The numerator is

"Dépôts," exclusive of "Comptes courants." The denominator is "Capital versé et réserves."

For Belgium, 3, among the 5, banks with the largest own resources in 1913 (Société Générale, Crédit Général Liègeois, Banque de Bruxelles; the other two largest banks were not included, the deviant Caisse Générale de Reports et de Dépôts because it was a pure deposit bank, and the Banque d'Outremer because I have no data), Chlepner 1930, pp. 96–99. The numerator includes "Capital" and "Réserves." The denominator includes "Obligations," "Dépôts à terme"; current accounts are excluded.

For Switzerland, 8 *grandes banques* (Société de banque suisse, Crédit Suisse, Banque populaire suisse, Union des banques suisses, Banque commerciale de Bâle, Banque fédérale [SA], Comptoir d'escompte de Genève, Société anonyme Leu & Co.), *La Suisse économique et sociale* 1927, pp. 326–27. The numerator includes "Capital versé et réserves." The denominator includes "Obligations," "Dépôts d'épargne," and "Autres dépôts"; creditor current accounts are excluded.

For Germany, 9 *Berliner Großbanken*, Deutsche Bundesbank 1976, table 1.01, pp. 56–59. The numerator includes "Kapital" and "Reserven." The denominator includes "Depositen," exclusive of creditor current accounts.

For Denmark, the 5 largest commercial banks, *Statistiske Undersøgelser 1969* 1969, pp. 23, 30, 32, 39, 58. The numerator includes "Aktiekapital" and "Reservefond." The denominator includes "Folio, indlån, kontokurant og sparekasseindskud"; it includes current accounts, overstating the liquidity of Danish banks.

For Sweden, all enskilda banks, *Statistisk Arsbok för Sverige* 1914, tab. 97, p. 115. The numerator includes "Fonder." The denominator includes "Innestäende pä sparkasseräkning" and "Innestäende pä depositions- och kapitalräkning."

For Norway, 119 commercial banks (in 1914), *Historisk Statistisk: 1968* 1975, tab. 252, pp. 492–93. The numerator includes "Aksjekapital" and "Fond." The denominator includes "Innskott på tid" (deposits subject to notice); it does not include "Innskott på anfordring" (demand deposits), most likely to be current accounts.

For the Netherlands, 5 largest (*algemene*) banks (Amsterdamsche Bank, Incassobank, Nederlandsche Handelmaatschappij, Rotterdamsche Bank, and Twentsche Bank), Nederlandsche Bank n.v. 1987, tab. 3c, p. 43. The numerator includes "Kapital en reserves." The denominator includes "deposito's" and "spaargelden" (current accounts excluded).

For Austria-Hungary, 4 largest Viennese great banks involved with the financing and founding of industrial firms (Österreichische Creditanstalt,

Table A4.1. *The equity–deposit ratio, 1913*

Country	Ratio	Country	Ratio
Spain	5.00	France	0.43
Austria-Hungary[a]	2.00	Australia	0.35
Netherlands	1.58	Denmark	0.32
Italy	0.88	Norway	0.25
Germany	0.73	United States	0.25
Belgium	0.72	Canada	0.19
Switzerland	0.56	United Kingdom	0.10
Sweden	0.45		

[a] Austria and the Czech Lands.

Allgemeine Bodenkreditanstalt, Niederösterreichische Escompte-Gesellschaft, and Wiener Bankverein), Nötel 1984, 154. The numerator includes share capital and reserves. The denominator includes deposits (current accounts excluded). I used Rudolph's 10:57 ratio to break down individual deposits from current accounts (Rudolph 1976, p. 84). That breakdown was established for the six largest Viennese great banks in 1912.

For Italy, 5 major commercial banks (Banca Commerciale Italiana, Credito Italiano, Banco di Roma, Societa Bancaria Italiana, Credito Provinciale); for the Credito Italiano, Confalonieri 1982, vol. I, p. 610; for the Banca Commerciale, Confalonieri 1976, p. 538; Banco di Roma, archival document; Credito Provinciale, archival document; Societa Bancaria, archival document. The numerator includes "Capitale sociale" and "Fondi di riserva." The denominator includes "Depositi in conto corrente ed a risparmio"; it was not possible to exclude current accounts from deposits. Consequently, the ratio overstates the liquidity of Italian banks.

For Spain, 3 Catalan (Banco de Barcelona, Sociedad Catalana General de Crédito, Banco de Cataluña), 3 Basque (Banco de Bilbao, Banco del Comercio, Banco de Vizcaya), and 1 Madrid (Banco de Castilla), Tortella 1974, pp. 234, 274, 286, 326, 394, 408, 418. The numerator includes "Capital desembolsado" and "Reserva." The denominator includes "Depósitos" and "Cuentas de ahorro"; creditor current accounts are excluded.

Appendix 5: Dataset for chapter 9

Table A5.1. *Dataset for chapter 9*

Country	(1)	(2)	(3)	(4)	(5)	(6)	(7)	(8)
Australia	0.71	1	0.92	0.50	1.26	17,280	2.55	0.11
Austria	0.68	0	0.36	0.17	2.11	20,550	5.56	0.15
Belgium	0.91	0	0.69	0.37	2.78	19,460	4.77	0.15
Canada	0.48	1	0.58	0.47	1.29	20,130	4.17	0.11
Denmark	0.70	0	0.47	0.37	2.46	24,680	4.69	0.16
Finland	0.72	0	0.67	0.12	2.68	23,490	7.02	0.14
France	0.81	0	0.53	0.29	2.63	20,500	6.95	0.14
Germany	0.48	0	0.27	0.26	1.76	21,490	6.98	0.15
Greece	0.95	0	0.62	0.14	3.87	8,290	5.88	0.14
Italy	0.91	0	0.40	0.15	3.95	18,850	8.34	0.15
Japan	0.64	0	0.45	0.93	1.29	27,200	2.90	0.13
Netherlands	0.89	0	0.54	0.49	2.28	18,870	6.02	0.13
New Zealand	0.92	1	0.66	0.34	1.66	12,050	7.62	0.11
Norway	0.83	0	0.41	0.21	3.19	26,800	5.89	0.16
Portugal	0.92	0	0.70	0.12	2.83	7,090	3.44	0.14
Spain	0.81	0	0.56	0.26	2.59	12,560	6.13	0.14
Sweden	0.62	0	0.42	0.44	1.51	25,620	7.75	0.18
Switzerland	0.38	0	0.70	0.77	2.08	34,060	5.40	0.15
UK	0.93	1	0.83	1.02	0.55	16,520	4.91	0.16
USA	0.56	1	0.46	0.61	0.85	22,800	3.33	0.13
Mean	0.74	0.25	0.69	0.40	2.18	19,915	5.52	0.14
Std. Dev.	0.17	0.44	0.18	0.26	0.92	6,556	1.67	0.02

Data description and sources: All data are for 1991.

(1) *State centralization* is described in appendix 3.

(2) *Common law* is a dummy variable, coded "1" for countries of common law origins, "0" otherwise.

(3) *Money center banks* is described in appendix 2.

(4) *Stock market capitalization* was calculated by FIBV *Annual Report 1992*. It is described as "the total number of issued shares of domestic companies, including their several classes, multiplied by their

respective prices." The figure excludes investment funds and "companies whose only business goal is to hold shares of other listed companies." The figures are expressed in percent of GDP. For Greece and Portugal, I used data from *Global Financial Data* 2000.

(5) *State control* is a ranking of twenty-one countries constructed by Nicoletti et al. (1999, p. 74) and described as capturing "public ownership" (in turn taking into account the "size" and "scope" of the public sector, "control of public enterprises by legislative bodies," and "special voting rights") and "(state) involvement in business operation" (in turn including "price controls" and "use of command and control regulations").

(6) *GNP per capita* in current US$: source is *World Development Indicators*.

(7) *State public pensions* in percent of GDP comprises all cash expenditures on old-age pensions within the public sphere; it is category 1.1 of the *Social Expenditure Database 1980–1996*.

(8) *Population aged 65 and above* in percent of total population was calculated using data from *World Development Indicators*.

Bibliography

Ackland, Robert and Ian R. Harper. 1992. "Financial Deregulation in Australia: Boon or Bane?" In *Microeconomic Reform in Australia*, edited by Peter J. Forsyth, pp. 45–71. St. Leonards, Australia: Allen & Unwin.

Akerlof, G. A. 1970. "The Market for Lemons: Qualitative Uncertainty and the Market Mechanism." *Quarterly Journal of Economics* 84: 488–500.

Albert, Elisabeth. 1995. "Les banques populaires de 1917 aux années 1950." In Lévy-Leboyer 1995, pp. 59–73.

Albrecht, Catherine. 1989. "Nationalism and Municipal Savings Banks in Bohemia Before 1914." *Slovene Studies* 11, 1–2: 57–64.

1990. "The Decision to Establish Savings Banks in Bohemia, 1825–1870." In Komlos 1990a, pp. 75–87.

Alesina, A. and E. Spolaore. 1997. "On the Number and Size of Nations." *Quarterly Journal of Economics* 112, 4: 1027–56.

Alt, James E. and Michael J. Gilligan. 1994. "The Political Economy of Trading States: Factor Specificity, Collective Action Problems, and Political Institutions." *Journal of Political Philosophy* 2: 165–92.

Alt, James E., Fredrik Carlsen, Per Heum, and Kåre Johansen. 1999. "Asset Specificity and the Political Behavior of Firms: Lobbying for Subsidies in Norway." *International Organization* 53, 1: 99–116.

Alt, James E., Jeffry Frieden, Michael Gilligan, Dani Rodrik, and Ronald Rogowski. 1996. "The Political Economy of International Trade: Enduring Puzzles and Agenda for Inquiry." *Comparative Political Studies* 29, 6: 689–717.

Americi, Laurence. 1997. "Les Caisses d'épargne françaises face aux crises (1850–1914)." In Vogler 1991b, pp. 103–12.

Andrews, David M. 1994. "Capital Mobility and State Autonomy: Toward a Structural Theory of International Monetary Relations." *International Studies Quarterly* 38: 193–218.

Annuaire Statistique de la Belgique. Institut National de Statistique. Ministère des Affaires Economiques.

Annual Abstract of Statistics. Central Statistical Office. Government Statistical Service. London: Her Majesty's Stationery Office.

Ashton, T. S. 1945. "The Bill of Exchange and Private Banks in Lancashire, 1790–1830." *Economic History Review* 15, 1: 25–35.

Australian Financial System: Interim Report of the Committee of Inquiry. May 1980. Canberra: Australian Government Publishing Service.

Bagehot, Walter. 1991 [1873]. *Lombard Street*. Philadelphia: Orion.

Bagnasco, Arnaldo. 1977. *Tre Italie*. Bologna: Il Mulino.

Bagnasco, Arnaldo and Charles F. Sabel, eds. 1995. *Small and Medium-Size Enterprises*. London: Pinter.

Bairoch, Paul. 1976. *Commerce extérieur et développement économique de l'Europe au XIXe siècle*. Paris: Mouton.

1993. *Economics and World History: Myths and Paradoxes*. Chicago: University of Chicago Press.

Bairoch, Paul and Maurice Lévy-Leboyer, eds. 1981. *Disparities in Economic Development Since the Industrial Revolution*. London: Macmillan.

Banca d'Italia. a. *Bolletino della Banca d'Italia*. Rome: Banca d'Italia.

Banca d'Italia. b. *Relazione annuale della Banca d'Italia*. Rome: Banca d'Italia.

Banco de España. 1996. *Cuentas financieras de la economía española 1986–1995*. Madrid: Banco de España.

Banerjee, A. V., T. Besley, and T. W. Guinnane. 1994. "Thy Neighbour's Keeper: The Design of a Credit Cooperative with Theory and a Test." *Quarterly Journal of Economics* May: 490–515.

Bank of Japan. *Economic Statistics Monthly*. Statistics Department.

Bank Profitability. Paris: OECD.

Bankaktiebolagen Fonkommissionärerna Fondbörsen och VPC. Sveriges officiella statistik. Bankinspektionen. Stockholm.

Bankstatistikk. Norges Offisielle Statistikk XI. 208. Oslo: Statistisk Sentralbyrå.

Banque de France. a. *Bulletin trimestriel de la Banque de France*. Paris.

Banque de France. b. *Statistiques monétaires et financières annuelles*. Paris.

Bänziger, Hugo. 1985. "Vom Sparerschutz zum Gläubigerschutz – die Entstehung des Bankengesetzes im Jahre 1934." In *Jubiläeumsschrift: 50 Jahre eidgenössische Bankenaufsicht*, edited by Urs Zulauf, pp. 3–81. Zürich: Schulthess.

Barrett Whale, P. 1968 [1930]. *Joint Stock Banking in Germany: A Study of the German Creditbanks Before and After the War*. London: Frank Cass & Co.

Baskin, Jonathon B. and Paul J. Miranti, Jr. 1997. *A History of Corporate Finance*. Cambridge: Cambridge University Press.

Bayliss, B. T. and A. A. S. Butt Philip. 1980. *Capital Markets and Industrial Investment in Germany and France*. Westmead: Saxon House.

Beckerath, Herbert von. 1954. *Grossindustrie und Gesellschaftsordnung*. Tübingen: J. C. B. Mohr.

Beckhart, B. Haggott, ed. 1954. *Banking Systems*. New York: Columbia University Press.

Beer, Samuel H. 1982. *Britain Against Itself*. New York: Norton.

Benston, George J. 1990. *The Separation of Commercial and Investment Banking*. London: Macmillan.

Benz, Gérard. 1987. "Un aspect du financement des chemins de fer en Suisse par le capital étranger." *Schweizerische Zeitschrift für Geschichte* 37, 2: 169–85.

Berendsen, Christiaan. 1999. "Global Ambitions, ABN AMRO Bank 1990–1999." In *Worldwide Banking: ABN AMRO Bank 1824–1999*, edited by Joh. De Vries et al., pp. 449–87. Amsterdam: ABN AMRO Bank.

Berger, A. N. and G. Udell. 1995. "Relationship Lending and Lines of Credit in Small Firm Finance." *Journal of Business* 65, 3: 351–81.

Berger, A. N., R. S. Demsetz, and P. E. Strahan. 1998a. *The Consolidation of the Financial Services Industry: Causes, Consequences, and Implications for the Future.* Bank of New York, Staff Reports 55, December 1998.

Berger, A. N., A. K. Kashyap, and J. M. Scalise. 1995. *The Transformation of the US Banking Industry: What a Long, Strange Trip It's Been.* Brookings Papers on Economic Activity 2. Washington, DC: Brookings Institution.

Berger, A. N., A. Saunders, J. M. Scalise, and G. Udell. 1998b. "The Effects of Bank Mergers and Acquisitions on Small Business Lending." *Journal of Financial Economics* 50: 187–229.

Bernis, Francisco. 1919. *La Hacienda Española.* Barcelona: Editorial Minerva.

Bingham, T. R. G. 1985. *Banking and Monetary Policy.* Paris: OECD.

BIS (Bank of International Settlements). 1989. *Payment Systems in Eleven Developed Countries.* Basle: BIS.

Bloomfield, Arthur L. 1968. *Patterns of Fluctuation in International Investment Before 1914.* Princeton Studies in International Finance No. 21. Princeton University.

Bloomfield, G. T. 1984. *New Zealand: A Handbook of Historical Statistics.* Boston: G. K. Hall & Co.

Board of Governors of the Federal Reserve System. a. *Annual Report.* Washington, DC: Board of Governors of the Federal Reserve System.

b. *Federal Reserve Bulletin.* Washington, DC: Board of Governors of the Federal Reserve System.

1943. *Banking and Monetary Statistics.* Washington, DC: Board of Governors of the Federal Reserve System.

1959. *All-Bank Statistics: United States, 1896–1955.* Washington, DC: Board of Governors of the Federal Reserve System.

Bollen, Kenneth A. and Robert Jackman. 1990. "Regression Diagnostics: An Expository Treatment of Outliers and Influential Cases." In *Modern Methods of Data Analysis,* edited by John Fox and J. Scott Long, pp. 257–91. Newbury Park, CA: Sage.

Borchardt, Knut. 1961. "Zur Frage des Kapitalmangels in der erstern Hälfte des 19. Jahrhunderts in Deutschland." *Jahrbucher für Nationalökonomie und Statistik* 173: 401–21.

1971. "Realkredit- und Pfandbriefmarkt im Wandel von 100 Jahren." In *100 Jahre Rheinische Hypothekenbank,* pp. 102–96. Frankfurt am Main: Fritz Knapp Verlag.

Bordo, Michael D. and Finn Kydland. 1995. "The Gold Standard as a Rule: An Essay in Exploration." *Explorations in Economic History* 32: 423–64.

Bordo, Michael D. and Hugh Rockoff. 1995. *The Gold Standard as a Good Housekeeping Seal of Approval.* National Bureau of Economic Research Working Paper No. 5340. November.

Bordo, Michael D. and Anna J. Schwartz. 1994. *The Specie Standard as a Contingent Rule: Some Evidence for Core and Peripheral Countries, 1880–1990.* National Bureau of Economic Research Working Paper No. 4860. November.

Bordo, Michael D. and Richard Sylla. 1995. *Anglo-American Financial Systems: Institutions and Markets in the Twentieth Century.* New York: Irwin.

Bordo, Michael D., Barry Eichengreen, and Jongwoo Kim. 1998. *Was There Really an Earlier Period of International Financial Integration Comparable to Today?* National Bureau of Economic Research Working Paper No. 6738. September.

Born, Karl Erich. 1983 [1977]. *International Banking in the 19th and 20th Centuries.* Leamington Spa: Berg Publishers.

Bouvier, Jean. 1968. *Naissance d'une banque: le Crédit Lyonnais.* Paris: Flammarion.

———— 1973. *Un siècle de banque française.* Paris: Hachette.

———— 1988. "The Banque de France and the State from 1850 to the Present Day." In *Central Banks' Independence in Historical Perspective*, edited by Gianni Toniolo, pp. 72–104. Berlin: Walter de Gruyter.

Boyd, J. H. and M. Gertler. 1993. *US Commercial Banking: Trends, Cycles and Policy.* C. V. Starr Center for Applied Economics. New York University, Economics Research Report No. 93–19.

Boyer, Robert and Daniel Drache, eds. 1996. *States Against Markets: The Limits of Globalization.* London: Routledge.

Brewer, John. 1989. *The Sinews of Power: War, Money and the English State, 1688–1783.* New York: Knopf.

Bröker, G. 1989. *Competition in Banking.* Paris: OECD.

Broz, J. Lawrence. 1997. *The International Origins of the Federal Reserve System.* Ithaca: Cornell University Press.

———— 1998. "The Origins of Central Banking: Solutions to the Free-Rider Problem." *International Organization* 52, 2: 231–68.

Brück, C. et al., eds. 1995. *Les Caisses d'épargne en Europe*, vol. I, *Les douze pays de l'Union européenne.* Paris: Les éditions de l'épargne.

Bryant, Ralph. 1987. *International Financial Intermediation.* Washington, DC: Brookings Institution.

Bunbury, D. 1997. "The Public Purse and State Finance: Government Savings Banks in the Era of Nation Building, 1867–1900." *Canadian Historical Review* 78, 4: 566–98.

Butlin, S. J., A. R. Hall, and R. C. White. 1971. *Australian Banking and Monetary Statistics 1817–1945.* Reserve Bank of Australia. Occasional Paper No. 4A. Sydney.

Cahill, J. R. 1913. *Report to the Board of Agriculture and Fisheries of an Inquiry into Agricultural Credit and Agricultural Cooperation in Germany.* London: His Majesty's Stationery Office.

Calder, Kent E. 1993. *Strategic Corporatism: Private Business and Public Purpose in Japanese Industrial Finance.* Princeton: Princeton University Press.

Calomiris, Charles W. 1995. "The Costs of Rejecting Universal Banking: American Finance in the German Mirror, 1870–1914." In *Coordination and Information: Historical Perspectives on the Organization of Enterprise*, edited by Naomi R. Lamoreaux and Daniel M. G. Raff, pp. 257–315. Chicago: University of Chicago Press.

Cameron, Rondo, ed. 1967. *Banking in the Early Stages of Industrialization: A Study in Comparative Economic History*. New York: Oxford University Press.
  ed. 1972. *Banking and Economic Development: Some Lessons of History*. New York: Oxford University Press.
  1991. "Introduction." In Cameron and Bovykin 1991, pp. 3–21.
  1992 [1965]. "Theoretical Bases of a Comparative Study on the Role of Financial Institutions in the Early Stages of Industrialization." Reproduced in *Financing Industrialization*, vol. I, edited by Rondo Cameron, pp. 1–20. Aldershot: Edward Elgar.

Cameron, Rondo and V. I. Bovykin, eds. 1991. *International Banking, 1870–1914*. New York: Oxford University Press.

Canada Year Book. Dominion Bureau of Statistics. Ottawa: Edmond Cloutier.

Capie, Forrest and Michael Collins. 1997. "Deficient Suppliers? Commercial Banks in the United Kingdom, 1870–1980." In Cottrell et al. 1997, pp. 164–83.

Capie, Forrest and Ghila Rodrik-Bali. 1982. "Concentration in British Banking 1870–1920." *Business History* 24: 280–92.

Caprio, Gerard Jr. and Dimitri Vittas, eds. 1997. *Reforming Financial Systems: Historical Implications for Policy*. Cambridge: Cambridge University Press.

Caranza, Cesare and Carlo Cottarelli. 1987. "Financial Innovation in Italy: A Lop-Sided Process." In *Changing Money: Financial Innovation in Developed Countries*, edited by Marcello de Cecco, pp. 172–211. Oxford: Basil Blackwell.

Cassis, Y., ed. 1992. *Finance and Financiers in European History 1880–1960*. Cambridge: Cambridge University Press.

Cassis, Youssef, Gerald D. Feldman, and Ulf Olsson, eds. 1995. *The Evolution of Financial Institutions and Markets in Twentieth-Century Europe*. Aldershot: Scholar Press.

Central Bank of Ireland. *Annual Report*. Dublin: Central Bank of Ireland.

Ceriani, L. 1962. "Italy. I. The Commercial Banks and Financial Institutions." In *Banking in Western Europe*, edited by R. S. Sayers, pp. 124–54. Oxford: Clarendon Press.

Cerny, Philip G. 1989. "The 'Little Big Bang' in Paris: Financial Market Deregulation in a Dirigiste System." *European Journal of Political Research* 17: 169–92.

Cesarini, Francesco. 1994. "The Relationship Between Banks and Firms in Italy: A Banker's View." *Review of Economic Conditions in Italy* 48, 1: 29–50.

Chhibber, Pradeep and Ken Kollman. 1998. "Party Aggregation and the Number of Parties in India and the United States." *American Political Science Review* 92, 2: 329–42.

Chlepner, B. S. 1926. *La banque en Belgique: étude historique et économique*. Brussels: Lamertin.
  1930. *Le marché financier belge depuis cent ans*. Brussels: Librairie Falk Fils.
  1943. *Belgian Banking and Banking Theory*. Washington, DC: Brookings Institution.

Cleveland, Harold van B. and Thomas F. Huertas. 1985. *Citibank 1812–1970*. Cambridge, MA: Harvard University Press.

Cohen, Benjamin J. 1996. "Phoenix Risen: The Resurgence of Global Finance."
    World Politics 48, 2: 268–96.
    1998. *The Geography of Money*. Ithaca: Cornell University Press.
Cohen, Jon S. 1967. "Financing Industrialization in Italy, 1894–1914: The
    Partial Transformation of a Late-Comer." *Journal of Economic History* 27,
    3 (September): 363–82.
Coleman, James S. 1990. *Foundations of Social Theory*. Cambridge, MA: Harvard
    University Press.
Coleman, William D. 1993. "Reforming Corporatism: The French Banking
    Policy Community, 1941–1990." *West European Politics* 16, 2: 122–43.
Collins, Michael. 1991. *Banks and Industrial Finance in Britain, 1800–1939*.
    London: Macmillan.
Commission Bancaire et Financière. 1990. *Statistiques 1990*. Brussels: Commis-
    sion Bancaire et Financière.
Confalioneri, Antonio. 1976. *Banca e industria in Italia (1894–1906)*, vol. III.
    Milan: Banca Commerciale Italiana.
    1982. *Banca e industria in Italia della crisi del 1907 all'agosto 1914*. 2 vols. Milan:
    Banca Commerciale Italiana.
Conference of State Bank Supervisors. 1988. *A Profile of State-Chartered Banks*.
    12th edn. Washington, DC: Conference of State Bank Supervisors.
Conseil National du Crédit. *Rapport Annuel*. Paris.
Conti, Giuseppe. 1993. "Finanza di impresa e capitale di rischio in Italia
    (1870–1939)." *Rivista di storia economica* 10, 3: 307–32.
Conti, Giuseppe and Giovanni Ferri. 1997. "Banche locali e sviluppo economico
    decentrato." In *Storia del capitalismo italiano dal dopoguerra a oggi*, edited by
    Fabrizio Barca, pp. 429–65. Rome: Donzelli editore.
Cottrell, P. L. 1980. *Industrial Finance 1830–1914: The Finance and Organization
    of English Manufacturing Industry*. London: Methuen.
    1992. "The Domestic Commercial Banks and the City of London,
    1870–1939." In Cassis 1992, pp. 39–62.
Cottrell, P. L. and Lucy Newton. 1999. "Banking Liberalization in England and
    Wales, 1826–1844." In Sylla et al. 1999, pp. 75–117.
Cottrell, P. L., Alice Teichova, and Takeshi Yuzawa, eds. 1997. *Finance in the Age
    of the Corporate Economy*. Aldershot: Ashgate.
Covill, Laura. 1998. "Landesbank Reform Hitch." *The Banker* November: 51–53.
Cox, Robert W. 1993. "Gramsci, Hegemony and International Relations: An
    Essay in Method." In Gill 1993, pp. 49–66.
Danthine, Jean-Pierre, Francesco Giavazzi, Zavier Vives, and Ernst-Ludwig
    von Thadden. 1999. *The Future of European Banking*. London: Centre for
    Economic Policy Research.
Davis, James A. 1985. *The Logic of Causal Order*. Beverly Hills: Sage Publications.
Davis, K. T. 1985. "Thrift Institutions." In *Australia's Financial Institution and
    Markets*, edited by M. K. Lewis and R. H. Wallace. Melbourne: Longman
    Cheshire.
Davis, Lance E. 1960. "The New England Textile Mills and the Capital Markets:
    A Study of Industrial Borrowing, 1840–1860." *Journal of Economic History*
    20 (March): 1–30.

Davis, Philip. 1995. *Pension Funds: Retirement-Income Security and Capital Markets: An International Perspective*. Oxford: Clarendon Press.

De Boissieu, Christian. 1990. "Recent Developments of the French Financial System: An Overview." In *Banking in France*, edited by Christian de Boissieu, pp. 1–25. London: Routledge.

De Cecco, Marcello. 1974. *Money and Empire*. Oxford: Basil Blackwell.

    1983. *Italian Monetary Policy in the 1980s*. Working Paper No. 64. European University Institute.

    ed. 1987a. *Changing Money: Financial Innovation in Developed Countries*. Oxford: Basil Blackwell.

    1987b. "Financial Innovations and Monetary Theory." In de Cecco 1987a, pp. 1–9.

De Long, J. Bradford. 1991. "Did J. P. Morgan's Men Add Value? An Economist's Perspective on Financial Capitalism." In *Inside the Business Enterprise: Historical Perspectives on the Use of Information*, edited by Peter Temin, pp. 205–36. Chicago: University of Chicago Press.

Deeg, Richard E. 1992. "Banks and the State in Germany: The Critical Role of Subnational Institutions in Economic Governance." Ph.D. diss., MIT, Cambridge, MA.

    1997. "Economic Globalization and the Shifting Boundaries of German Federalism." *Publius* 26, 1: 27–52.

    1999. *Finance Capitalism Unveiled: Banks and the German Political Economy*. Ann Arbor: University of Michigan Press.

Deeg, Richard and Susanne Lütz. 2000. "Internationalization and Financial Federalism: The United States and Germany at the Crossroads." *Comparative Political Studies* 33, 3: 374–405.

Deutsche Bundesbank. *Monatsberichte der Deutschen Bundesbank*. Frankfurt.

    1976. *Deutsches Geld- und Bankwesen in Zahlen, 1876–1975*. Frankfurt am Main: Fritz Knapp.

Diamond, Douglas W. 1984. "Financial Intermediation and Delegated Monitoring." *Review of Economic Studies* 51, 166: 393–414.

    1991. "Monitoring and Reputation: The Choice Between Bank Loans and Directly Placed Debt." *Journal of Political Economy* 99, 4: 689–721.

Dickson, P. G. M. 1967. *The Financial Revolution in England: A Study in the Development of Public Credit, 1688–1756*. London: Macmillan.

Diwok, Fritz. 1982. *Struktur des Bankwesens in Österreich*. Frankfurt am Main: Fritz Knapp.

Donaubauer, K. A. 1988. *Privatbankiers und Bankenkonzentration in Deutschland von der Mitte des 19. Jahrhunderts bis 1932*. Frankfurt am Main: F. Knapp.

Downs, Anthony. 1957. *An Economic Theory of Democracy*. New York: Harper and Row.

Drees, Burkhard and Ceyla Pazarbasioglu. 1995. *The Nordic Banking Crises: Pitfalls in Financial Liberalization?* Working Paper 95/61. International Monetary Fund.

Drummond, Ian M. 1991a. "Banks and Banking in Canada and Australia." In Cameron and Bovykin 1991, pp. 189–213.

    1991b. "Why Canadian Banks Did Not Collapse in the 1930s." In Harold James et al. 1991, pp. 232–50.

Duet, Daniel. 1991. *Les Caisses d'Epargne*. Paris: Presses Universitaires de France.

Dunning, John H. 1992. *Multinational Enterprises and the Global Economy*. New York: Addison-Wesley.

Edelstein, Michael. 1982. *Overseas Investment in the Age of High Imperialism: The United Kingdom, 1850–1914*. New York: Columbia University Press.

Edwards, Jeremy and Sheilagh Ogilvie. 1996. "Universal Banks and German Industrialization: A Reappraisal." *Economic History Review* 49, 3: 427–46.

Egge, A. 1983. "Transformation of Bank Structures in the Industrial Period: The Case of Norway 1830–1914." *Journal of European Economic History* 12, 2: 271–94.

Eisfeld, C. 1916. *Das niederländische Bankwesen*. The Hague: Martinus Nijhoff.

Emery, H. C. 1908. "Ten Years of Regulation of the Stock Exchange in Germany." *Yale Review* May: 5–23.

Engberg, Holger L. 1981. *Mixed Banking and Economic Growth in Germany, 1850–1931*. New York: Arno Press.

Estatística Financeiras. Instituto Nacional de Estatística. Portugal.

European Commission. 1989. *First Survey on State Aids in the European Union in the Manufacturing and Certain Other Sectors*. Brussels: European Commission.

1990. *Second Survey on State Aids in the European Union in the Manufacturing and Certain Other Sectors*. Brussels: European Commission.

1992. *Third Survey on State Aids in the European Community in the Manufacturing and Certain Other Sectors*. Brussels: European Commission.

1995. *Fourth Survey on State Aids in the European Union in the Manufacturing and Certain Other Sectors*. Brussels: European Commission.

1997a. *Communication from the Commission. European Capital Markets for Small and Medium-Sized Enterprises: Prospects and Potential Obstacles to Progress*. 05/05. Brussels: European Commission.

1997b. *European Economy. Supplement A*. No. 7, July. Brussels: European Commission.

1997c. *European Economy. Supplement A. Economic Trends*. No. 12, December. Brussels: European Commission.

European Commission, DGII. 1998. Business Accounts Harmonised Databank (BACH). Brussels.

FDIC (Federal Deposit Insurance Corporation). 1991. *Historical Statistics on Banking. A Statistical History of the United States Banking Industry: 1934–1991*. Washington, DC: FDIC.

Feinstein, C., ed. 1995. *Banking, Currency, and Finance in Europe Between the Wars*. Oxford: Clarendon Press.

Feldman, Gerald D. 1991. "Banks and the Problem of Capital Shortage in Germany, 1918–1923." In Harold James et al. 1991, pp. 49–79.

FIBV (International Federation of Stock Exchanges). *Annual Report*. Paris: FIBV.

Financial Institutions. Quarterly. Ottawa: Statistics Canada.

Financial Statistics. Central Statistical Office. London: Her Majesty's Stationery Office.

Financial Statistics: Methodological Supplement. Paris: OECD.

Fitch-IBCA. 2001. *BankScope*. CD-ROM, update 129.2. London: Bureau van Dijk.

Flora, P. 1983. *State, Economy, and Society in Western Europe, 1815–1975*, vol. I. London: Macmillan.

Fohlin, Caroline. 1997. "Universal Banking Networks in Pre-war Germany: New Evidence from Company Financial Data." *Research in Economics* 51, 3: 201–25.

Forsyth, D. J. and T. Notermans, eds. 1997. *Regime Changes: Macroeconomic Policy and Financial Regulation in Europe from the 1930s to the 1990s*. Providence, RI: Berghahn Books.

Francke, Hans-Hermann and Michael Hudson. 1984. *Banking and Finance in West Germany*. London: Croom Helm.

Freixas, Xavier and Jean-Charles Rochet. 1998. *Microeconomics of Banking*. Cambridge, MA: MIT Press.

Frieden, J. 1991. "Invested Interests: The Politics of National Economic Policies in a World of Global Finance." *International Organization* 45: 425–52.

Frieden, J. and R. Rogowski. 1996. "The Impact of the International Economy on National Policies: An Analytical Overview." In *Internationalization and Domestic Politics*, edited by R. O. Keohane and H. V. Milner, pp. 25–47. New York: Cambridge University Press.

Fries, Steven M. 1993. *Japanese Banks and the Asset Price "Bubble."* Working Paper 93/85. International Monetary Fund.

Frowen, Stephen F. and Dietmar Kath. 1992. *Monetary Policy and Financial Innovations in Five Industrial Countries*. London: Macmillan.

Fujita, Masahisa, Paul Krugman, and Anthony J. Venables. 1999. *The Spatial Economy: Cities, Regions and International Trade*. Cambridge, MA: MIT Press.

Fukuyama, Francis. 1995. *Trust: The Social Virtues and the Creation of Prosperity*. London: Hamish Hamilton.

Gall, Lothar. 1995. "The Deutsche Bank from Its Founding to the Great War 1870–1914." In *The Deutsche Bank, 1870–1995*, edited by Lothar Gall et al., pp. 1–129. London: Weidenfeld & Nicolson.

Gallarotti, Giulio M. 1995. *The Anatomy of the Gold Standard: The Classical Gold Standard, 1880–1914*. New York: Oxford University Press.

Ganne, Bernard. 1995. "France: Behind Small and Medium-Size Enterprises Lies the State." In Bagnasco and Sabel 1995, pp. 115–33.

Gardener, Edward P. M. and Philip Molyneux. 1990. *Changes in Western European Banking*. London: Unwin Hyman.

Garofalo, Paolo and Daniela Colonna. 1999. "Statistiche creditizie." In *Stabilita e sviluppo negli anni cinquanta*, vol. III, *Politica bancaria e struttura del sistema finanziario*, edited by Franco Cotula, pp. 885–941. Rome-Bari: Laterza.

Gerschenkron, Alexander. 1962 [1952]. *Economic Backwardness in Historical Perspective: A Book of Essays*. Cambridge, MA: Belknap.

Gertler, Mark and Simon Gilchrist. 1994. "Monetary Policy, Business Cycles, and the Behavior of Small Manufacturing Firms." *Quarterly Journal of Economics* 109, 2: 309–40.

Gill, Stephen, ed. 1993. *Gramsci, Historical Materialism and International Relations*. Cambridge: Cambridge University Press.

Gill, Stephen and David Law. 1993. "Global Hegemony and the Structural Power of Capital." In Gill 1993, pp. 93–125.

Gille, Bertrand. 1965–67. *Histoire de la Maison Rothschild.* 2 vols. Geneva: Droz.

Global Financial Data. CD-ROM, update January 2000. Los Angeles: Global Financial Data.

Goldsmith, Raymond W. 1958. *Financial Intermediaries in the American Economy Since 1900.* Princeton: Princeton University Press.

———. 1969. *Financial Structure and Development.* New Haven: Yale University Press.

———. 1971. "The Development of Financial Institutions During the Post-War Period." *Quarterly Review* 17: 129–92.

———. 1975. "Some Reflections on the Past, Present and Future of Financial Institutions." In *Current Problems of Financial Intermediaries,* edited by P. Frantzen, pp. 77–90. Rotterdam: Rotterdam University Press.

———. 1985. *Comparative National Balance Sheets: A Study of Twenty Countries, 1688–1978.* Chicago: University of Chicago Press.

Golob, Eugene O. 1944. *The Méline Tariff: French Agriculture and Nationalist Economic Policy.* New York: Columbia University Press.

Goodhart, Charles. 1988. *The Evolution of Central Banks.* Cambridge: MIT Press.

Goodman, John and Louis Pauly. 1993. "The Obsolescence of Capital Controls Economic Management in an Age of Global Markets." *World Politics* 46: 50–82.

Green, Alan and M. C. Urquhart. 1976. "Factor and Commodity Flows in the International Economy of 1870–1914: A Multi-Country View." *Journal of Economic History* 36: 217–52.

Gueslin, A. 1992. "Banks and State in France from the 1880s to the 1930s: The Impossible Advance of the Banks." In Cassis 1992, pp. 63–91.

Gueslin, A. and M. Lescure. 1995. "Les banques publiques, parapubliques et cooperatives françaises (vers 1920–vers 1960)." In Lévy-Leboyer 1995, pp. 45–57.

Guex, Sébastien. 1993. *La politique monétaire et financière de la Confédération suisse, 1900–1920.* Lausanne: Payot.

———. 1997. "Au carrefour de l'économie et de la politique: la genèse des banques cantonales en Suisse et leur développement jusqu'à la première guerre mondiale." In *Des personnes aux institutions: réseaux et cultures du crédit du XVIe au XXe siècle en Europe,* edited by L. Fontaine, G. Postel-Vinay, J.-L. Rosenthal, and P. Servais, pp. 332–47. Louvain-la-Neuve: Bruylant-Academia.

Guinnane, Timothy W. 1994. "A Failed Transplant: Raffeisen's Credit Cooperatives in Ireland, 1894–1914." *Explorations in Economic History* 31: 38–61.

———. 1995. *Diversification, Liquidity, and Supervision for Small Financial Institutions: Nineteenth-Century German Credit Cooperatives.* Economic Growth Center. Yale University. Center Discussion Paper No. 733, October.

———. 1997. "Regional Organizations in the German Cooperative Banking System in the Late 19th Century." *Research in Economics* 51, 3: 251–74.

Haggard, S. and C. H. Lee. 1993. "The Political Dimension of Finance in Economic Development." In *The Politics of Finance in Developing Countries,* edited by S. Haggard, C. H. Lee, and S. Maxfield, pp. 3–22. Ithaca: Cornell University Press.

1995. "Introduction: Issues and Findings." In *Financial Systems and Economic Policy in Developing Countries*, edited by S. Haggard and C. H. Lee, pp. 1–30. Ithaca: Cornell University Press.

Hall, Peter and David Soskice, eds. 2001. *Varieties of Capitalism: The Institutional Foundations of Comparative Advantage*. Oxford: Oxford University Press.

Hansen, Joseph. 1906. *Gustav von Mevissen: ein rheinisches Lebensbild 1815–1899*. 2 vols. Berlin: Georg Reimer.

Hansen, Per H. 1991. "From Growth to Crisis: The Danish Banking System from 1850 until the Interwar Years." *Scandinavian Economic History Review* 39: 20–40.

Hansen, S. A. 1982. "The Transformation of Bank Structures in the Industrial Period: The Case of Denmark." *Journal of European Economic History* 3: 575–603.

Harrington, Richard. 1987. *Asset and Liability Management by Banks*. Paris: OECD.

Harris, Stephen L. 1996. "The Politics of Financial Services Liberalization: The Case of the Canadian Investment Dealer Industry." Paper prepared for the annual meeting of the American Political Science Association, San Francisco, September.

Hartmann, Alfred. 1947. *Der Konkurrenkampf zwischen den schweizerischen Grossbanken und Kantonalbanken*. Zürich: Kommerzdruck- und Verlag AG.

Heald, David. 1989. "The United Kingdom: Privatisation and Its Political Context." In *The Politics of Privatisation in Western Europe*, edited by John Vickers and Vincent Wright, pp. 31–48. London: F. Cass.

Helleiner, Eric. 1994. *States and the Reemergence of Global Finance: From Bretton Woods to the 1990s*. Ithaca: Cornell University Press.

Helpman, Elhanan and Paul R. Krugman. 1985. *Market Structure and Foreign Trade*. Cambridge, MA: MIT Press.

Herrigel, Gary. 1996. *Industrial Constructions: The Sources of German Industrial Power*. Cambridge: Cambridge University Press.

Hertner, Peter. 1999. "Central Banking and German-Style Mixed Banking in Italy, 1893/5–1914: From Coexistence to Cooperation." In Sylla et al. 1999, pp. 182–209.

Hiler, D. 1993. "De la Caisse d'épargne à la banque universelle: l'exemple de la caisse d'épargne de Genève." In *Banques et crédit en Suisse (1850–1930)*, edited by Youssef Cassis and Jakob Tanner, pp. 185–98. Zürich: Chronos Verlag.

Hiscox, Michael J. 1997. "The Trade War at Home: Factor Mobility, International Trade, and Political Coalitions in Democracies." Ph.D. diss., Harvard University, Cambridge, MA.

2000. "International Capital Mobility and Trade Politics: Capital Flows and Political Coalitions." Mimeo. Department of Political Science, University of California, San Diego.

Historical Statistics of the United States: Colonial Times to 1970. 1975. Washington, DC: US Department of Commerce, Bureau of the Census.

Historisk Statistisk: 1968. 1975. Microfilm edn. Norge Statistisk Centralbyra. Cambridge: Chadwyck-Healey.

Holmström, Bengt and Jean Tirole. 1997. "Financial Intermediation, Loanable Funds, and the Real Sector." *Quarterly Journal of Economics* 112, 3: 663–91.

Horne, H. Oliver. 1947. *A History of Savings Banks*. Oxford: Oxford University Press.

Hu, Y.-S. 1984. *Industrial Banking and Special Credit Institutions: A Comparative Study*. Policy Studies Institute, No. 632. London.

IMF (International Monetary Fund). 1962. *International Monetary Statistics*. Washington, DC: IMF.

1995. *International Financial Statistics*. Washington, DC: IMF.

Institutional Investors: Statistical Yearbook. Paris: OECD.

Ireland Statistical Abstract. Central Statistics Office. Dublin: Stationery Office.

Irwin, Douglas A. 1995. "Industry or Class Cleavages over Trade Policy? Evidence from the British General Election of 1923." National Bureau of Economic Research, Working Paper No. 5170.

James, Harold, Hakan Lindgren, and Alice Teichova, eds. 1991. *The Role of Banks in the Interwar Economy*. Cambridge: Cambridge University Press.

James, John A. 1978. *Money and Capital Markets in Postbellum America*. Princeton: Princeton University Press.

1995. "The Rise and Fall of the Commercial Paper Market, 1900–1929." In Bordo and Sylla 1995, pp. 219–59.

Johansen, Hans Christian. 1985. *Dansk Historisk Statistik 1814–1980*. Copenhagen: Gyldendal.

1991. "Banking and Finance in the Danish Economy 1870–1914." In Cameron and Bovykin 1991, pp. 159–73.

Jones, J. R. 1994. "Fiscal Policies, Liberties, and Representative Government During the Reigns of the Last Stuarts." In *Fiscal Crises, Liberty, and Representative Government, 1450–1789*, edited by Philip T. Hoffman and Kathryn Norberg, pp. 67–95. Stanford: Stanford University Press.

Jonker, Joost. 1991. "Sinecures or Sinews of Power? Interlocking Directorships and Bank–Industry Relations in the Netherlands, 1910–1940." *Economic and Social History in the Netherlands* 3: 119–32.

1995. "Spoilt for Choice? Banking Concentration and the Structure of the Dutch Capital Market, 1900–1940." In Cassis et al. 1995, pp. 187–208.

1996a. "Between Public and Private Responsibility: The Relations Between the Nederlandsche Bank and the Commercial Banks in the Netherlands, 1900–1940." *Financial History Review* 3, 2: 139–52.

1996b. *Merchants, Bankers, Middlemen: The Amsterdam Money Markets During the First Half of the 19th Century*. Amsterdam: Neha.

Kane, E. 1981. "Accelerating Inflation, Technological Innovation, and the Decreasing Effectiveness of Banking Regulation." *Journal of Finance* 36, 2 (May): 355–67.

Katzenstein, Peter. 1985. *Small States in World Markets*. Ithaca: Cornell University Press.

Kauch, P. 1950. *The National Bank of Belgium 1850–1918*. Brussels: Société Belge d'Imprimerie Sobeli.

Kaufman, George G., ed. 1992. *Banking Structures in Major Countries*. Boston: Kluwer Academic Publishers.

Keating, Michael. 1997. "The Political Economy of Regionalism." In *The Polit-ical Economy of Regionalism*, edited by Michael Keating and John Loughlin, pp. 17–40. London: Frank Cass.

Kelly, Janet. 1976. *Bankers and Borders: The Case of American Banks in Britain*. Cambridge, MA: Ballinger.

Kinghorn, J. R. and J. V. Nye. 1996. "The Scale of Production in Western Economic Development: A Comparison of Official Industry Statistics in the United States, Britain, France, and Germany, 1905–1913." *Journal of Economic History* 56, 1: 90–112.

Knodell, Jane. 1998. "The Demise of Central Banking and the Domestic Ex-changes: Evidence from Antebellum Ohio." *Journal of Economic History* 58, 3 (September): 714–30.

Knutsen, Sverre. 1995. "Phases in the Development of the Norwegian Banking System, 1880–1980." In Cassis et al. 1995, pp. 78–121.

1997. "Post-War Strategic Capitalism in Norway: A Theoretical and Analytical Framework." *Business History* 39 (4): 106–27.

2000. "Why Didn't Universal Banks Develop in Norway, and Did It Really Matter? Banks and Economic Change in the European Periphery 1870–1913." Paper presented at the conference on the Origins of Universal Bank-ing. European University Institute. San Domenico di Fiesole. March 2–4.

Komlos, John, ed. 1990a. *Economic Development in the Habsburg Monarchy and in the Successor States*. New York: East European Monographs.

1990b. "Financial Innovation and the Demand for Money in Austria-Hungary, 1867–1913." In Komlos 1990a, pp. 115–32.

Koning, Niek. 1994. *The Failure of Agrarian Capitalism: Agrarian Politics in the UK, Germany, the Netherlands and the USA, 1846–1919*. London: Routledge.

Köver, G. 1991. "The Austro-Hungarian Banking System." In Cameron and Bovykin 1991, pp. 319–44.

Kregel, Jan A. 1997. "The Role of 1930s Regulations in the Development of Financial Markets in Postwar United States, Germany, and Great Britain." In Forsyth and Notermans 1997, pp. 256–309.

Kroszner, R. S. and G. R. Rajan. 1994. "Is the Glass–Steagall Act Justified? A Study of the US Experience with Universal Banking Before 1933." *American Economic Review* 84, 4: 810–32.

Krugman, Paul. 1991. "Increasing Returns and Economic Geography." *Journal of Political Economy* 99, 3: 483–99.

Kydland, Finn E. and Edward Prescott. 1977. "Rules Rather Than Discretion: The Inconsistency of Optimal Plans." *Journal of Political Economy* 85: 473–91.

Kymmel, J. 1996. *Geschiednis van de algemene banken in Nederland, 1860–1914*, vol. II. Amsterdam: NIBE.

La Porta, Rafael, Florencio Lopez-De-Silanes, and Andrei Shleifer. 1998. "Law and Finance." *Journal of Political Economy* 106, 6: 1112–55.

La Porta, Rafael, Florencio Lopez-De-Silanes, Andrei Shleifer, and Robert Vishny. 1997a. "Legal Determinants of External Finance." *Journal of Finance* 52, 3 (July): 1131–50.

1997b. "Trust in Large Organizations." *American Economic Review* 87, 2 (May): 333–38.

Lamoreaux, Naomi R. 1994. *Insider Lending: Banks, Personal Connections and Economic Development in Industrial New England*. New York: Cambridge University Press.

Lange, Even. 1994. "The Norwegian System of Banking Institutions Before and After the Interwar Crises." In *Universal Banking in the Twentieth Century*, edited by A. Teichova et al., pp. 12–21. Aldershot: Edward Elgar.

Laufenburger, H. 1940. *Enquête sur les changements de structure du crédit et de la banque, 1914–1938: les banques françaises*, vol. I. Paris: Sirey.

League of Nations. 1939a. *Money and Banking 1937/38*, vol. I, *Monetary Review*. Geneva: League of Nations.

1939b. *Money and Banking 1937/38*, vol. II, *Commercial Banks*. Geneva: League of Nations.

Lebovics, Herman. 1988. *The Alliance of Iron and Wheat in the Third French Republic, 1860–1914*. Baton Rouge and London: Louisiana State University Press, 1988.

Lescure, Michel. 1995. "Banking in France in the Inter-War Period." In Feinstein 1995, pp. 314–36.

1999. "Conclusion." In Lescure and Plessis 1999, pp. 323–31.

Lescure, Michel and Alain Plessis, eds. 1999. *Banques locales et banques régionales en France au XIXe siècle*. Paris: Albin Michel.

Levy, Jonah D. 1999. *Tocqueville's Revenge: State, Society, and Economy in Contemporary France*. Cambridge, MA: Harvard University Press.

Lévy-Leboyer, Maurice. 1976. "La spécialisation des établissements bancaires." In *Histoire économique et sociale de la France. Tome III: L'avènement de l'ère industrielle (1789–années 1880)*, vol. I, edited by Fernand Braudel and Ernest Labrousse, pp. 431–71. Paris: Presses Universitaires de France.

ed. 1995. *Les banques en Europe de l'Ouest de 1920 à nos jours*. Paris: Ministère de l'économie et des finances.

Loriaux, M. 1991. *France After Hegemony: International Change and Financial Reform*. Ithaca: Cornell University Press.

Lütz, Susanne. 1998. "The Revival of the Nation-State? Stock Exchange Regulation in an Era of Internationalized Financial Markets." *Journal of European Public Policy* 5, 1: 153–68.

2000. *From Managed to Market Capitalism? German Finance in Transition*. Discussion Paper 00/2. Cologne: Max Planck-Institut für Gesellschaftsforschung.

Lynn, Matthew. 1999. "Europe's Big Stock Bias." *International Herald Tribune*, January 8.

Mabe, William F. Jr. 2000. "The Political Origins of Financial Systems." Paper presented at annual meeting of the American Political Science Association, Marriott Wardman Park, Washington, DC. August 30–September 3.

Maddison, Angus. 1991. *Dynamic Forces in Capitalist Development: A Long-Run Comparative View*. Oxford: Oxford University Press.

Magee, Stephen. 1980. "Three Simple Tests of the Stolper–Samuelson Theorem." In *Issues in International Economics*, edited by Peter Oppenheimer, pp. 138–53. London: Oriel Press.

Marshall, Alfred. 1920. *Principles of Economics*, 8th edn. London: Macmillan.

Martin-Aceña, Pablo. 1994. "Spain During the Classical Gold Standard Years, 1880–1914." In *Monetary Regimes in Transition*, edited by Michael Bordo and Forrest Capie, pp. 135–72. New York: Cambridge University Press.

1995. "Spanish Banking in the Inter-war Period," In Feinstein 1995, pp. 502–27.

März, Eduard. 1984. *Austrian Banking and Financial Policy: Creditanstalt at a Turning Point, 1913–1923*. London: Weidenfeld and Nicolson.

Matre, Hege Imset. 1992. *Norske kredittinstitusjoner 1850–1990: en statistisk oversikt*. Research on Banking, Capital and Society. Report No. 42. Oslo.

Merrett, D. T. 1997. "Capital Markets and Capital Formation in Australia, 1890–1945." *Australian Economic History Review* 37, 3: 181–201.

Mexia, Antonio and Antonio Nogueira Leite. 1992. *The Pattern of Banking Liberalization in Portugal: 1984–1990*. Working Paper 187. Universidade Nova de Lisboa.

Michel, Bernard. 1976. *Banques et banquiers en Autriche au début du 20è siècle*. Paris: Presses de la Fondation Nationale de Sciences Politiques.

Michie, Ranald C. n.d. "Finance and the Making of the Modern Capitalist World 1830–1931: Stock Exchanges and the Finance of Economic Growth, 1830–1939." Mimeo. Department of History, University of Durham.

1985. "The London Stock Exchange and the British Securities Market, 1850–1914." *Economic History Review* 38, 1: 61–82.

1988a. "The Canadian Securities Market, 1850–1914." *Business History Review* 62, 1 (Spring): 35–73.

1988b. "Different in Names Only? The London Stock Exchange and Foreign Bourses, c. 1850–1914." *Business History* 30, 1 (January): 46–68.

1998. "The Invisible Stabiliser: Asset Arbitrage and the International Monetary System Since 1700." *Financial History Review* 15: 5–26.

Mitchell, B. R. 1983. *International Historical Statistics: The Americas and Australasia*. Detroit: Gale Research Company.

1992. *International Historical Statistics: Europe 1750–1988*, 3rd edn. New York: Stockton Press.

Mondello, Andrea. 1994. "The Relationship Between Banks and Firms: An Industrialist's View." *Review of Economic Conditions in Italy* 48, 1: 191–205.

Monthly Statistical Bulletin. Statistical Service of Greece. Athens.

Mooney, Christopher Z. and Robert D. Duval. 1993. *Bootstrapping: A Nonparametric Approach to Statistical Inference*. London: Sage.

Moran, Michael. 1991. *The Politics of the Financial Services Revolution: The USA, UK and Japan*. London: Macmillan.

1994. "The State and the Financial Services Revolution: A Comparative Analysis." In *The State in Western Europe: Retreat or Redefinition?* edited by Wolfgang C. Müller and Vincent Wright, pp. 158–77. Portland: Frank Cass.

Moss, Michael. 1997. "L'exemple du Royaume-Uni (1810–1914)." In Vogler 1997, pp. 133–46.

Moster, Antoine and Bernard Vogler. 1996. "France." In *History of European Savings Banks*, edited by Jürgen Mura, pp. 75–104. Stuttgart: Wissenschaftsförderung der Sparkassenorganisation eV.

National Accounts. Paris: OECD.

National Monetary Commission. 1911. *German Bank Inquiry of 1908–1909. Stenographic Reports: Proceedings of the Entire Commission on Point VI of the Question Sheet,* vol. II. Washington, DC: Government Printing Office.

Neal, Larry. 1994. "The Finance of Business During the Industrial Revolution." In *The Economic History of Britain Since 1700,* 2nd edn., vol. I, *1700–1860,* edited by Roderick Floud and Donald McCloskey, pp. 151–81. Cambridge: Cambridge University Press.

Nederlandsche Bank n.v. *Annual Report.* Dordrecht: Kluwer Academic Publishers.

——— 1987. *Financiële instellingen in Nederland 1900–1985: balansreeksen en naamlijst van handelsbanken.* DNB Statistische Cahiers No. 2. Amsterdam.

Neufeld, E. P. 1972. *The Financial System of Canada: Its Growth and Development.* Toronto: Macmillan Company of Canada.

New Zealand Official Yearbook. Department of Statistics. Wellington.

Newton, Lucy A. 1996. "Regional Bank–Industry Relations During the Mid-Nineteenth Century: Links Between Bankers and Manufacturing in Sheffield c. 1850 to c. 1855." *Business History* 38: 64–83.

Nicoletti, G., S. Scarpetta, and O. Boylaud. 1999. *Summary Indicators of Product Market Regulation and Employment Protection Legislation for the Purpose of International Comparisons.* OECD Economics Department Working Paper No. 226. Paris.

Nishimura, Shizuya. 1995. "The French Provincial Banks, the Banque de France, and Bill Finance, 1890–1913." *Economic History Review* 48, 3: 536–54.

Nordvik, Helge W. 1993. "The Banking System, Industrialization and Economic Growth in Norway, 1850–1914." *Scandinavian Economic History Review* 41, 1: 51–72.

North, Douglass C. and Barry R. Weingast. 1989. "Constitutions and Commitment: The Evolution of Institutions Governing Public Choice in Seventeenth-Century England." *Journal of Economic History* 49, 4: 803–32.

Nötel, Rudolf. 1984. "Money, Banking and Industry in Interwar Austria and Hungary." *Journal of European Economic Review* 13, 12: 137–202.

Nunes, Ana Bela, Carlos Bastien, and Nuno Valério. 1994. *Caixa Económica Montepio Geral: 150 Anos de História 1844–1994.* Lisbon: Caixa Económica Montepio Geral.

Nygren, I. 1983. "Transformation of Bank Structures in the Industrial Period: The Case of Sweden 1820–1913." *Journal of European Economic History* 1: 29–68.

O'Brien, Richard. 1992. *Global Financial Integration: The End of Geography.* New York: Council on Foreign Relations.

OECD (Organization for Economic Co-operation and Development). 1992. *Industrial Support Policies in OECD Countries 1986–1989.* Paris: OECD.

——— 1996. *Public Support to Industry: Report by the Industry Committee to the Council at Ministerial Level.* Paris: OECD.

——— 1999. *Revenue Statistics.* Paris: OECD.

Official Year Book of Australia. Australian Bureau of Statistics. Canberra.

Official Year Book of the Commonwealth of Australia 1901–1907. 1908. Commonwealth Bureau of Census and Statistics. Melbourne: McCarron, Bird & Co.

Ollerenshaw, Philip. 1997. "The Business and Politics of Banking in Ireland 1900–1943." In Cottrell et al. 1997, pp. 52–78.

Olsson, Ulf. 1997. *At the Centre of Development: Skandinaviska Enskilda Banken and Its Predecessors 1856–1996.* Stockholm: Skandinaviska Enskilda Banken.

Österreichische Nationalbank. *Statistisches Monatsheft: Zahlungsbilanz Österreichs.* Vienna.

Parker, William. 1920. *The Paris Bourse and French Finance.* New York: Columbia University Press.

Passion, Luc. 1991. "La Caisse d'épargne de Paris: 1818–1848." In Vogler 1991b, pp. 89–109.

Pauly, Louis W. 1988. *Opening Financial Markets: Banking Politics on the Pacific Rim.* Ithaca: Cornell University Press.

Pauly, Louis W. and Simon Reich. 1997. "National Structures and Multinational Corporate Behavior: Enduring Differences in the Age of Globalization." *International Organization* 51, 1: 1–30.

Pecchioli, R. M. 1983. *The Internationalisation of Banking: The Policy Issues.* Paris: OECD.

Pempel, T. J. 1998. "Structural Gaiatsu: International Finance and Political Change in Japan." Paper prepared for the annual meeting of the American Political Science Association. Boston, September 2–6.

Pérez, Sofía A. 1997a. *Banking on Privilege: The Politics of Spanish Financial Reform.* Ithaca: Cornell University Press.

    1997b. "'Strong States' and 'Cheap' Credit: Economic Policy Strategy and Financial Regulation in France and Spain." In Forsyth and Notermans 1997, pp. 169–220.

Petersen, Mitchell A. and Raghuram G. Rajan. 1994. "The Benefits of Lending Relationships: Evidence from Small Business Data." *Journal of Finance* 49, 1: 3–37.

    1995. "The Effect of Credit Market Competition on Lending Relationships." *Quarterly Journal of Economics* 110, 2: 407–43.

Piore, Michael and Charles F. Sabel. 1984. *The Second Industrial Divide: Possibilities for Prosperity.* New York: Basic Books.

Platt, D. C. M. 1984. *Foreign Finance in Continental Europe and the USA, 1815–1870.* London: George Allen & Unwin.

Plender, John. 1987. "London's Big Bang in International Context." *International Affairs* 1: 39–48.

Plessis, Alain. 1985. *La politique de la Banque de France de 1851 à 1870.* Geneva: Droz.

    1999. "Les banques locales, de l'essor du Second Empire à la crise de la Belle Epoque." In Lescure and Plessis 1999, pp. 202–32.

Polsi, Alessandro. 1993. *Alle origini del capitalismo italiano: stato, banche e banchieri dopo l'Unità.* Turin: Einaudi.

    1996. "Financial Institutions in Nineteenth-Century Italy: The Rise of a Banking System." *Financial History Review* 3: 117–37.

    1997. *Il mercato del credito a Piacenza.* Piacenza: Banca di Piacenza.

2000. "The Origins of Italian Mixed Banks in an Adverse Institutional Context (1850–1914)." Paper presented at the conference on the Origins of Universal Banking. European University Institute. San Domenico di Fiesole. March 2–4.

Porter, Michael E. 1992. "Capital Disadvantage: America's Failing Capital Investment System." *Harvard Business Review* September–October: 65–83.

Posner, Elliot. 2001. "Financial Change and European Union Politics: The Origins of Europe's 'Market of Nasdaq Marketplaces.'" Ph.D diss. draft (September). Department of Political Science, University of California, Berkeley.

Posner, M. V. and S. J. Woolf. 1967. *Italian Public Enterprise*. London: Gerald Duckworth & Co.

Powell, Ellis T. 1966 [1915]. *The Evolution of the Money Market 1385–1915*. London: Frank Cass.

Pressnell, L. S. 1956. *Country Banking and the Industrial Revolution*. Oxford: Clarendon Press.

Pringle, Robin. 1975. *Banking in Britain*. London: Methuen.

Putnam, Robert. 1993. *Making Democracy Work: Civic Traditions in Modern Italy*. Princeton: Princeton University Press.

Quinn, Dennis P. and Carla Inclán. 1997. "The Origins of Financial Openness: A Study of Current and Capital Account Liberalization." *American Journal of Political Science* 41, 3: 771–813.

Rajan, Raghuram G. and Luigi Zingales. 1999. "The Politics of Financial Development." Mimeo. University of Chicago.

Reinicke, Wolfgang H. 1995. *Banking, Politics and Global Finance: American Commercial Banks and Regulatory Change, 1980–1990*. Aldershot: Edward Elgar.

Riesser, Jacob. 1977 [1911]. *The Great German Banks and Their Concentration*. New York: Arno Press.

Ritter, Gretchen. 1997. *Goldbugs and Greenbacks: The Antimonopoly Tradition and the Politics of Finance in America*. Cambridge: Cambridge University Press.

Ritzmann, Franz. 1973. *Die Schweizer Banken*. Bern: Paul Haupt.

Rodrik, Dany. 1995. "Political Economy of Trade Policy." In *Handbook of International Economics*, vol. III, edited by G. M. Grossman and K. Rogoff, pp. 1457–94. Amsterdam: Elsevier.

1997. *Has Globalization Gone Too Far?* Washington, DC: Institute for International Economics.

Rogowski, R. 1989. *Commerce and Coalition*. Princeton: Princeton University Press.

Rokkan, Stein and Derek W. Urwin. 1983. *Economy, Territory, Identity: Politics of West European Peripheries*. London: Sage.

Root, Hilton L. 1994. *The Fountain of Privilege: Political Foundations of Markets in Old Regime France and England*. Berkeley: University of California Press.

Rosenbluth, F. McCall. 1989. *Financial Politics in Contemporary Japan*. Ithaca: Cornell University Press.

Rudin, Donald. 1990. *In Whose Interest? Quebec's Caisses Populaires, 1900–1945*. Montreal: McGill-Queen's University Press.

Rudolph, Richard L. 1976. *Banking and Industrialization in Austria-Hungary: The Role of Banks in the Industrialization of the Czech Crownlands, 1873–1914.* London: Cambridge University Press.

Rybczynski, Tad M. 1988. "Financial Systems and Industrial Re-Structuring." *National Westminster Bank Quarterly Review* November: 3–13.

Sabel, Charles F. and Jonathan Zeitlin. 1985. "Historical Alternatives to Mass Production: Politics, Markets and Technology in Nineteenth-Century Industrialization." *Past and Present* 108: 133–76.

eds. 1997. *World of Possibilities: Flexibility and Mass Production in Western Industrialization.* New York: Cambridge University Press.

Sabel, Charles F., John R. Griffin, and Richard E. Deeg. 1993. "Making Money Talk: Towards a New Debtor–Creditor Relation in German Banking." Paper presented at conference on Relational Investing. Center for Law and Economic Studies. Columbia University School of Law. New York. May 6–7.

Sartori, Giovanni. 1976. *Parties and Party Systems: A Framework for Analysis.* Cambridge: Cambridge University Press.

Saunders, Anthony and Ingo Walter. 1994. *Universal Banking in the United States.* New York: Oxford University Press.

Saurel, Maurice. 1901. *Sociétés de crédit contre banques locales.* Paris: Arthur Rousseau.

Sayers, R. S., ed. 1962. *Banking in Western Europe.* Oxford: Clarendon Press.

1976. *The Bank of England 1891–1944*, vols. I and II. Cambridge: Cambridge University Press.

Schmoller, Gustav. 1904. *Grundriss der allgemein Volkswirtschaftslehre.* Leipzig: Duncker und Humblot.

Schön, Lennart. n.d. "Capital Imports, Credit Market and Industrialisation in Sweden 1850–1910." Mimeo. University of Lund, Sweden.

Schonhardt-Bailey, Cheryl M. 1991. "Lobbying for Free Trade in 19th-Century Britain: To Concentrate or Not." *American Political Science Review* 85: 37–58.

Schonhardt-Bailey, Cheryl M. and Andrew Bailey. 1995. "The Buck in Your Bank Is Not a Vote for Free Trade: Financial Intermediation and Trade Preferences in the United States and Germany." In *Preferences, Institutions, and Rational Choice*, edited by Keith Dowding and Desmond King, pp. 179–210. Oxford: Clarendon Press.

Schweizerische Nationalbank. *Das Schweizerische Bankwesen.* Zürich: Orel Füssli.

Sheppard, D. K. 1971. *The Growth and Role of UK Financial Institutions 1880–1962.* London: Methuen & Co.

Sheppard, D. K., K. Guerin, and S. Lee. 1990. "New Zealand Monetary Aggregates and the Total Assets of Leading Groups of Financial Institutions. 1862–1982." Discussion Paper 11. Victoria University of Wellington, Money and Finance Association.

Shonfield, Andrew. 1965. *Modern Capitalism.* Oxford: Oxford University Press.

Sinclair, Timothy J. 1994. "Between State and Market: Hegemony and Institutions of Collective Action Under Conditions of International Capital Mobility." *Policy Sciences* 27: 447–66.

Sinn, Hans-Werner. 1999. *The German State Banks: Global Players in the International Financial Markets.* Cheltenham: Edward Elgar.

Smith, Adam. 1976 [1776]. *The Wealth of Nations*. Chicago: University of Chicago Press.

Snowden, Kenneth A. 1995. "Mortgage Securitization in the United States: Twentieth-Century Developments in Historical Perspective." In Bordo and Sylla 1995, pp. 261–98.

Sobel, Andrew C. 1994. *Domestic Choices, International Markets: Dismantling National Barriers and Liberalizing Securities Markets*. Ann Arbor: University of Michigan Press.

Social Expenditure Database 1980–1996. CD-ROM. Paris: OECD.

Société des nations. 1931. *Mémorandum sur les banques commerciales 1913–1929*. Service d'études économiques. Geneva: Société des nations.

Statistical Abstract of the United States. Washington, DC: US Department of Commerce, Bureau of the Census.

Statistical Year-Book of Canada. Department of Agriculture. Ottawa: Brown Chamberlin.

Statistical Year-Book of Canada for 1889. 1890. Department of Agriculture. Ottawa: Brown Chamberlin.

Statistical Yearbook of Finland. Central Statistical Office. Helsinki.

Statistical Yearbook of the Netherlands. Netherlands Central Bureau of Statistics. The Hague: SDU Publishers.

Statistisches Handbuch für die Republik Österreich. Statistisches Zentralamt. Vienna.

Statistisches Jahrbuch der Schweiz. Eidgnössisches Statistisches Amt. Basel: Birkhäuser.

Statistisches Jahrbuch für die Bundesrepublik Deutschland. Statistisches Bundesamt. Stuttgart: Kohlammer.

Statistisk Årbog. Danmark statistik. Copenhagen.

Statistisk Årbok. Statistisk Sentralbyrå. Oslo.

Statistisk Arsbok för Sverige. Statistiska Centralbyran. Stockholm.

Statistiske Undersøgelser 1969. No. 24. Kreditmarkedsstatistik. Danmarks Statistik. Copenhagen.

Steinherr, Alfred and Pier-Luigi Gilibert. 1989. *The Impact of Financial Market Integration on the European Banking Industry*. Research Report No. 1. Centre for European Policy Studies, Brussels.

Stewart Patterson, E. L. 1932. *Canadian Banking*. Toronto: Ryerson Press.

Stigler, George J. 1971. "The Theory of Economic Regulation." *Bell Journal of Economics and Management Science* 2, 1 (Spring): 3–21.

Stiglitz, J. E. and A. Weiss. 1981. "Credit Rationing in Markets with Imperfect Information." *American Economic Review* 71, 3: 393–410.

Stolper, Wolfgang and Paul Samuelson. 1941. "Protection and Real Wages." *Review of Economic Studies* 9: 58–73.

Story, Jonathan. 1997. "Globalisation, the European Union and German Financial Reform: The Political Economy of 'Finanzplatz Deutschland.'" In Underhill 1997b, pp. 245–73.

Story, Jonathan and Ingo Walter. 1997. *Political Economy of Financial Integration in Europe: The Battle of the Systems*. Cambridge, MA: MIT Press.

Strange, Susan. 1986. *Casino Capitalism*. Oxford: Basil Blackwell.

La Suisse économique et sociale. 1927. Département Fédéral de l'Economie Publique. Zürich: Benziger and Cie.

Svennilson, Ingvar. 1954. *Growth and Stagnation in the European Economy.* Geneva: United Nations, Economic Commission for Europe.

Sveriges officiella statistik Bankinspektionen. Bankaktiebolagen Fondkommissionärerna Fondbörsen och VPC. Sveriges officiella statistik. Bankinspektionen. Stockholm.

Sveriges Riksbank. *Statistical Appendix to the Annual Report.* Stockholm.

Sylla, Richard. 1997. "The Rise of Securities Markets: What Can Government Do?" In Caprio and Vittas 1997, pp. 198–215.

——— 1999. "Shaping the US Financial System, 1690–1913: The Dominant Role of Public Finance." In Sylla et al. 1999, pp. 249–70.

Sylla, Richard and George David Smith. 1995. "Information and Capital Market Regulation in Anglo-American Finance." In Bordo and Sylla 1995, pp. 179–207.

Sylla, Richard and Gianni Toniolo. 1991. "Introduction: Patterns of European Industrialization During the Nineteenth Century." In *Patterns of European Industrialization: The Nineteenth Century,* edited by Richard Sylla and Gianni Toniolo, pp. 1–28. New York: Routledge.

Sylla, Richard, Richard Tilly, and Gabriel Tortella, eds. 1999. *The State, the Financial System, and Economic Modernization.* Cambridge: Cambridge University Press.

Tamaki, Norio. 1995. *Japanese Banking: A History, 1859–1959.* Cambridge: Cambridge University Press.

Thomas, Kenneth P. 1997. *Capital Beyond Borders: State and Firms in the Auto Industry, 1960–1994.* New York: St. Martin's Press.

Thomes, Paul. 1995. "German Savings Banks as Instruments of Regional Development up to the Second World War." In Cassis et al. 1995, pp. 145–64.

Thompson, John K. 1995. *Securitisation: An International Perspective.* Paris: OECD.

Tilly, Richard. 1966. *Financial Institutions and Industrialization in the Rhineland, 1815–1870.* Madison: University of Wisconsin Press.

——— 1967. "Germany, 1815–1870." In *Banking in the Early Stages of Industrialization: A Study in Comparative Economic History,* edited by Rondo Cameron, pp. 151–82. New York: Oxford University Press.

——— 1986. "German Banking, 1850–1914: Development Assistance for the Strong." *Journal of European Economic History* 15, 1: 113–52.

——— 1991. "International Aspects of the Development of German Banking." In Cameron and Bovykin 1991, pp. 90–112.

Titos Martinez, Manuel. 1995. "Les Caisses d'épargne en Espagne." In Brück et al. 1995, pp. 105–24.

Tortella, Gabriel. 1974. *La Banca Española en la Restauracion,* vol. II, *Datos para una Historia Economica.* Madrid: Servicio de Estudios del Banco de España.

Treisman, Daniel. 2000. "Decentralization and Inflation: Commitment, Collective Action, or Continuity?" *American Political Science Review* 94, 4: 837–57.

Underhill, Geoffrey R. D. 1997a. "The Making of the European Financial Area: Global Market Integration and the EU Single Market for Financial Services." In Underhill 1997b, pp. 101–23.

ed. 1997b. *The New World Order in International Finance*. New York: St. Martin's Press.

Urquhart, M. C. and K. A. H. Buckley, eds. 1965. *Historical Statistics of Canada*. Cambridge: Cambridge University Press.

Van der Wee, Herman. 1982. "La politique d'investissement de la Société Générale de Belgique, 1822–1913." *Histoire, Economie et Société* 1, 4: 603–19.

Van Gor, Linda and Jaap Koelewijn, 1995. "Le système bancaire néerlandais: étude rétrospective." In Lévy-Leboyer 1995, pp. 153–75.

Vanthemsche, Guy. 1991. "State, Banks and Industry in Belgium and the Netherlands, 1919–1939." In Harold James et al. 1991, pp. 104–21.

Vatter, Barbara. 1961. "Industrial Borrowing by the New England Textile Mills, 1840–1860: A Comment." *Journal of Economic History* 21 (June): 216–21.

Verdier, Daniel. 1994. *Democracy and Trade: Britain, France, and the United States, 1860–1990*. Princeton: Princeton University Press.

1995. "The Politics of Public Aid to Private Industry: The Role of Policy Networks." *Comparative Political Studies* 28, 1 (April): 3–42.

1997. "Universal Banking and Bank Failures Between the Wars." EUI Working Paper SPS No. 97/11.

1999. "Domestic Responses to Free Trade and Free Finance in OECD Countries." *Business & Politics* 1, 3: 279–316.

2000. "The Rise and Fall of State Banking in OECD Countries." *Comparative Political Studies* 33, 3 (April): 283–318.

2002. "How and Why Financial Systems Differ: A Survey of the Existing Literature." EUI Working Paper SPS No. 02/2. Florence.

Vittas, Dimitri. 1997. "Thrift Deposit Institutions in Europe and the United States." In Caprio and Vittas 1997, pp. 141–79.

Vogler, Bernard. 1991a. "Les Caisses d'épargne en Alsace de 1831 à 1870." *Bankhistorisches Archiv* 17: 82–98.

ed. 1991b. *L'histoire des Caisses d'épargne européennes*, vol. I, *Les origines des Caisses d'épargne 1815–1848*. Paris: Les éditions de l'épargne.

ed. 1997. *L'histoire des Caisses d'épargne européennes*, vol. III, *Conjoncture et crises 1850–1914*. Paris: Les éditions de l'épargne.

Wade, Robert. 1985. "East Asian Financial Systems as a Challenge to Economics: Lessons from Taiwan." *California Management Review* 27, 4: 106–26.

Wallace, R. H. 1964. "The Australian Savings Banks." In *Studies in the Australian Capital Market*, edited by E. R. Hirst and R. H. Wallace, pp. 231–302. Melbourne: Cheshire.

Weingast, Barry R. 1995. "The Economic Role of Political Institutions: Market-Preserving Federalism and Economic Development." *Journal of Law, Economics, and Organization* 11, 1: 1–31.

White, Eugene Nelson. 1986. "Before the Glass–Steagall Act: An Analysis of the Investment Banking Activities of National Banks," *Explorations in Economic History* 23: 33–55.

1998. "Were Banks Special Intermediaries in Late Nineteenth-Century America?" *Review of the Federal Reserve Bank of St. Louis* May/June: 13–25.

White, R. C. 1973. *Australian Banking and Monetary Statistics 1945–1970.* Occasional Paper No. 4B. Reserve Bank of Australia, Sydney.

Witte, Els. 1991. "Les origines des Caisses d'épargne en Belgique: 1825–1850." In Vogler 1991b, pp. 169–89.

Woo, J.-E. 1991. *Race to the Swift: State and Finance in Korean Industrialization.* New York: Columbia University Press.

World Development Indicators. CD-ROM. New York: World Bank.

Wotherspoon, G. 1979. "Savings Banks and Social Policy in New South Wales 1832–1871." Supplement to *Australian Economic History Review* 19: 141–63.

Wysocki, Josef. 1997. "Croissance et conjoncture (1850–1914)." In Vogler 1997, pp. 17–28.

Yearbook of National Accounts Statistics, vol. I. New York: United Nations.

Zeitlin, Jonathan. 1995. "Why Are There No Industrial Districts in the United Kingdom?" In Bagnasco and Sabel 1995, pp. 98–114.

Ziegler, Dieter. 1990. *Central Bank, Peripheral Industry: The Bank of England in the Provinces 1826–1913.* London: Leicester University Press.

1991. "The Origins of the 'Macmillan Gap': Comparing Britain and Germany in the Twentieth Century." London School of Economics, Business History Unit, Papers in Business History, vol. 9, Report from the BHU International Conference 1991, mimeo. September 11–14.

Zimmerman, R. 1987. *Volksbank oder Aktienbank? Parlamentsdebatten, Referendum und zunehmende Verbandsmacht beim Streit um die Nationalbankgründung 1891–1905.* Zürich: Chronos Verlag.

Zysman, John. 1983. *Governments, Markets, and Growth: Financial Systems and the Politics of Industrial Change.* Ithaca: Cornell University Press.

Citations index

Subject index